*With the pl[easure]
of a first meeting
and conversation,
& looking forward
to more.*

MARKETS

of Dispossession

Politics, History, and Culture

A series from the International Institute at the University of Michigan

Series Editors

George Steinmetz and Julia Adams

Series Editorial Advisory Board

Fernando Coronil

Mamadou Diouf

Michael Dutton

Geoff Eley

Fatma Müge Göcek

Nancy Rose Hunt

Andreas Kalyvas

Webb Keane

David Laitin

Lydia Liu

Julie Skurski

Margaret Somers

Ann Laura Stoler

Katherine Verdery

Elizabeth Wingrove

Sponsored by the International Institute at the University of Michigan and published by Duke University Press, this series is centered around cultural and historical studies of power, politics, and the state—a field that cuts across the disciplines of history, sociology, anthropology, political science, and cultural studies. The focus on the relationship between state and culture refers to both a methodological approach—the study of politics and the state using culturalist methods—and a substantive approach that treats signifying practices as an essential dimension of politics. The dialectic of politics, culture, and history figures prominently in all the books selected for the series.

MARKETS
of Dispossession

NGOS,

ECONOMIC DEVELOPMENT,

AND THE STATE IN CAIRO

Julia Elyachar

DUKE UNIVERSITY PRESS

Durham and London

2005

Printed in the United States of America on acid-free paper ∞

Designed by Teresa Bonner

Typeset in Minion by Keystone Typesetting, Inc.

Library of Congress Cataloging-in-Publication Data appear on the last printed
page of this book.

An earlier version of chapter 3 appeared as "Mappings of Power: The State,
NGOS, and International Organizations in the Informal Economy of Cairo," in
Comparative Studies in Society and History 45, no. 3 (2003): 571–605. Reprinted
with the permission of Cambridge University Press. © Society for the
Comparative Study of Society and History.

To the memory of Avraham Zloczower

Contents

ACKNOWLEDGMENTS

This book has taken many years to complete. I have incurred many debts in the long process, and it is a pleasure to acknowledge some of them here. The book grows out of research that I conducted for my doctoral dissertation at Harvard, and I would like to acknowledge the following institutions whose support made that research possible: the Fulbright Commission, Institute of International Exchange, Egypt, 1993–94; the Sheldon Fellowship of Harvard University, 1993; and the Social Science Research Council and MacArthur Foundation Program in International Peace and Security in a Changing World, 1994–96. The Center for Middle Eastern Studies under the directorships of Roy Mottahedeh and William Graham provided me with Foreign Language Area Studies Grants, a Mellon Foundation Grant, and a special Center grant that made possible my studies at Harvard. Also at Harvard, I would like to thank Tosun Arıçanli, Cemal Kafadar, Arthur Kleinman, Zachary Lockman, David Maybury-Lewis, Roger Owen, Stanley Tambiah, and Nur Yalman for their support. I am indebted to my advisor and thesis chair, Sally Falk Moore, for her sharp critical eye and unwavering support: both have had a decisive impact on my work. Michael Herzfeld has been a generous source of advice on matters both intellectual and practical since we met during my last year at Harvard.

I am also grateful to the following individuals and institutions for helping me acquire some level of mastery of the Arabic language. The Mellon Foundation funded my study at Middlebury College in 1990, and the Center for Arabic Studies Abroad of Georgetown University awarded me a fellowship for an intensive course at the American University of Cairo in 1991–92. I was privileged to study with two teachers of Arabic,

'Abbas al-Tonsi and Samira Khalil, whose skills are unparalleled and whose passion for Arabic language and literature is unmatched. 'Abbas al-Tonsi in particular gave me the key for my learning of Arabic and Egyptian dialect, and for understanding much more about Arabic literature and culture. Laila Moustafa helped many times over the years with various aspects of Arabic language, and Essam Fawzi was a constant tutor during the two years of our work together in Cairo.

The committee members of the Program in International Peace and Security in a Changing World during my tenure between 1994 and 1996 shaped my research in important ways. Ashraf Ghani gave generously of his time and insights over the years of my graduate studies. Avraham Zloczower, to whom this book is dedicated, gave me my first education in anthropology and social theory. He supported this project in its early stages, even though it seemed to move in directions away from what he had taught me. His pathbreaking approach to theory of the state, class, and citizenship in the context of Israel/Palestine has had an impact in the world that he did not live to see.

The support of a number of individuals and institutions in Cairo was crucial to the success of this research. Throughout my stay I was privileged to have the institutional support of the Cairo Fulbright Commission. I remember with gratitude the unfailing kindness and professionalism of the entire Fulbright staff. Ann Radwan and Nevine Gad el-Mawla in particular facilitated my research in important ways, even after my formal association with the Fulbright Commission had ended. Samia el-Khashab of the Sociology Department of Cairo University was extremely helpful and generous while overseeing my project during my tenure with the Fulbright Commission. Asef Bayat of the American University of Cairo provided intellectual support and kind friendship. I also have an immense debt of gratitude to my friend and doctor, Milijana Vucicevic-Salama of Sarajevo and Cairo, for restoring my health on more than one occasion.

I wrote the first of many versions of this book and completed the final revisions while living in Ljubljana, Slovenia. I am grateful to the Scientific Research Centre of the Slovene Academy of Sciences and Arts of Ljubljana and its director, Oto Luthar, for providing me with visiting fellowships in 1997–98 and 2004–5. My thanks to the Institute of Anthropological and Spatial Studies of the Scientific Research Centre, and its director Ivan Šprajc, for hosting me in 2004–5. I would also like to thank

Borut Telban and Božidar Jezernik for their intellectual companionship and many efforts on my behalf, Katarina Drenik for making the impossible possible, and Melita Pisek for her kindness and help. In New York I thank Tsewang Dolma for her loving care and friendship.

It would be impossible for me to thank every individual who has helped me over the many years it has taken me to research and write this book. Among those who have helped me with their friendship, support, and comments are Mirielle Abelin, Talal Asad, Ragui Assaad, Kamran Asdar Ali, Kelly Askew, Jean-François Bayart, Rosemarie Bernard, the late Avriel Botowsky, Koray Çaliskan, John Comaroff, Virginia Dominguez, James Ferguson, Julie Graham, Béatrice Hibou, Charles Hirschkind, Marion Katz, Petra Kuppinger, Yahya M. Madra, Cameel Makhoul, Achille Mbembe, Timothy Mitchell, Hiro Miyozaki, Dorothea von Moltke, Laila Moustafa, Hudita Mustafa, Eve Troutt Powell, Moustafa 'Abd el-Rahman, Annelies Riles, Janet Roitman, Shahnaz Rouse, Kristin Sands, Eileen Setzman, Bashir al-Siba'i, Cliff Simms, Mara Thomas, 'Abbas al-Tonsi, Thomas Trauttman, Ruth Turner, and the editors and anonymous readers of *American Ethnologist*, *Comparative Studies in Society and History*, and *Public Culture*.

This book took its final shape during the three years that I spent as an assistant professor, faculty fellow, and director of graduate studies at the Kevorkian Center for Near Eastern Studies at New York University. I had the pleasure there of working under two outstanding directors. Timothy Mitchell brought me to NYU and helped me in countless ways. I will always be deeply grateful to him. Zachary Lockman, who assumed the directorship of the Kevorkian Center during the last year of my stay at NYU, took time from a very busy schedule to read the entire manuscript of this book and to offer invaluable comments. Michael Gilsenan was generous with his time and interest. I am also grateful to Shiva Balaghi, Bill Carrick, and Barbara Pryce, the staff of the Kevorkian Center, for their help and friendship. Without Bill Carrick, I would have accomplished much less and with much less pleasure.

For their comments on earlier versions of the entire manuscript, my thanks to Walter Ambrust, Bill Fisher, and Diane Singerman. At Duke University Press, I am indebted to the editors of this book series, Julia Adams and George Steinmetz, for their probing and critical comments on an earlier version of this book, and for their confidence in taking me on when this book was far from ready for publication. Julia Adams in particular has been a source of help far beyond the call of duty. Raphael Allen, who has since left Duke University Press, expressed early confidence in the project, and Ken Wissoker, who took over the project at a late stage, has been a source of much understanding and helpful advice. Fred Kameny edited the manuscript with graceful precision, improved it immensely, and expertly oversaw production of the book. Two anonymous readers for the Press contributed insightful comments. The University of Michigan International Institute provided generous financial support for the publication of this book.

Four colleagues read this book in its entirety when I thought it almost finished and showed me how to improve its final shape. Michel Callon twice helped me see what I was doing before I realized it myself. Bill Maurer forced me to sharpen my argument when I equivocated, helped me to restructure the book, and caught a number of errors and omissions. Zachary Lockman helped me to understand what was important and how to communicate it better. My debt to Essam Fawzi is immense. I discuss his contribution and the nature of our working relationship in chapter 1. Essam believed in my project and its importance before I did. He shared with me his genius for ethnography and wealth of knowledge about Cairo and its people. Our rich conversations over the course of this research continue to animate my mental world.

My debts to those with whom this research was conducted are immense. I could have accomplished nothing without the kindness and generosity of countless residents of el-Hirafiyeen and other neighborhoods of Cairo. Some took risks to speak openly about controversial matters. Even if I cannot thank them here by name because of concerns about privacy, I would like to note my gratitude to all of those in el-Hirafiyeen who were so kind as to spend many hours talking with me, and who welcomed me into their homes, workshops, micro-enterprises, and offices. I am equally grateful to all of those in USAID, Cairo; the Industrial Development Bank of Egypt; the National Bank for Development; the Governorate of Cairo; the Local Government of el-Salam; Environment Quality International; and Integrated Development Associates who spoke to me and offered important chances to understand more about their work and lives. Others in Cairo who offered assistance in various stages of this research also requested anonymity; to them I am grateful as well.

My expression of gratitude to Tomaž Mastnak comes last because he is first. My debts to him go beyond thanks for his readings of, and comments on, countless versions of what became this book. Those readings have been so many, and his comments so extensive, that his thinking is woven into every page. He often knew what I wanted to say before I did, figured out how to say it when I could not, and always calmed me when I was desperate that I would never finish. I am grateful to Elijan and Martín Mastnak for lending me their pencils and pencil sharpeners during book revisions, and for making life such a joy.

To all those who influenced my work over the many years it has taken me to complete this book, and whom I forgot to mention here by name, I offer my gratitude and my apologies. Despite my countless debts to others, responsibility for remaining errors is mine alone.

A Note on Transliteration

I have tried to use a system of transliteration that would provide some ease to the reader who has no familiarity with the Arabic language. When transliterating words and phrases from Egyptian spoken Arabic, I have retained the language in its original form. As for words familiar to a foreign reader, I have used spellings that are more familiar rather than those that are technically correct. Otherwise, I have deleted the initial hamza, notation of long vowels, and diacritics in the hope that the speaker of Arabic will already recognize the words under discussion and that the non-Arabic speaker will be able to read with less puzzlement. At the time of this fieldwork, the value of the Egyptian pound was approximately 3.3 LE for one U.S. dollar.

1. Introduction: The Power of Invisible Hands

The Generation of Structural Adjustment

It's a Ramadan evening, February 1995, in the streets of a neighborhood in Cairo called "Madinet el-Hirafiyeen," literally Craftsmen's Town. An hour after the break of the fast observed by Muslims during the holy month of Ramadan, most of the workshop doors are still closed. Families are inside, workshop masters are still drinking their tea. For those who commute across long distances of the megacity, home to seventeen million or more, Ramadan also means a shift in the rhythms of the working day. Customers come at different times; buses and microbuses tear through the streets at a different hour. Food is served, if discreetly, to these migrant workers in their own land.

Let me describe my path of movement on that evening around that small span of Cairo: Into an empty apartment built for a craftsman's family where a state employee, an "entrepreneur" in his off-time, sits with two telephones at hand, pondering the reopening of his "microenterprise marketing office." Into the unfurnished, unpainted apartment of a woman whose sharp mind peers out from behind her body's folds of resignation, and off to the workshop where her husband works away late into the night. Down streets lit by small lamps hung on car hoods, illuminating the backs of five boys and three teens—workers all—hunched over a car engine that waits to be revived. To the doors of a coffeehouse flung open at night after the fast, where the budding flowers of child laborers' faces glow in the warmth of dancing girls and great actors whose laughs and shouts from television screens mark the return of

1

Ramadan, its annual nightly television series followed closely around the country and the Arab world.

Men and women make Ramadan their own in a few spots of warmth. Lanterns and paper chains, such as those found throughout Cairo during this holy month, play quietly in the dark outside apartments gleaming with laughter. A few workshops resound with the sounds of eating and drinking far into the night. Some kilometers away, in the workers' dormitory town of Madinet el-Salam, still within the bounds of the megacity, the streets are emptier still. Men and women sit quietly at home together with a child, maybe two, around the nuclear family's television screen. Cousins and grandparents and aunts of these families, who were also evicted from apartments downtown after the earthquake of 1993, watch the same programs in other neighborhoods on other outskirts of town.

A car passes by, stops, and backs up: Be sure to come tonight! Come and see us! Come and see Mahmoud el-Sherif (former governor of Cairo)! So Essam Fawzi, my partner in the conduct of most of this fieldwork, and I get into the first microbus that passes through el-Hirafiyeen to complete its fare before heading downtown. Seats are filled with big women veiled, sleepy children on laps, and thin, tired men heading back to visit family and friends in downtown neighborhoods from which natural disaster and the state evicted them in 1993. The microbus moves fast but then, as we move into what used to be the heart of the city, where the joyous mood of Ramadan becomes most intense, traffic slows down.

From far away comes the roar of the celebration in Hussein, the neighborhood known to foreigners as Khan el-Khalili. We walk up the street toward the Eastern Cemeteries, toward exhibition halls owned by the governorate. This Ramadan, the halls have been given over to the "Exhibition of the Products of the Youth Micro Industries funded by the Social Fund" (itself an organization funded by the World Bank). Loudspeaker voices boom into the street, in the scratchy sound of the Friday call to prayer. But this time it's a call to build the future through the market and debt. Words call out in steady rhythm: "the banks," "our youth," "social needs," "production." A few steps further, and boom! The lights are blaring, television cameras are running, and men stand gathered under the dyed red colors of tents that imitate the great hand-embroidered craft still practiced by a few old men near Bab Zuwaylah, built by the Fatimids in A.D. 1092, not far from here.

2

Gathered around this impromptu stage were some of my informants from el-Hirafiyeen, including past and present officials of two nongovernmental organizations (NGOS) in town established to support small productive enterprises. Small enterprises are central to Egypt's economy—one estimate put them at 99 percent of private sector economy units in Cairo (World Bank 1994, 3). From the outside those enterprises all look the same. They are small spaces facing the street in which a few men (rarely women) and children work. They are sometimes called microenterprises because they are so small. But few Egyptians would call a workshop (*warsha*) a microenterprise (*mashruʿ saghir*). A microenterprise denotes a place established with loans from development agencies to reduce unemployment, empower the poor, and support the free market. Those funded microenterprises represent a minuscule proportion of Cairo's small enterprises. Most of these places of work are, rather, workshops. A workshop denotes a place run by a man who learned his trade in childhood. A workshop master learned by doing, not from books or in school. Unlike the microenterprise owner, he is not a mere student (*telmidh*). His knowledge resides, as one master put it, in his body and his brain. Workshop masters are by and large deeply integrated into what is known as Egyptian popular culture.

The first of the two NGOS in el-Hirafiyeen had been established by craftsmen moved from other neighborhoods of Cairo. The second NGO had been established for youth graduates (*al-shabab al-kharigiyeen*) who had received loans from the Social Fund for Development to open microenterprises. The president of the youth graduates was the first invited to speak: "We were the children of socialism. We were brought up to go to school and then wait for an appointment from the State. And then structural adjustment hit us. We didn't know what to do at first. We had to learn to depend on ourselves, that we couldn't sit and wait for the State to take care of us, that we had to do something. And that's what we've done. Now, we make things happen for ourselves, we don't wait for someone to come to us. Now, we are the generation of Structural Adjustment." The president of the craftsmen's NGO was next. His speech was filled with flowery reminders of the importance of small craft workshops in the history of Egypt. His talk elicited yawns and sneers. It was not workshops and the popular culture of which they were part that were being celebrated, but rather the values associated with microenterprises—market culture, individualism, and self-discipline. Craftsmen,

3

the ones who had made the goods that marked out the cultural practices of Cairo since its Fatimid rulers built their great gates, had no real place here. The sense that something was off increased when the former governor of Cairo, now a cabinet minister, the very one whom they called the father of el-Hirafiyeen, took his turn to speak. He evoked the vision of the "children of structural adjustment." The previous speaker from the Social Fund had just announced the release of an additional 15 million LE (about $5 million US) given by the World Bank, the EEC, and others for microenterprise projects in Hirafiyeen and elsewhere in Cairo. He too wanted to talk about the young entrepreneurs, whom he compared to the "craftsmen" and for whom he was said to have built that model town. "You young entrepreneurs are not just craftsmen who make a piece of something and that's it. You are small businessmen: You have to learn administration, marketing, how to run a business. And you have to be ready for GATT, when the trade barriers of Egypt will come down."

These "microentrepreneurs" had come into existence as a social group when the World Bank designated a new funding category, and set into motion new hybrid forms of organizational power that stretched the bounds of the state, international organizations, and the NGO.[1] These young microentrepreneurs were to embody the new, vigorous market economy that would take Egypt forward in the era of neoliberalism and the ITO. They were not, the speaker wanted to make clear, the old-style craftsmen of Egypt who "make a piece of something and that's it." Although they had been born to rely on the state, they had reemerged from a chrysalis of debt and training to become entrepreneurs. They would embody the free market.

Rethinking the Market

This book challenges prevailing notions of the market. That task is urgent in an age when the market is so triumphant. By the beginning of the twenty-first century, there was no place devoid of the market. The question of whether the market was a good thing had become politically moot. The market was all there was. Planned socialist economies were, with isolated exceptions, a thing of the past. In these circumstances to challenge the idea of the market became not only urgent but also difficult.

It is always hard to challenge prevailing realities and ideas. But it is especially hard to challenge the idea of the market because it is complicated and contested. That it is contested is important to remember in the face of the apparent unanimity of thinking about the market. I have no intention of covering the entire spectrum of ideas about the market in this book. I do not even intend to cover the spectrum of the best-marketed ideas about the market, or the contests and struggles involved in advocating and implementing those ideas. Instead I will focus on one idea about how to rejuvenate the market and extend its scope. That idea is to reconstitute the social networks and cultural practices of the poor as part of the free market. Networks and practices that used to be seen as lying outside the market (or perhaps as a necessary environment for the market) became a key ingredient of market success.

To my mind, this process of free-market expansion is one of the more important transformations under way in the world today. It is at the center of myriad processes discussed under the rubric of globalization, development, forms of power, and new agencies or subjectivities emerging with the decline of the state-centered political order of the last century. It is at the center of new policies implemented by global powers and organizations such as the World Bank, as well as at the center of anti-globalization movements. In this book, based on my ethnographic research in Cairo, I study the ways in which networks and social practices of the poor have been incorporated into the market. I believe that what I observed there in the mid-1990s was typical of, or at least intimately related to, processes under way in other parts of the world. A comparative project analyzing processes of incorporation in different parts of the world would be of great interest. But already in light of my research in Cairo, I maintain, prevailing ideas of the market can be judged inadequate.

Ideas of the market do not reside in the realm of pure theory. They are practical as well. I will thus show how ideas about extending and rejuvenating the market by incorporating the social networks and cultural practices of the poor have evolved in the context of ongoing social experiments. Those experiments have entailed the implementation of quite practical measures and social technologies. In what follows, it will often be hard to distinguish between what lies on the level of "ideas of the market" and what lies on the level of "market practices." In my view, drawing clear distinctions of that sort is unwise and often unworkable. Ideas about the market are inextricable from the implementation of new social technologies, and the spread of new social practices. In the period covered in this book, market practices of the poor were studied, analyzed, and recreated as raw materials for implementing social experiments. Those experiments then became the subject of social science research. In what follows, I will deal with new ideas about the market on all of the levels that I have discussed. That includes the unintended consequences of a multifaceted endeavor to turn community resources of the poor into a source of profit.

That ideas about the market do not exist in the realm of pure theory is very clear in the Middle East. There the idea of the free market (and of free trade, as in nineteenth-century debates) has long been used to justify the overt use of violence. As one of the oldest and greatest cities of the world, Cairo has witnessed many interventions in the name of the market (Mitchell 2002). The assumption that the Middle East must be opened up to the free market has most recently been used to justify the war on and occupation of Iraq. The Middle East is not unique in this regard. Violence has often lain in the background of efforts to create and maintain free markets around the world. In this book, for example, I will discuss how what Marx referred to as "primitive accumulation," which involves the explicit use of force, is integral to the functioning of the free market. At the same time, the particular way that the free market has been imposed on Iraq is not typical of neoliberalism. The invisible hand of the market is usually imposed not through violence but rather through more subtle processes. In this book I will focus largely on those processes, through which the working poor in Cairo, Harlem, or Lima come to accept one version of the market as the only possible market.

I have said that with regard to the market the question of "whether" had become moot by the end of the twentieth century. At the same time, the question of "which market" had taken on new urgency. The United States and international organizations such as the World Bank and the IMF went to great lengths to impose a specific, neoliberal vision of the free market on other countries. Struggles to resist that vision of the market became more common. In many parts of the world people began to ask: What kind of market do we want? What does the market produce, and for what ends? All this brings to mind the old anthropological literature about markets, which pointed to the existence of many different kinds of markets, with different modes of social integration. Increasingly, such differences among forms of the market took on political import as well.

The Anthropology of Value

I will approach the political import of different kinds of markets by means of the anthropology of value. My approach to value is in the spirit of Chris Hann's call (1998, 32) for an anthropology of value that is not an end in itself but rather is tied into broader debates about power in society. At the same time, I think that Hann was wrong to think that a focus on symbol and meaning is contradictory to an analysis of power or property. There need be no contradiction between the two. The anthropology of value, which has a strong focus on symbolic meaning, can have politics at its center as well (Graeber 2001, 88; Turner 1978; Turner 1979; Myers and Brenneis 1991, 4–5). In my approach to an anthropology of value in Cairo, I draw on the work of Nancy Munn to discuss how the popular classes of Egypt in general, and workshop masters in particular, seek "to create the value [they] regard as essential to [their] community viability" (Munn 1986, 3). Again inspired by Munn, I view that value creation in tandem with "antithetical transformations that, in the perception of the community, specify what undermines this value or define how it *cannot* be realized" (3). I call this value produced in workshop exchanges "relational value," since it expresses the positive value attached to the creation, reproduction, and extension of relationships in communities of Cairo. I argue that workshop masters seek to intensify the production of this value through ongoing exchanges in a spatio-temporal template of their neighborhood, in Cairo, in Egypt, and in some cases throughout the region as a result of cycles of circular migration to the Gulf states. The production of value in workshops is naturalized in metaphors of kinship and a cosmology of the workshop order with deep historical roots. I look at the production of this positive value in tandem with the creation of negative value in workshop life, as embodied in the notion of the evil eye.

In the period that I study in this book, the practices of craftsmen in workshops in Cairo were conceptualized as informal economy, microenterprise, and then social capital. As I have made clear above, those conceptual shifts were not merely a matter of ideas. The conceptual shift—away from the terms in which workshop masters discussed their own networks of exchange (which are deeply rooted in the long history of organized craft production in Egypt), and toward a conceptual system based on the notions of informal economy, microenterprise, and social capital—was part of a broader process of incorporating the social practices of the poor into the free market. I analyze that process of incorporation as simultaneously a process of dispossession. Part of what is being dispossessed, in my view, is the power to decide what matters or, in other terms, what is value.

Systems of categories are, from an anthropological point of view, but one side of a system of action (Graeber 2001, 254). Society itself can be seen as an active project or set of projects. Value, in turn, "is the way actions become meaningful to the actors by being placed in some larger social whole, real or imagined" (254). From this perspective, the incorporative project that I analyze in this book is a struggle over value as well. In what follows, I will analyze the system of categories through which craftsmen in Cairo discuss their exchanges, and show how that system of categories is simultaneously a system of action rooted in a larger, meaningful, social whole. The contours of that larger social whole are rooted in the "popular culture" of Cairo.

The category of "popular culture," or "popular classes," has always been ill defined. What is the relation of the "popular classes" to class structure? How does a category that is expressed through cultural practice, rather than through relations of production, intersect with class. This broad theoretical question is of practical urgency for anyone doing social analysis in Egypt. I believe that an anthropological approach to value could be a fruitful way to address this dilemma. Such an ambitious project is of course a collective one. In this book, what matters is that efforts to reshape the categories through which workshop masters organize their knowledge, action, and meaning in their market life is a highly political undertaking. The politics at stake are about more than money: they are about the power to act and to create meaning as well. They are the politics of value.

In an anthropological approach to value, the reader might have already noticed, the central analytic concept—value—can easily become a metaphor for too many things at the same time. Are we talking about economic value, cultural values, or moral values? It is easy for those three to become murky. That is a pity. Value in politics, value in ethics, and value in economy are different things; the distinctions among them should, and can, be upheld. The distinctions matter in this book in particular, because of the strange ways in which these different kinds of value have been bound together in the subject matter of this book. In it

I show how an attempt to extract new *economic* value has been carried out by transforming social networks and culture *into* value. (A term used by Marx, *Verwertung*, which can be translated as "making-into-value," is useful here.) This process of extracting new economic value by transforming culture into value, or making-into-value, has been marketed, moreover, *in terms* of value. This time I refer to value as ethical value. For the incorporation of social networks into the free market has usually been presented as a matter of bringing new ethics to the (willing) victims of the project. Adapting to the market has been presented as an ethical imperative. Broad political support, from surprising circles, has been given to a project of squeezing more value out of the as yet unexploited cultural possessions of the poor. Since there is "value" involved in all the aspects of the story I am telling here (even if—analytically speaking— they are not the same kind of value), it is important to keep these distinctions in mind.

I will argue that the value produced in workshops of Cairo became of immense importance in the late twentieth century. That importance was, first, strategic. In conditions of structural adjustment where jobs and futures were no longer being provided by the state to citizens of poor countries around the world, social scientists and development planners realized that important sectors of the population could be left to take care of themselves. A talent for self-help among the poor could no longer be neglected. Those who had to survive on their own and would be cast to the mercies of the market were reconfigured as a sector of the economy. They became "the informal economy." The most important thing they produced was survival itself.

The discovery of the strategic importance of this survival capacity of the working poor in the workshops of Cairo and sister megacities around the globe added a new dimension to workshop production. The value rooted in the networks of sociality and ongoing exchange among the poor acquired new meaning. Developments in the social sciences facilitated the theorization of this value in terms of social capital. Social capital came to be viewed as indispensable to economic success. It became central to ideas about the market in general. Social practices that had been a local resource for survival, and had often been viewed as an obstacle to economic development, were now seen, in the guise of social capital, as a resource for reproducing global markets, maintaining global stability, and achieving economic growth.

9

The conceptual transformation of social networks among the poor into an economic resource for capital entails, I have said, a process of dispossession. A vast amount of labor is involved in persuading people that they should embrace markets of dispossession. The ethnographic field through which I studied that vast project included the work of social scientists such as anthropologists, sociologists, and economists, and the labor of officials and clerks of states and international organizations. It included a broad set of material devices and organizational forms such as NGOs, new state ministries, bank departments, training sessions, and financial devices.

NGOs, the Evil Eye, and Neoliberalism

Social experiments lead to unexpected outcomes. Attempts to incorporate the social networks and cultural practices of the poor into the market as a source of profit have unexpected outcomes as well. In Cairo one of those outcomes was a striking convergence between neoliberal market visions and evil eye beliefs.[2] Such a convergence might be surprising. The two would seem to be miles apart. The evil eye is usually seen as part of popular religion or superstition. But the evil eye is as integral to workshop markets as money or a craftsman's tools. Attacks of the evil eye among craftsmen mark their victims as selfish pursuers of short-term gain. The evil eye marks out those who neglect the production of positive relational value and concentrate only on individual, immediate gain. The very behaviors that provoked the evil eye in workshop markets were actively being promulgated by NGOs in el-Hirafiyeen.

The NGOs that I discuss in this book were of a particular kind. They were established for the market. Such NGOs are quite common. Around the world, NGOs are established to provide small loans for microenterprises. They usually provide training to member entrepreneurs in marketing, accounting, and banking. Usually they promote a view of the market as a potential ally of the poor. The Grameen Bank of Bangladesh is probably the most famous purveyor of this NGO model. In practice, as others have noted, NGOs do not always serve the interests of the poorest members of their communities. In the NGO of workshop masters in el-Hirafiyeen, this was certainly the case.

This NGO was an organization through which wealthy members of the community could intensify their pursuit of individual short-term gain.

10

Through the NGO, wealthy masters could pursue contacts with officials in the local government; those contacts were necessary for their economic expansion. The meaning of the NGO in the community, in other words, was quite different from that advanced by Appadurai, who has argued for the importance of NGOS as a site of "grassroots globalization" (Appadurai 2000). Rather than oppose the "capital-state nexus" (Appadurai 2000), NGOS in el-Hirafiyeen furthered it. NGOS facilitated individual projects to extract rents in the name of informal economy and microenterprise, and to forge exchange relations with local state officials. Those projects sometimes went awry. Modes of negative value production associated with the NGO could elicit a strike of the evil eye, or the eruption of a scandal (*fadiha*) that would wipe out the positive value production marked in the community by the "name" or personality of the workshop master. Attacks of the evil eye had material effects—masters got into car accidents, lost customers, and saw their workshops mysteriously go up in fire.

This individualized agent of short-term gain in the marketplace was exactly the subjectivity being advanced during my fieldwork in the name of the free market. The group called the "youth graduates," around which NGOS were organized, was supposed to embody that subjectivity of the invisible hand and the market. The members of the "generation of structural adjustment" had been designated by the World Bank, and adopted by the state, as dynamic agents of entrepreneurship. But the kind of market they were meant to foster was an abstraction to which they could not sell. They searched for "the market" but could rarely find it. With few exceptions, they could not create the kind of markets crafted by their neighbors. Their enterprises failed. The microenterprise experiment in Cairo—of which el-Hirafiyeen was repeatedly claimed a centerpiece—was thus often deemed a failure.

Development organizations tried to learn the lessons of those failures and to improve their efforts to instill the market through debt and education. During my fieldwork, for example, my informants in development agencies and NGOS were concerned to begin teaching their borrowers about marketing. An earlier generation of NGO funders had not thought much about the market—they had focused on loans and production. And yet the extensive failure of the microenterprise project was itself productive. It provided an endless stream of rents to officials of all the NGOS, international organizations (IOs), and state organizations involved. Even more, it produced a widespread sense that what had failed was something specific to Egypt—the youth were lazy, the officials were corrupt, the banks were too rigid, and marketing had been neglected. It was not the market that was flawed—Egypt was flawed. A more critical observer might say that development was flawed. Every failure, in other words, reinforced the power of the free market.

Egypt for the Egyptians or Backwards Culture?

Contests over markets have a long history in Egypt. Foreigners were granted immense economic privileges in Egypt centuries before formal occupation of the country. Long-standing arrangements between the Ottoman Porte and western powers, called the "capitulations," became more extensive and widespread in 1740. Under the regime of capitulations, foreigners in Ottoman lands had been exempted from most forms of local property law. Local non-Muslims, moreover, were often granted certificates of protection (*berats*), which accorded to most of them the privileges of foreign nationals. The Ottoman Public Debt Administration, established in 1881, gave European holders of Ottoman bonds property rights over important tax revenues in the region until the debt was repaid. Egypt was forced to accept a similar scheme in 1876. Also in Egypt, "mixed courts" arbitrated all property disputes in which foreigners or holders of berats were involved—a regime that only ended together with the capitulations in 1937.

Ongoing resentment about foreign exploitation of the local economy took new expression at the beginning of the twentieth century, when 'Abdallah al-Nadim and others conceptualized local markets as a bulwark of defense against foreign occupation. The market, in this view, was not an abstract place where strangers met to buy and sell. It marked out a space of Egyptian cultural practice that included language, forms of production, and patterns of consumption. This is well illustrated in one issue of *al-Ustadh*, a newspaper founded by al-Nadim, in which he describes the rich texture of traditional Egyptian life, in all its social and economic aspects (al-Nadim 1994). He presents a vision of the market as the material crystallization of traditional modes of urban and rural life in Egypt. His lucid writing traces the movement of commodities throughout Egypt, from the workshops where they were produced to the homes where they were consumed. By following the movement of commodities, al-Nadim draws a spatial image of the market as a set of practices. We see the markets in which the craftsmen make and sell their products, and the interactions between those who sell and those who buy. We move with the products to the houses where they are consumed, through the villages and towns of Egypt, in a vivid map of a national market that must be preserved against colonial domination, together with the Arabic language and the cultural identity of Egyptians.

After the British occupied Egypt in 1882 to crush the 'Urabi rebellion of which al-Nadim was a leader, Lord Cromer became the effective ruler of Egypt until 1907 (although the Ottoman Empire retained nominal sovereignty). For him those indigenous market practices were something that progress and free trade—imposed with the help of British rule—would sweep away. An outspoken defender of the doctrine of "free trade" who is often blamed for blocking the development of local industry in Egypt (Vitalis 1995, 39–40), Cromer welcomed the destruction of the "native trades" at the hands of progress. In one often-cited report, he lists the many occupations that were steadily collapsing because of cheap imports, infrastructural change, shifting consumption patterns, the competition of European subject artisans in Egypt, and the "lethargy" and "fatalism" of the indigenous traders themselves. "Quarters that were formerly hives of busy workmen—spinning, weaving, braiding, tassel making, dyeing, tent-making, embroidering, slipper making, gold and silver working, spice crushing, copper beating, water skin making, saddle making, sieve making, wooden-bolt making, lock making, etc. have shrunk to attenuated proportions or have been entirely obliterated. Cafés and small stores retailing European wares are now to be found where productive workshops formerly existed" (United Kingdom, House of Commons, 1906, 572).

Cromer welcomed shifts in the consumption patterns of Egyptians from local workshop commodities to those produced by European capitalist firms as a sign of progress. According to the historian Roger Owen, Cromer made many statements that contradicted his more famous quote (personal communication, 3 April 2001), and by the end of his rule he was willing to compromise on free trade enough to intervene in behalf of joint venture sugar-refineries (Owen 1969, 343–44; see also Vitalis 1995, 39–40). But his views against the traditional native trades, and thus workshops, remain a vital illustration of how economic theories of free trade helped legitimize British informal colonial rule.[3] Al-Nadim argued for the importance of local markets as a way to defend Egypt for the Egyptians; Cromer welcomed their decline as a sign of progress. But despite the expectations of Lord Cromer, workshops and local market practices did not disappear with "modernization." Nor did they help form the basis for defending Egypt for the Egyptians, as hoped by al-Nadim.

On the level of policy making, however, Cromer was victorious. Economic policy in Egypt, at least since the British occupation of 1882, was defined in terms of "modern" forms of economic activity in which large industry was central, and the market was guided by either the invisible hand or the state. Historiography reflected that bias.[4] Workshops and the craftsmen who ran them were considered traditional and backward. The markets that craftsmen made were small, local, and insignificant. Of course "traditional crafts" were not completely ignored and were occasionally the subject of study and discussion, even under British rule (Koptiuch 1999, 82–86; Lockman ed. 1994). But in modernist projects to build national economy, from whatever political perspective, modern industry and national markets were seen as essential for national development.[5] Modernization theory after the Second World War only consolidated the trend. The political project of modernization around the world underplayed indigenous cultural practices, which were usually seen as an obstacle to development. In a period of modernization and nation-state building, craftsmen, the workshop, and workshop markets became identified with what was backward and thus needed to be overcome for Egypt to become part of the "modern world." By the same token, historians of labor in Egypt focused on workers in large-scale industries, and tended to see craftsmen as the remnants of a decaying past that would inevitably collapse in the face of modernization and progress.[6]

As such, while it did not disappear in practice, the workshop was marginal to dominant discourses of economy and the market in Egypt through most of the twentieth century. Consistent arguments for indigenous forms of economic practice and local market models would not rise to prominence again until the discussions of "informal economy" in the 1970s.[7] In the 1980s the focus then shifted to "microenterprise" as a way to talk about workshops in Egypt. With that move, economic practices characteristic of the workshop were given full recognition as a legitimate mode of economic activity, not as a block to economic development.

At the beginning of the twenty-first century, in other words, Cromer's conviction that indigenous economic practices were antithetical to progress had been decisively refuted. Local economic practices as a wellspring of cultural strength and independence came, once again, to be explicitly defended. But this time, not as a way to defend Egypt for the Egyptians, as hoped for by al-Nadim, but as a way of maintaining global economic order. This time, local practices were championed by IOs eager to benefit from indigenous cultural practices, and international development experts who saw in those practices a new form of "social capital." Workshops, and the social networks in which they were embedded, came to be highly valued and emulated as well. A new field of power had emerged in which a direct link was being forged among the economic practices of marginal groups, NGOs, states, and IOs like the World Bank, through the mediation of finance and debt.[8] Shared among the actors was talk of the market.

Ethnography of the Market and the Invisible Hand

The notion of the market is so familiar that we tend to take it for granted. But like so many things we take for granted, we don't really know what it is. "The market" functions as a folk concept more than a scientific term. The folk concept of the market is intimately connected to the image of the invisible hand. The connection functions as a central trope in popular thinking and talking about the market. But sometimes power is mobilized in quite visible ways in the name of the market and the invisible hand. Moving toward "the market" is a political goal in the name of which invasions are launched and regimes overthrown. The end of communism was supposed to lead to the triumph of the market; the spread of the WTO is supposed to lead to open markets; development projects carried out by bilateral and multilateral funders are supposed to improve the functioning of the market; the invasion of Iraq was supposed to bring free markets and thus democracy to the Middle East.

In this book, I take on prevalent images of the market through my ethnographic research in Cairo. My research focused on the neighborhood of el-Hirafiyeen, which was built for workshops and their markets. El-Hirafiyeen was a virtual laboratory in which contrasting views of "the market" were set into motion: those of the workshop masters, those enacted through microenterprise, and those grounded in a more community-oriented idea of the informal economy. It was a place where abstract concepts of "the state," "the World Bank," "IOs," and "the informal economy" appeared as concrete actors. Carrying out ethnographic research in this context required the study of many institutional powers interacting in one site. Following the evolution of el-Hirafiyeen, as it was constructed by the state as a site for small workshops, and then adopted by the World Bank Social Fund as a home for its microenterprise project, offered a valuable environment in which to interrogate the usefulness of common binary oppositions of global and local, state and nonstate, IO and NGO. In this light, el-Hirafiyeen functioned in two ways as a field site. It was a local community of the traditional kind studied by anthropologists since the "Malinowskian revolution."[9] But it was also a locality that was useful as a "strategically situated single site ethnography" (Marcus 1998, 95). This community was formed by decisions of both the state and IOs, exercising their power to set the rules of the game for social action. As that new community became a reality, it was reshaped by the actions of individuals within those institutions—and those affected by their decisions—leading to a set of outcomes quite different from those planned. El-Hirafiyeen could thus also be a starting point for a different kind of "multi-sited ethnography" (Marcus 1998, 95). From the site of this one small part of Cairo, I had to "study up" (Nader 1969) the various institutions—of the state, IOs, and NGOs—that were implicated in producing and reproducing this one locality. And, likewise, I had to "study down" how the intentions of states and IOs were subverted by the objects of large institutions' development actions. As Sally Falk Moore has argued, fieldwork about attempts to "plan the future" must look at far more than just the intended effects of states or IOs. An "extended milieu" that includes unintended impacts must be part of the story as well (Moore 2005).

There are other reasons for the importance of an ethnography of this neighborhood. El-Hirafiyeen was designated a home base of the Social Fund, established by the World Bank. Seeing what happened there, and contrasting the results with the happy pictures of the Social Fund's or World Bank's development reports, can tell us much about the nature—and limits—of tactical and structural power. Many issues other than those which planners of the state, or the World Bank had thought through come to the fore in the actual practice of development projects. The forces that are out of their control are myriad and must form the subject of our research together with—not marginalized from—an ethnography of the state or IO.

My paths of movement to study the market experiments carried out in el-Hirafiyeen went well outside the bounds of this small community, into bank offices, consulting firms, office buildings, NGOS, and the neighborhoods from which masters had been moved into el-Hirafiyeen. Only thus could I study the intensive labor involved in creating markets. The immense labor involved in the multiple and contrasting projects to construct markets that I found over the course of my fieldwork provides a marked contrast to pervasive images of the market as a given, thanks to the invisible hand and the human "propensity to truck, barter, and exchange one thing for another" (Smith 1976b, I:25).[10]

The Invisible Hand in the Heavens and on Earth

The notion of the invisible hand, I have said, is a central folk concept of our times. "Adam Smith's ideas have had odd secular destinies, and the twentieth century was the epoch of the invisible hand" (Rothschild 1991, 116). Economists have claimed that the invisible hand is "surely the most important contribution [of] economic thought to the understanding of social processes." In the words of James Tobin, it is "one of the great ideas of history and one of the most influential."[11]

But what is the invisible hand? Despite a wealth of new work in anthropology that involves rethinking the market, finance, and economy, there has been little discussion of this central term around which the politics of the market have been shaped. The secular manifest destiny of the invisible hand, it turns out, does not have its origins in the practical matters of the market that we usually associate with the grandfather of neoclassical economics. In fact Adam Smith first used the term "the invisible hand" in "The History of Astronomy" (III.2). In the relevant passage he is not discussing market life but witches, demons, savages, heathens, and the god Jupiter: "vulgar superstition. . . . ascribes all the irregular events of nature to the favour or displeasure of intelligent, though invisible beings, to gods, daemons, witches, genii, fairies. For it may be observed, that in all Polytheistic relations, among savages, as well as in the early ages of Heathen antiquity, it is the irregular events of nature only that are ascribed to the agency and power of their gods. Fire burns, and water refreshes; heavy bodies descend, and lighter substances fly upwards, by the necessity of their own nature; nor was the invisible hand of Jupiter ever apprehended to be employed in those matters" (Smith 1980, 49).[12]

In *The Theory of Moral Sentiments* (1759), his first book, Smith turns to more earthly matters. He condemns the "natural selfishness and rapacity" of the rich and their tendency to "only select from the heap what is most precious and agreeable"; the "sole end which they propose from the labours of all the thousands whom they employ, be the gratification of their own vain and insatiable desire." And yet, in a famous passage, he notes that the rich "are led by an invisible hand to make nearly the same distribution of the necessaries of life, which would have been made, had the earth been divided into equal portions among all its inhabitants, and thus without intending it, without knowing it, advance the interest of the society, and to the multiplication of the species" (Smith 1976a, 184–85).

The invisible hand seemed to descend from the skies as the solution to a divine predicament: when "providence divided the earth among a few lordly masters," what would happen to those "who seemed to have been left out in the partition" (Smith 1976a, 185)? In this passage Smith refers to a key debate in the tradition of natural jurisprudence philosophers framed by Aquinas, who "set the terms of the argument on the origins and limits of property right in the grain-trade debates of mid-eighteenth century Catholic Europe" (Hont and Ignatieff 1983, 26). For Aquinas, the world was God's property and had been given to the human species for collective stewardship. This was the first "competence" of humans as trustees of the world's resources. Private property was legitimate as a second "competence" of human beings to care for and distribute those resources, since it is under private possession that "each person takes more trouble to care for something that is his sole responsibility than what is held in common by many."[13] According to Hont and Ignatieff, the history of European natural law "can be understood as a series of attempts to re-arrange the elements of the puzzle left by Aquinas" (27). How could the rights of private property be reconciled with the rights of the poor to reclaim their original share in the community of goods in a time of famine? Could those rights to the original share override the rights of private property? This moral dilemma, which is understood in the western tradition as stemming from God's donation of the world in exclusive dominion to Adam and his heirs, and subsequent individuation which "made possible a responsible and productive management of God's estate," was central to the evolution of natural jurisprudence (Hont and Ignatieff 1983, 42).

The Wealth of Nations is usually placed in a genealogy of the history of economic thought and read in relation to economic pamphlets circulating in the 1690s (Hont and Ignatieff 1983, 42). But the central question of The Wealth of Nations is not economic. The book is an attempt to solve the problems set out in Smith's earlier work of moral philosophy.[14] It grows out of Smith's immersion in debates of moral philosophy about the rights of private property versus the rights of the excluded. Smith sought to transcend the terms of that debate in The Wealth of Nations by "finding a market mechanism capable of reconciling inequality of property with adequate provision for the excluded" (Hont and Ignatieff 1983, 2). He did so by arguing for the possibility of an "economy of abundance" (2) in which application of the division of labor would provide plenty for all. In that economy of abundance in commercial society, a "workman, even of the lowest and poorest order," could enjoy "a greater share of the necessaries and conveniences of life than it is possible for any savage to acquire" (Smith 1976b, I:10). Smith's constitutive move in the making of classical political economy, whereby the division of labor overcomes the lack of abundance in society from which those moral dilemmas sprang, did not grow out of his reading of economic pamphlets.

The story I have just told complicates popular images of Smith and the invisible hand, images that have been so important in justifying western interventions into the Middle East in the name of the market. Let me complicate that picture a bit further. The formative debates of western philosophy that shaped Adam Smith cannot be confined to the West. They were formed within a discursive universe in which Islamic philosophy was central.[15] Aquinas posed the puzzle that moral philosophy would attempt to unravel through to Smith. But Aquinas's thought was deeply shaped by Islamic philosophy, notably the work of the philosopher ibn Rushd, also known as Averroes and often simply as "the commentator," so famous and important were his commentaries on Aristotle.[16] Ibn Rushd was the most important Islamic philosopher of his time, and his translations of Aristotle and commentaries on his work were central to the formation of western political thought. In the words of Alasdair MacIntyre, "the encounter of Islam with Aristotle provides the crucial background to thirteenth-century European intellectual history" (MacIntyre 1990,105). Concepts of the free market and the invisible hand, in sum, are deeply enmeshed in a broader intellectual climate in which "the West" cannot be opposed to "the Islamic world."

Throughout this book, I will place concepts such as the invisible hand, social capital, and the informal economy in the context of the broader web of thought in which they are rooted, to see the very practical measures and actions to which they are linked. Already we can see that the concept of the invisible hand is not part of a recipe book for how to grow markets. Instead these concepts are enmeshed in broader networks of thought that are implicated in the development of specific kinds of expertise and knowledge forms.

In the course of my fieldwork, I found that lending programs to the "informal economy" and supporting microenterprise in Cairo in the 1990s were a very Smithian exercise. But the Smith whom they invoke is not a comic-book hero of the free market. Lending programs to the informal economy and microenterprise did not implant robust neoclassical subjectivities loath to rely on the state. They were a new attempt to square the circle that Smith thought he had transcended once and for all: how can a system of private property rights be reconciled with the moral rights of the poor to survive? In *The Wealth of Nations* the solution was simple: given the application of the division of labor in commercial society, an economy of plenty would overcome the contradiction between these two forms of rights. In programs for the informal economy, the cultural practices of the poor were reformulated as robust market activity. Once again, the market became an all-encompassing device of positive moral attributes.

In the story told by Smith, the state was the category against which the market had to gain its freedom. The two volumes of *The Wealth of Nations* are often concerned with oppressive state measures that impede the workings of the market and imperil the pure rights of property.[17] In the 1990s, however, the state was not the sole "container of power" relevant to the problem of reconciling the private property rights of the wealthy with the need of the poor to survive.[18] IOs and NGOs were central to that exercise as well. As with the political economists of the twentieth century (Perelman 2000), reconceptualizing the market to economize practices once denigrated as backwards culture did not proceed in the realm of pure theory. Anthropology was central to the endeavor.

20

The Gift and the Market in the Middle East

Anthropology's special expertise was, for some time, the gathering of knowledge about primitive society. That image of primitive society, as I have already indicated, was important in foundational texts of the market in the West as well. Smith first used the phrase "invisible hand," the reader may recall, in a discussion of primitive society. Later, he opened *The Wealth of Nations* with the following paradox: How was it that a "workman, even of the lowest and poorest order" in England could enjoy "a greater share of the necessaries and conveniences of life than it is possible for any savage to acquire"? (Smith 1976b, I:10). In commercial society, an "industrious and frugal peasant" lived better than an "African king, the absolute master of the lives and liberties of 10,000 naked savages" (Smith 1976b, I:23–24). The image of "primitive society" in the Americas was central to thinking about property and the market in the eighteenth century. "Savage kings" in American and African colonies of Great Britain were seen to preside over a wealth of natural resources in a condition of indolence.

Such images merged with a longer experience in England of commerce during the Moghul and Ottoman Empires. The Levant Company, to cite just the institutional structures for that commerce, was founded in England in 1583 (Wood 1964). The experiences in the Levant and India were part of, not external to, the formation of what became political economy (Elyachar 1991), as can be seen by reading the works of such political economists as Nassau Senior and Robert Malthus.[19] The image of the Indian prince or the Turkish king often served the same function as that of the African king in foundational texts of western social theory. In an economic pamphlet of John Locke's day, for example, one finds the following: "Among the wild Indians of America, almost every thing is the labourer's, 99 parts of a 100 are to be put upon the account of Labour. In England perhaps the Labourer has but 2/3 of all the conveniences of Life, but then the Plenty of these Things is so much greater here that a King of India is not so well lodg'd and fed and cloathed as a Day Labourer of England."[20]

Those primitive societies that form the backdrop to Locke and Smith were the places that would become the province of anthropologists. In anthropology they came to the foreground alongside the "archaic societies" that Mauss studied together with the primitive.[21] They did so in a period very different from that of *The Wealth of Nations*. The rise of commercial society had been superseded as a subject of debate by the need to assuage the ill effects of a firmly entrenched capitalist economic system. The invisible hand, which was invented with the image of primitive society in the backdrop, itself became a backdrop for thinking about primitive society. This can perhaps be seen most clearly in the foundational text of the gift, by Marcel Mauss, first published in 1925 (Mauss 1990). In primitive society, according to Mauss, "exchanges and contracts take place in the form of presents; in theory these are voluntary, in reality they are given and reciprocated obligatorily" (Mauss 1990, 3). Mauss newly recognized that "one section of humanity, comparatively rich, hard-working, and creating considerable surpluses, has known how to, and still does know how to, exchange things of great value, under different forms and for reasons different from those with which we are familiar" (33).

Different as the logics of gift exchange may be from market society as analyzed by Mauss, Malinowski, and others, the theory of the gift was a direct echo of Smith's invisible hand, "in so far as it operates where the latter is absent" (Douglas 1990, xiv). The gift cycle became the "theoretical counterpart to the invisible hand" (xiv). Lying behind both concepts—the gift and the invisible hand—is, Annette Weiner has argued, a shared assumption of reciprocity. In her view, an assumption shared in political philosophy from Hobbes to Locke to Smith is that reciprocity is a fundamental principle of human society. In debates of the eighteenth century about the free market, that assumption was cited "to justify the rise of a free-market economy without state interventions" (Weiner 1992, 28). In the twentieth century that same assumption of reciprocity was seen as the essence of what made primitive society work. Malinowski, we are reminded by Weiner, never resolved for himself "the dilemma of whether Trobrianders (and by extension, all 'primitives') represented the alter ego or the antithesis of Western *Homo oeconomicus*" (Weiner 1992, 31). In his ethnography, "custom" becomes the driving force in the prevailing norm of reciprocity (31).

"Custom" has often been seen as the driving force of life in the Middle East as well as honor and religion. Thus, for example, in anthropology the Middle East was long associated with three theoretical concerns: Islam, segmentation, and the harem (Abu-Lughod 1989). Economic anthropology of the Middle East barely exists (Elyachar 2005). This neglect is all the more striking when we recall the region's importance in the genesis of commercial society in England, let alone the long history of markets in the Middle East. The Middle East was globalized long before globalization; circuits of migration for pilgrimage and labor have inscribed the region since the rise of Islam; markets are highly monetized and have been for millennia. The long history of cities, markets, and complex economies in the region might suggest that economics rather than economic anthropology would be the dominant theoretical paradigm. However, in both urban and rural settings in the Middle East the gift and nonmonetary exchanges are crucial to the economy writ large. Economic interest does not stand starkly revealed in ways assumed by economic theory and the principle of *homo economicus*. Exchanges of gifts, in the broadest anthropological sense, can be central to market as well as social life. In other words, in the economies of the Middle East both the "gift" and the "commodity" are relevant and intertwined. These points should not be taken to indicate Middle Eastern exceptionalism, however. I am suggesting instead that taking on the theoretical challenges in the Middle East can contribute to the broader project of rethinking the market and the nature of market society in the era of neoliberalism, when the name of Adam Smith and the image of the invisible hand have been so important the world round.

The Work of Making Markets

The idea that markets are a spontaneous outcome of the instinct to truck, barter, and exchange should have disappeared in the 1990s after the collapse of communism in the Soviet Union and Eastern Europe. Scholars who studied the region in the 1990s began to shed light on the work of making markets, and the power relations that this work involves (Stark and Bruszt 1998, Mandel and Humphrey 2002, Humphrey 1996–97, Verdery 1998, Buraway and Verdery 1999). The lessons they had to teach have implications far beyond the countries that emerged from behind the iron curtain. Transition from socialism was supposed to be a transition to "market society." But it turned out that there was no there there. "Market society" as such did not exist. In its place hybrids emerged in which property was a "recombinet" that drew together elements of various property regimes and forms of markets from the remnants of the old system (Stark 1998, 128). Forms of the market that did emerge, moreover, were so diverse that not only "market society" but even a unitary "post-socialism" came to seem like misleading terms (Mandel and Humphrey 2002, 2–3). As Roy Dilley pointed out in 1992, there is no such thing as "the market" outside specific historical circumstances in specific countries and cultures (Dilley 1992, Mandel and Humphreys 2002). If there was an invisible hand, then it was quite a bricoleur, combining elements of diverse origins in new and unexpected fashion. Rather than the market, we need to think about a multiplicity of markets that are the outcomes of specific forms of labor, culture, technological mixes, and modes of organization specific to time and place (Callon 1998). The old anthropological adage that economy is embedded in society (Polanyi 1957c) is thus not of great help.

Market economies are at least as embedded in the social sciences. Accounting and finance have often been bracketed off from the more prestigious field of economics, just as "development" has been bracketed off from the more prestigious field of anthropology (Peters 1996; Ferguson and Gupta 1997). But once practical subdisciplines are included inside the definition of what a discipline such as economics or anthropology is, we gain a far richer picture of what the social sciences do. For social science includes the implantation, as well as the conceptual theorization, of social technologies that shape subjectivities and have practical effects in the organization of knowledge and the channeling of financial resources. As has been pointed out by Nikolas Rose, the calculative regimes of accounting and finance are central to the governing of advanced liberal democracies (Rose 1996, 54). Those calculative regimes have to be installed and internalized.

The labor of making particular forms of markets is also the labor of politics. It is about power. Attempts to teach the poor of Cairo to budget their time and money with more streamlined methods resembling those of capitalist firms, and to learn accounting, "the language of business" (Davidson, Schindler, and Weil 1982), are more than ethnographic anomalies. They are attempts to reshape the nature of power and subjectivities as well as to create particular forms of markets. Too often, the question of power is missing from the new research on markets inspired by Callon. What forms of power are involved in the work of making markets? How do the form and content of markets and economies in the Middle East affect thinking about the market in general? What can we learn about the market in a context where concepts such as honor and the gift have been assumed to be more pervasive than economic rationality? How does the labor that goes into making "the gift" affect our thinking about the labor of making economies? How can we study in a unified fashion practices that we have tended to associate with the market on the one hand and the gift on the other?

Once we remember that there is no great divide between societies of the gift and those of the market, it is possible to think more creatively about how groups actually do exchange in and out of markets. We can turn to the different kind of "calculative agencies" (Callon 1998) that exist in market and gift exchange as well. Egyptian craftsmen are by definition involved in markets, they sell their services for money, they produce commodities, and they hire wage labor. And yet their exchanges with one another and with their neighbors invoke modalities of gift exchange. Workshop masters are constantly engaged in giving. That giving does not include the exchange of money. It emphasizes people and relations more than things, but it is certainly calculative. The calculative agencies are highly sophisticated. They are enmeshed in distinct modalities of power and value creation within craftsmen's communities. They lie outside the market as it was defined until recently but are essential to the masters' success in the market. Calculative agencies of the gift do not take away from the calculative agencies of traditional market exchanges. Craftsmen are emphatic that this is so, and their practice bears them out.

These calculative agencies can be analyzed in connection with the various networks of workshop life. The markets of workshop masters can usefully be conceived of as networks, or as actor-networks, despite all the problems with that term (Latour 1999; Law 1999). Masters talk about their markets as literal extensions of their selves. As such, an actor-network perspective is extremely useful for understanding how it is that markets are created among workshop masters. It is also useful for understanding the nature of networks among workshop masters, and for understanding how those networks can be transformed into something quite different when joined to NGOs and IOs and infused with finance originating in global financial institutions.

The Centrality of Marginality in the Age of the NGO

Consider the following scenes from my fieldwork in Cairo. A group of men in their thirties, become "youth" by virtue of having received loans for "youth microenterprise" from the Social Fund funded by the World

Bank, sit in the office of a closed-down workshop, figuring out how to establish a new NGO that could outmaneuver their competitors for influence with state officials and funding from the World Bank and other donors. Meanwhile, the sister of a workshop owner mobilizes her neighbors and kids to hunt up women—wives, sisters, workers—for a women's NGO meeting, at which women to be empowered in the informal sector of Upper Egypt will be "trained" by women in the neighborhood for the benefit of bilateral and IO funders.

In another part of Cairo, an official of the governorate mediates between the head of a mosque (another state official) and one of the youth NGO leaders from el-Hirafiyeen about governorate land recently allotted for a marketing center for youth microenterprise products subsidized by NGOs and IOs, but now squatted on by an official state mosque. The solution includes putting the state mosque official on the NGO. In a consulting office that is also home to a few Egyptian NGOs in an élite Cairo neighborhood, a microenterprise consultant complains about the state of the state in Egypt and lauds the situation in Latin America, where microenterprise opened the way to peace, and where after ten years of banking sponsored by IOs and NGOs put money in people's pockets, the power base of the informal economy has taken off and the state has come down. In a downtown hotel, trainers from the U.S. Agency for International Development (USAID), some on leave from their main work teaching America's poor to open up microenterprises in their homes, teach a group of Arab NGO leaders that the family is a microenterprise, the homeworker an entrepreneur, and microenterprise the way forward to a strong civil society independent of the state.

What draws together these seemingly disparate ethnographic moments? None seem to have anything to do with workshops or the common images of craftsmen in medieval Cairo producing traditional items for sale. These moments mark, rather, the genesis of a new field of power set into motion when IOs studied the social realities of Cairene workshops, called them "the informal economy," and set out to promote that informal economy with new funding and a new set of organizing concepts. In that vision of society, finance channeled by international financial organizations (IFOs) and bilateral development institutions would directly engage "the people" in relations of debt. That debt would "set free" the social networks and practices through which the poor had survived in the margins of national economy. The proletariat of old had been created when rural and urban freeholders were set free from their autonomous relations to the means of production. Now the proletariat was being set free from its subsumption to capital and recreated as microentrepreneurs. This liberation was also from the national economy that had been built up by the state over the course of the twentieth century. National economy was being dismantled by structural adjustment policies (SAPs) that were being enforced by those same IFOs who wanted to empower the poor through debt and microenterprise. Indigenous economic practices of the poor had lain in the remote margins of modernist images of national economy. Now those practices were being dusted off to assume central place in a new political economy of Egypt. Previously marginalized economic practices had a new political value in the era of neoliberalism. The "generation of structural adjustment" was being taught to fend for itself. Survival strategies were given a morally uplifting cast. Through the mediation of NGOs, through new instruments of debt, and through social technologies to foster social capital, and in a larger climate where financial and economic discipline were being imposed by international financial organizations and the state, those cultural resources and survival strategies were integrated into the core of global political economy through the financialization of indigenous social practices. The social theorist David Harvey has recently characterized such processes as "accumulation by dispossession" (Harvey 2003).

In the first volume of Marx's *Capital*, the concept of primitive accumulation refers to the state's use of direct force to evict peasants from their land and separate them from ownership of their means of production. The chapter titled "The So-Called Primitive Accumulation" illustrates the processes through which vast numbers of peasants and townspeople are turned into a landless proletariat, "free" to sell their labor-power to capitalists for a wage. Marx coined the term "primitive accumulation" in response to Adam Smith's "original accumulation." Marx wanted to refute Smith's claim that capital accumulation was set into motion through the previous savings of the capitalist. He emphasized instead the centrality of the direct use of violence and forced dispossession to create the conditions necessary for capitalist production in England. As independent ways to survive outside market relations grew more scarce, along with alternatives to wage labor, proletarianized workers were forced into ever deteriorating working conditions and conditions of life. Those deteriorating conditions were extremely profitable for the emerging bourgeoisie of England.

This process of primitive accumulation also entailed the commoditization of what the anthropologist Annette Weiner has called "inalienable possessions"—possessions that bear collective identity and meaning. Land, the foremost of these possessions, was commoditized through the forcible conversion of "the commons" into the private property of wealthy individuals.[22] As such, primitive accumulation was not an economic or even political process alone. From an anthropological point of view, we can see how it undermined historically constituted forms of collective identity and cosmology as well.

Marx's chapter on "the so-called primitive accumulation" is one of the more historically oriented chapters of the first volume of *Capital*. In a book in which mode of presentation is central to communicating theoretical argument, the discursive tone of the chapter is striking. Primitive accumulation lies at the margins of Marx's analytic frame. Throughout, there seem to be two arguments: first, that violent dispossession is central to capitalist reproduction, and second, that primitive accumulation is part of the past, not the present, of capitalism (Perelman 2000). In that second, more dominant argument, in the same vein as the Adam Smith whom Marx is critiquing, primitive accumulation appears as the "original sin" of capitalism that gets the system going. Once that engine is going, the violence that lies at the heart of exploitation under capitalism becomes hidden under a veneer of legality enforced through the state and its regulation of the key commodities of labor power and money.

More recently two important books have renewed the debate about primitive accumulation (Perelman 2000; Harvey 2003). Those books were published in a climate in which a term on the margins of theorizing in Smith and Marx seemed to be moving to the center of political debate. The political activist and writer Arundhati Roy (2001), in a reference to the concept of primitive accumulation, regularly criticized globalization as a process of "privatizing the commons."[23] In the period of neoliberalism, David Harvey has recently suggested, direct forms of dispossession and devastation have become central to the reproduction of political order. Harvey draws on the writings of Rosa Luxemburg and Hannah Arendt to argue that so-called primitive or original accumulation is in fact constant and central to the ongoing ability of capitalism to reproduce itself. In Harvey's view, accumulation by dispossession always exists in tension with accumulation by expanded reproduction. In his view, during the period after 1973 that many characterize as post-Fordist, "accumulation by dispossession" grew in importance, as did "financialization," the growing reach and depth of finance capital in new areas of the globe and social life. Finance capital and institutions of credit backed by the state were the "umbilical cord that ties together accumulation by dispossession and expanded reproduction" (Harvey 2003, 152). I propose in this book that valorizing the cultural practices of the poor as a form of social capital, and financializing their social networks through relations of debt mediated by NGOs, is an important aspect of accumulation by dispossession. I will argue that this mode of accumulation by dispossession, a mode that speaks the language of empowering the poor, is yet another side of more familiar forms of dispossession encouraged by neoliberal economic policies such as enforced privatization and structural adjustment programs.

Harvey's focus, like that of Marx, is on the state as an agent of accumulation by dispossession. In this book, by contrast, I argue that the state is not an adequate unit of analysis for understanding such processes of dispossession. Instead, practices carried out by diverse institutional forms such as the state, IOs, and NGOs need to be studied together in one field of power.[24] In my own work, I look at how "financialization of the globe" (Spivak 1999) weaves together agents of the state, IOs, and NGOs in projects of what I have called "empowerment debt." Empowerment debt is a mode of fiscal relations that links IOs and NGOs with individuals outside of their relation to the state as citizens. It is also, I will argue, an important mode of "accumulation by dispossession" through which indigenous forms of production, markets, and sociability are transformed into resources for reproducing dominant forms of power. As Harvey has pointed out, primitive accumulation "entails appropriation and co-optation of pre-existing cultural and social achievements" (Harvey 2003, 146) as well as overt forms of suppression and displacement. At the same time, the broad range of movements known under the rubric of anti-globalization have been in large part movements against accumulation by dispossession, as opposed to earlier forms of political organization in the period when expanded reproduction was dominant. The goals of these movements have included reducing the crippling debt of third world countries and defending "the authenticity of local production systems" (Harvey 2003, 166) such as those found in the workshops of

Cairo. Much about the anti-globalization movement can be criticized, such as its implicit support of microenterprise as a counterweight to top-down, state-led development, an attachment that dovetails nicely with the agendas of the World Bank and the economic analysis of many on Wall Street (Elyachar 2002). But these minor points do not undercut Harvey's argument for the importance of accumulation by dispossession. Dispossession took many forms in many places in the 1990s. In the former Soviet Union, Caroline Humphrey has shown, the end of socialism saw huge sectors of the population transformed into a new social group she called "the dispossessed." The coming of the free market dispossessed many individuals of property, work, and entitlements. In post-Soviet Russia, moreover, the dispossessed were also "themselves no longer possessed" (1996–97, 70). They were left isolated from the collective domains that remained in practice still "the key units disposing of property and people in Russia" (70). Dispossession is more than an economic process. It strips individuals of their political identity and their psychic well-being as well.

In this book I show how attempts to implant new market forms in Cairo were also a process of dispossession. Accumulation by dispossession in Cairo, I suggest, works on a number of levels. First, the economic discipline imposed on Egypt in the 1990s by global financial institutions such as the IMF and the World Bank, and the widespread unemployment that resulted, created a vast pool of Egyptians "freed" from their reliance on the state or national economy. That vast pool was freed into the space dubbed the "informal economy," where its members could become vibrant entrepreneurs simply by surviving. At the same time, I suggest, programs to support the informal economy and microenterprise have a paradoxical effect on the indigenous forms of culturally grounded production that they purport to champion. Such dynamic interaction between the levers of financial discipline on the one hand and small-scale efforts to champion threatened local economic forms on the other is not without historical precedent. In the Great Depression, for example, more than the credit system facilitated the destruction of the family farm in the United States. State institutions set up to preserve family farming "played a subversive role in facilitating the transition they were supposed to hold back" (Harvey 2003, 156). The historical parallel is telling even if we do not accept the contention that Egypt or anywhere else was undergoing a transition to another "stage" of production in the 1990s. But the potential for converting local networks into a channel for mining resources produced by the Egyptian people is contained in the very nature of networks themselves.

Networks, Ethnography and the Third

Studying networks encouraged me to think about the nature of networks formed in the course of fieldwork. Networks, it should be remembered, are formed by three members or more. As Georg Simmel first pointed out, relationships of threes are completely different from those of two: "the triad is a structure completely different from the dyad" (Simmel 1950, 141). Only when the third partner of a relationship is involved can the relationship between the first two become visible and intelligible.[25] "One need simply add a third party, C, and adopt its point of view, for the relationship between A and B to become analyzable and comprehensible" (Callon 1998, 9). After three members, however, there is no significant sociological shift from the incorporation of a fourth or a fifth. Networks potentially are endlessly incorporative. Such is the case with workshop networks as well. New kinds of exchange partners can easily be integrated into the networks of workshop masters. That includes ethnographers.

Ethnographers enter the field in different ways. In Egypt, where much of social life is organized around social networks, ethnographers often enter into social networks, and thus the field, through exchanges of gifts both material and intangible. Some of this dynamic is general to fieldwork in any setting. Ethnographers bring in resources that can be crucial to the survival of the people being studied. Since ethnographers are usually reluctant to enter into direct market exchanges of money for knowledge, they usually turn to modalities of gift exchange which, despite all of our writing on the gift, we still tend to treat as less problematic than the exchange of money for information or sociability. (It is certainly noteworthy that anthropologists often reproduce in their epistemological practices the division between the market and the gift that they critique in their writings.) When we enter into exchanges with informants, we can become partially absorbed in the social networks that we want to study. That is an important goal of carrying out participant observation, and achieving the "native point of view." The sociality generated in the social networks in turn becomes a resource for the production of knowledge and the professional advancement of the ethnographer. It can also become a resource for reproducing dominant global power relations.

Despite the partial absorption of the ethnographer into the social networks that he or she is studying, the relationship between the ethnographer on the one hand and "the field" on the other remains essentially dyadic. Such a relationship, following Simmel, can limit our ability to make intelligible the actions and identities that we study in the field. If we take Simmel's point to heart, then we need to think about whether the relationship between the ethnographer and the field can be rendered comprehensible without the addition of a third.[26] That raises questions about the often silent presence in the field of the research assistant.[27] These questions cannot be answered simply by adding explicit acknowledgments at the beginning of our ethnographies. The issues are epistemological as well.

One important ethnography to open up this issue of the assistant's presence is Vincent Crapanzano's *Tuhami*, which draws on Simmel's notion of the third to do so.[28] In Crapanzano's analysis, the presence of his assistant, Lhacen, significantly altered the nature of his interaction with his informant, Tuhami. The assistant Lhacen was, in Simmel's terms, the third for Tuhami and Crapanzano, the one who rendered their relationship comprehensible (Crapanzano 1980, 148). Looking back over years of fieldwork, Crapanzano realized that the fieldwork he had collected with a field assistant present had an "intimacy of tone and detail" that he did not obtain when he worked alone (Crapanzano 1980, 144). He attributes this difference to the presence of the assistant as the third in the ethnographic encounter, and notes that the implications of the assistant's presence have not been adequately addressed in anthropological research (Crapanzano 1980, 143). Twenty-five years later, that lacuna remains. For the postmodernist move in anthropology focused on the writing of ethnography at the expense of the issues involved in producing ethnographic knowledge.[29]

There is much that is questionable about Crapanzano's use of his fieldwork experience to draw this conclusion about the third. As one reads further in Crapanzano's text, it turns out that Lhacen's presence also rendered Tuhami comprehensible in the most pragmatic of ways. Crapanzano did not speak much Arabic, could not comprehend what Tuhami said, and probably missed much of what was going on when he worked alone—thus already accounting for the lack of intimacy and tone that he notes in the fieldwork he conducted alone. When we do not speak the language of our informants, then the nature of the third in the ethnographic encounter with the field is quite different from what it is when both ethnographer and assistant interact with informants and then discuss what they learned and experienced in the field. And yet the questions that Crapanzano raised in his ethnography of Tuhami deserve a second look. For if Simmel is correct, then the presence of the third does drastically alter the nature of the ethnographic experience, and transforms a one-to-one interaction of individual with field into a dynamic social terrain where a different kind of learning can take place and a different kind of knowledge can be produced.[30]

This book is based on three years of ethnographic research I carried out in Cairo between 1993 and 1996.[31] I defined my ethnographic field as an analytical problem: I wanted to study the interaction of the state, IOs, and NGOs in the social field of the informal economy. I was intrigued by the phenomenon of IOs and NGOs undertaking to develop a social field which, as I saw it at the time, negated the sovereignty of the state. Given my analytical interests, I found el-Hirafiyeen a fascinating place in which to work. From there I moved out into different institutions and locations throughout Cairo that were players in producing this particular ethnographic locale. In practice, this meant that my field included the offices of banks, consulting firms, state agencies, and NGOs around Cairo as well as the workshops, homes, and streets of el-Hirafiyeen. For various periods over the course of two years, I carried out this research together with Essam Fawzi.[32] He was an invaluable interlocutor for my thinking throughout my research, and my partner in key parts of the fieldwork. My ethnographic research gained a great deal of depth not only from Essam's outstanding ethnographic skills and deep knowledge of Egyptian society but also because his presence shifted my relationship to the field from dyadic to triadic. This was especially important in research on workshop life, since it is organized through social networks that are themselves predicated on a triadic relationship. I believe that this triadic relation of the field also made me much better aware of how social networks in workshop communities could be refigured when they absorbed new elements that were linked to a broader field of power.

The issues raised by Simmel and Crapanzano concerning the triad versus the dyad are relevant for any form of ethnographic production.

But the way I defined my field made these issues more urgent and less abstract. In a project that attempted to grasp the different forms of power acting on one ethnographic setting such as el-Hirafiyeen, multiple perspectives on that ethnographic reality were imperative. No one perspective on the complex reality that was el-Hirafiyeen was adequate. Debates about "the local" versus "the global" made little sense there. If only one person were conducting fieldwork in such a site, the ethnographic picture that would result would be severely limited. This in addition to the inevitable shaping of reality imposed by the concepts that we mobilize in the conduct of fieldwork, as well as in the process of analyzing and writing.

In the field, ethnographers are viewed by their informants through particular lenses. No matter how long the ethnographer stays in the field, and no matter if language and culture are shared, informants have their independent views of ethnographers that shape their presentations of self. The ethnographer can personify different forces to informants, even as a shared intersubjective reality is built over time. Essam and I attempted to make tactical decisions at every stage about how we should approach the subjects of this research in terms of these subjectivities that we embodied to our informants, especially with informants with whom we worked for a short time. In my case, many of my informants in banks and development organizations assumed that I was carrying out research for USAID or another such institution, since it is so common for anthropologists to produce research on economic issues such as the informal economy for development organizations. If I were attached to a development organization or NGO in some way, then I was likely to personify development funding as well. Rather than attempt to overcome these perceptions, we would often consciously mobilize them in the conduct of fieldwork. Each perceived subjectivity would elicit a different response from the informant. Each response was valuable, and none was total. When put together, those different interactions produced a far richer picture of reality than would a monolithic dual interaction between one ethnographer and "the field."

That field was a rich one. It would have been easy to reduce one component of it or another to a caricature, either of the illiterate craftsmen, or of World Bank consultants. Critiques of development, for example, sometimes read as if there were a monolithic character "The World Bank" that can be blamed for all ills. To state a banality, that is not the case. The bank and USAID are not as monolithic or powerful as perhaps they might like to believe. What matters here is something else. A field like that offered in this ethnography offers an opportunity to study the investments that need to be made in any set of circumstances to reshape economic subjectivities and impose new calculative tools.[33] The labor involved in such projects makes explicit issues that often go unstated. In a context like the one that I present in what follows, interventions to impose the "invisible hand" can trigger debates among all kinds of informants about processes that often go unremarked where the invisible hand has been seen as the organizing force of society for a much longer time. As such, the apparent oddities of el-Hirafiyeen were of enormous epistemological value for understanding the work of building "the market."

Essam and I did not always work together. When I conducted interviews with officials in banks and development institutions or with consultants, in Arabic or English, I usually did so alone. I lived part of the week in el-Hirafiyeen, which afforded me the perspective that can only come with long-term participant observation. As many female ethnographers have noted, being a woman offers particular advantages, since one can live reality from a woman's perspective while still being given access, as a foreigner, to activities normally closed to women. There were two occasions when Essam conducted interviews alone when informants wanted to talk about corruption, which they did not feel comfortable discussing in front of a foreigner. When we conducted extended interviews in el-Hirafiyeen with workshop masters and employees, and with male youth entrepreneurs, we always worked together. In institutions where we did not have a long time to work, like state bureaucracies or local government offices, we worked together as well.[34] In such settings, the dual presence of the high-prestige foreign researcher together with a local person who had the cultural capital necessary to make a functionary at home and willing to produce the information that was technically not ours to see was extremely important.

In the course of our research, we sometimes undertook to bring together individuals who might not otherwise have met to see what kinds of networks developed out of the meetings. We were also repeatedly sought out by informants who hoped to benefit from our own networks to further their own projects. The outcomes of these interactions were always extremely instructive. Some have told me that it might be unethical to treat informants "like objects."[35] But such an objection is misguided. My informants were already being treated as the objects of experiments—by the state agencies that had moved them into el-Hirafiyeen, and by the myriad agencies that were experimenting with the creation of new market forms and strategies to inculcate new economic subjectivities. It was not we who created them as the object of experiment. We merely brought that objectification more clearly into view. In many instances, we helped those who were treated as the object of market experiments to forge their own variant of responses to that process of objectification, with varying outcomes. The speed with which discrete networks forged links—across the boundaries of NGOs, development organizations, businesses, and state organizations—indicated important features of the market in the age of neoliberalism. What we uncovered during this fieldwork was not an exception and was clearly not about the particular failures or peculiarities of Egypt and its corrupt society. Rather, what we found taught us a great deal about the market itself.

A note about my level of Arabic when I conducted this research: I was fluent in Egyptian dialect and modern standard Arabic during the course of my fieldwork. However, when I began to work with craftsmen I often found myself at a loss. Just as the American English spoken in the halls of Columbia University is different from the language spoken on the streets of Harlem right next door, in Cairo, the register of Arabic spoken by the educated is quite different from that of the often illiterate craftsmen of the popular classes. The times when I "misunderstood" what informants were saying were often the richest in terms of ethnographic material, because of the condensed symbolic form of the informants' speech when they dealt with concepts integral to their forms of interaction. Similarly, my need to translate and explain interviews that I conducted alone in English to Essam, including the social technologies and concepts of my informants in banks, NGOs, and IOs, added another important layer to our research. At the same time, the ethnography that follows can in no way capture the richness of what I was privileged to study. For as Marilyn Strathern has so aptly put it, ethnographies are the analytical constructions of scholars; the people they study are not. It is part of the anthropological exercise to acknowledge how much larger is their creativity than what any particular analysis can encompass (Strathern 1988, xii).

2. A Home for Markets

Two Neighborhoods in Plan and Practice,
1905–1996

Moving through the Megacity

Daily life in Cairo is shaped by the realities of moving around the megacity. Invisible maps of power can be traced out in the value of real estate and modes of transport. This social geography of transport can be traced out in the buses, minibuses, and microbuses of the city. For the crowds storming onto the buses for 10 piasters, the minibus at 25 piasters can be out of reach. To those pushing their way onto the minibus for 25 piasters, 80 piasters for the microbus might be a great luxury. Some have no choice but to pay those high prices. Microbuses serve the outskirts of the city that are served only spottily by public transport. Drivers of those microbuses have many stories to tell. Like that of the migrant worker back from Libya who bought a microbus to drive on an unregulated route, but can't afford the price of a payoff to the official who grants access to the new official starting point. Others might tell of the loans they have taken out from the banks, and the long hours they work driving across Cairo to pay them back. The boys, or *subian*, who work for the drivers tell silent stories in the agility with which they negotiate the cramped spaces of the microbus, and lean out far into the street on the lookout for new passengers to fill their fare.

The microbus station is a meeting point for individual maps of movement through the city. Destinations mark social class. Clothes, language, and demeanor differ according to route. On the ride to el-Salam, my own destination, everyone can afford to pay one Egyptian pound (about 30 cents in 1996), but no one pays it lightly: only rarely does someone get out along the way. The microbus brings together people living the same stresses of daily life. Complaints or secrets which might endanger an ongoing social relation can be let out in the assurance of understanding and anonymity. As a young woman sitting next to me put it one day: after half an hour, everyone will go off on his own path and never see the others again. Those riding together have something in common before a word is spoken, and yet are assured of anonymity in the megacity of seventeen million.

People climb in one by one or in twos and threes and sit down. The choice seats go first, and only after all others are filled do people squeeze into those in the middle of a row. A woman might ask to sit against the wall even if a man got there first, or a group of three traveling together might be accommodated. "Let them sit so we can all get going!" someone might call out. Taking off from the lot, amid calls back and forth between the drivers and the conversational honking of horns, the driver passes money to a man sitting at the entrance and takes a ticket. This system exists around the city, but works slightly differently depending on whether the lot, and the driver, are registered with state agencies. Those who do not have a legal right to operate their microbuses out of the lot pay the ticket seller a higher price.

On the road, as we approach the northern reaches of Cairo we speed past the corpses of factories, downsized metal factories whose work is now spread out in little workshops around the city. Some time later the driver pulls over for a moment, along the highway road leading to the Isma'iliyya road just ahead, and lets me out. Across the street, the desert blooms plots of housing marked out owner by owner, bank by bank, all empty, waiting to be sold, resold, held over time. Cars stream by, eager to get onto the airport road. I walk across the six-lane highway to the other side, where silence reigns. Past the workers building private housing units, past the new five-story houses along the access road, past the flocks of goats sitting at the road's edge, past the signs enforcing informal property rights in land, and on to my destination—the main square of the neighborhood, where buildings mark the official presence of the state: the official mosque, a telephone central (rarely open), and the state-owned Bank for Industrial Development. A cloth banner hangs over the telephone central next to the bank: "Program for the Development of Madinet el-Hirafiyeen, in Cooperation with the Social Fund and the Industrial Bank for Development."

Snapshots and Soundscapes of a Market Workshop

El-Hirafiyeen was a place marked by sounds and silences. The silences came mainly from "youth graduate microenterprises," which had been established with loans provided by the Social Fund for Development, established by the World Bank. By the time I started working there in 1994, many of those microenterprises were closed down. Those that were open were relatively quiet places of work. One produced suitcases for export to the Arab Gulf: it was said that this microenterprise was really owned by an outside businessman enjoying the tax advantages accorded by the state to youth microenterprises. Another, a large, two-room microenterprise, was owned by the president of the NGO established for the "youth graduates," the owners of those microenterprises. This workplace was occupied by three large looms, whose shuttles were largely silent: The owner was busy full time with his NGO business. His assistant kept the workshop open, sat on his chair, and was ready to talk to any potential visitors who came by. A number of workshops were in the business of making clothes: one, owned by another member of the youth graduates' NGO, was open periodically, and employed fifteen workers when there was money to pay them.

The dominant sounds and sights emanated from the workshops of the craftsmen who had been evicted from other locations in northern Cairo. Some of these had closed down as well, or sold out to new owners who sometimes had no previous experience in the trade. Those who had survived their move into el-Hirafiyeen and reconstructed their markets and businesses were busy working inside the workshop or outside on the adjoining street. The workshops were constructed around the edge of eight open squares, the space of which was available to the workshop owners to work in as well. They worked long hours in trades that had everything possible to do with cars—painting, remaking the bodies, balancing, fixing engines, and making spare parts. Others took junk metal and refashioned it into spare parts for machinery. A few carpentry workshops were still open. The workshop owners called "buyers-in" were busy as well: these men had not grown up working in workshops; they gained their mastery over their place of work through cash pure and simple, and gained knowledge of the trade on the job.

Noise, banging, cutting, drilling, forging, yelling, driving. Mainly the incessant banging of metal on metal. This was the background to walking, talking, thinking, sleeping in el-Hirafiyeen. Sounds of the work outside were not kept out by the walls. For some time, when sitting inside the apartment that I lived in part of the week, I would jump up thinking that something had happened inside the apartment, only to realize that the sound had come from the outside. Women told me that they were jumping up like that for months when they first came. Sounds changed at night. The incessant sound of metal on metal gradually faded, and voices became more audible. Sounds became individual. You could tell which workshop over there was still open, at ten o'clock at night. Gunshots and shouts might come from a soundtrack. Those could be the faraway sounds of a video playing at the coffeehouse, where some fifty-odd boys and young men often sat around in chairs watching the show. Sound might blare from a TV whose flashing pictures peeped out from behind half-closed wooden shutters.

Sound and movement were shaped by the rhythms of the working day. The streets of the neighborhood woke up slowly. The early morning hours were inhabited by the young—children on the way to school, dressed in uniforms, book bags on their backs, escorted by women in bright-colored scarves with heads bent over, to the road where they could catch a bus, a good fifteen-minute walk away. Other children walked down the streets as well. These were the subian, child workers or so-called apprentices. Small groups of these children might stand huddled together in front of pushcarts, intently eating their morning bowls of *ful*. Walking into town from el-Salam you might also see a group of young women workers walking and laughing on the way to jobs in the clothing workshops and plastics workshops of the microenterprises.

Life on Main Street woke up slowly. Main Street was main not for its size but for its landmarks. An important one for the women was the one greengrocer in town. Another was the telephone central, from which workers sometimes placed calls after their long day ended, to families who would see them again only on a weekly Sunday visit home. There was the cafeteria that made sandwiches for workers in the workshops, boys, and teenagers, and sold bread and washing soap to the women. There was the coffeehouse that was often open long into the night, and where time was marked by shifting waves of customers, from the night-time video shows to young boys after work, to the morning's tea for the early morning workers with a moment to spare.

Each night of the week had its own sounds. Thursday was payday in the workshops. The sounds outside were of young men with money in their pockets, yelling and talking and playing. On Saturday night human voices faded away, as workers took off in minibuses and microbuses bound for their homes outside Cairo, in Zagazig and Sharqiyya. Some sounds of presence and absence were constant through the week. Most owners disappeared every night as they took off in their own or their customers' cars to the nearby neighborhoods of Heliopolis or Nasr City or el-Zeitoun, where many kept their homes even after their workshops were moved. An hour or two after the human sounds faded away, dogs would venture onto the streets from the receding boundary of the desert, which was slowly being encroached on by the persistent tide of real estate.

A Home for Noise and Disorder

The Egyptian state ministry, the governorate of Cairo, created el-Hirafiyeen by administrative fiat. It was built to house workshops evicted from three neighborhoods of northern Cairo: el-Zeitoun, Nasr City, and Heliopolis. The workshops were moved, it was said, because they had caused noise, disorder, and congestion in these residential neighborhoods. Some of those workshops had been "informal" from the start; others were made so when the Cairo Municipality revoked their licenses by administrative order. Even the most casual observer could realize, however, that these three neighborhoods were by Cairo's standards uncongested. As for noise and disorder, those are subjective criteria: whether they prompt countermeasures tends anywhere to be closely linked to who experiences them.

Those offended by these workshops had the power to set the state to work. Madinet Nasr is a seat of the Egyptian army and state bureaucracy, and by the early 1990s it had perhaps the most highly valued real estate in Cairo. Masr el-Gedida, or Heliopolis, is another neighborhood of Cairo closely linked to the name of the state. El-Zeitoun lies to its west, next to the "informal" area of Gesr el-Suez Street that borders Masr el-Gedida. Given that Madinet Nasr contains some of the most expensive real estate in Cairo, the remaining public housing from the era of Gamal Abdel-Nasser, and those workshops that gave some of its inhabitants work, were a stark anomaly. The evictions were not only about real estate values. They were also about power and its exercise in Cairo. Why one workshop area was shut down and another left standing seemed random to many of those affected. The logic may have boiled down to what one urban planner told me: those workshops were an eyesore in the way of the president when his motorcade passed.

The Governorate of Cairo revoked workshop licenses in parts of these neighborhoods in 1989. Workshop masters were informed that they had to shut down and would be compensated with a new workshop and an apartment in a new neighborhood exclusively for workshops, called Madinet el-Hirafiyeen. The decision to close down workshops in these three neighborhoods was not met with equanimity. The order was at first seen by many workshop masters as simply imposing a new business expense in the form of fines for disregarding the order. No one packed up and moved just like that. For a man who sometimes grossed 1000 LE a day (about $300) in a workshop, as a wealthy master from Nasr City reported earning, or for a carpenter from Heliopolis who reported making 80 LE a day from small repairs alone, a daily fine of 30 LE for operating without a license was a small expense, in comparison to moving out to the desolate reaches of the desert, far from any customers. Eventually the workshop masters were forced to move but soon enough, according to neighborhood residents, some of the workshops were operating again with different owners. In Madinet Nasr and el-Zeitoun workshop labor moved onto the street, where the same trades were practiced by former apprentices right in front of the old workshops, but now in "the informal economy."

El-Hirafiyeen is at the northern edge of Cairo, not far from Cairo International Airport. It is built on state-owned land allocated to the Governorate of Cairo, a state ministry directly under the president of the Republic. This area is near strategic sites of the state and its military: the airport, army bases, and army industries.

The 1983 Master Plan for Greater Cairo designated the area as part of an industrial zone in the further reaches of Northern Cairo. Nearby are other "New Settlements" built by the state, in various stages of occupancy.[1] Slightly to the north of el-Hirafiyeen lay one of these planned developments, or "cities," Madinet el-Salam. This neighborhood, also built by the governorate, consisted of approximately forty apartment blocks, each five stories high. In contrast to el-Hirafiyeen, which was for "craftsmen," it was built as a neighborhood for "the working class." It was largely unoccupied until the earthquake of 1993 forced many residents of downtown Cairo to leave their homes and accept compensation from the governorate in the form of subsidized apartments in el-Salam. According to one of the engineers who worked on both projects, the hope of providing work for the residents of el-Salam City was a motivation for building el-Hirafiyeen: "We [in the governorate] had already made el-Salam. We had that experience behind us, and thought also that we could get work for those people in the city of el-Hirafiyeen." Indeed, el-Salam was home to many workers in el-Hirafiyeen. (Most of those workers were children, but that's another story.) Government services for el-Hirafiyeen were available in el-Salam as well. While there was a small police office (*nu'ta*) in el-Hirafiyeen that was rarely open, the police station that mattered was in el-Salam. There was no hospital, first-aid station, or post office in el-Hirafiyeen. There was a bank—the Industrial Bank of Egypt—a state-owned enterprise that had been chosen as a financial mediator for the Social Fund project.

Who Lives Where When There's Nothing There

Initial sketches for el-Hirafiyeen were made by engineers in the governorate at the time of the decision to move the workshops out of northern Cairo. Those sketches were preliminary: they show blocks of five-story apartment buildings, arranged around twelve squares of empty land, each with workshops lining the bottom floor.

One engineer claimed for himself and a colleague credit for the town's design. The original plan for the project bypassed the tricky problem of land use on neighboring property (for example, an army-owned poultry farm squatted on land nearby). Another map of this period was a rudimentary affair, consisting of little more than sketches on paper held together with scotch tape. This map grappled with the problem of other users of the land in the area but left out any details. The plans sat for six months in the governorate when the fact that the poultry farm was squatting on some of the designated land was discovered. After negotiations the poultry farm was moved down the road, although it stayed on some of the land designated for el-Hirafiyeen.

The illegal houses of local state officials on what was supposed to be the main access road to the neighborhood were also a problem: there the road was constricted a bit. The houses remained, and became the subject of debate through 1994. Other illegal buildings on the allocated land were dealt with differently: they were being "used by people who have no legal status," people who "didn't cause any problems when we moved them out because they're Bedouin who migrate ['Arab ruhal']." They were offered apartments as compensation in the neighborhood of el-Salam.

Three state institutions were in control of the making and running of el-Hirafiyeen. The governorate did the basic planning of the project. The actual building of el-Hirafiyeen was carried out by the Cairo General Company for Contracting, which then subcontracted to other companies. Meanwhile, the governorate oversaw the installation of electricity and water, and the building of an access road to the town. The project was funded from state money, but the funds for public utilities were to be paid for by the selling at auction of rights to service shops in the town.[2] Constructing the neighborhood involved many state institutions, contracting companies, and subcontractors. Plans for el-Hirafiyeen were made more concrete, and its size expanded, in the course of the actual building of the workshop town, managed by the Cairo Public Company for Contracting (*Shirket el-Qahira el-'Ama lil-muqawalat*). After the town was built, responsibility for its operations was handed over in full to the local government in el-Salam City.

A long negotiation, managed by the governorate, marked the process of settling people and workshops into el-Hirafiyeen and deciding who would live where, who would work where. People in the neighborhood mentioned the sums they paid to get access to the apartments or workshops they wanted. About two years after the neighborhood was first built in 1989 things began to settle down, according to most accounts. Many workshops had already closed their doors by 1991, especially those of craftsmen who served people in homes—like carpenters and window makers. Some workshops that did metal work found new customers in neighboring factories of the industrial zone.

The neighborhood became known as a place for cars, for all kinds of repair and maintenance work for cars. But the masters of small workshops who had worked on the low end of the business had a bad time. There was a shakeout in the business of painting cars in particular: those who had the money to invest in more sophisticated equipment kept customers who were willing to travel the extra distance to el-Hirafiyeen. But it wasn't worth it for customers to travel all that distance for a hand-sprayed *duko* job. They just went to the new "workshops" that had opened up "on the street" in the old neighborhoods to get the job done, in the words of one master, "any old way and on the cheap."

Meanwhile, the plan to clean up northern Cairo of its workshops and polluting industries was never fully carried out. A few targeted neighborhoods were cleansed of their workshops, but matters never went beyond that. Closing down the workshops did not change the character of northern Cairo, or even clean up target neighborhoods of polluting industrial workshops. The orders did provide a pause, a glitch, in the relentless flow of life in a few streets in Cairo. But soon enough, the unceasing determination of Cairenes to live and to work and to survive in their own way, and not as regulated by a factory owner or state official, reasserted itself. Workshops reopened, but now on the street. New owners appeared, if perhaps less skilled than those who had been moved out. Workshops stayed padlocked for a few months, but then reopened. Markets for labor and commodities reasserted themselves, with less regard for the rule of law than before.

One direct outcome of the state's exercise of its organizational power was the creation of landed property in el-Hirafiyeen. How that site evolved was not, however, subject to administrative fiat. Many workshops and apartments in el-Hirafiyeen stood empty years after the neighborhood was built. Those who could afford to do so just held onto the workshops or apartments and "put them in cold storage," to let the magic of the booming real estate market do its work. The future of el-Hirafiyeen was changed when the Social Fund decided to make the neighborhood a center of its operations. If the establishment of the neighborhood illustrated the organizational power of the state, the way it evolved over time also showed the limits of its power. Those limits could be seen first of all in absences—craftsmen who didn't move in, neighborhoods that weren't rid of workshops, workshops that stood empty. The empty spaces paved the way for a second mobilization of organizational power on the part of IOs, which established the Egyptian Social Fund and designated el-Hirafiyeen one of its principal locations. That second phase of intervention put this small neighborhood on an international map and made it a place of broader significance.

The impact of the IOs could be discerned in the most mundane categories shaping daily life in el-Hirafiyeen. Given the importance of real estate and its values, these categories became part of daily conversation in a number of ways. Apartments and workshops had been designed by engineers of the governorate for "the craftsmen." When the Social Fund took over the empty apartments and workshops, they acquired a new name among the residents of the neighborhood. Now spaces that had been called "workshops" became "small enterprises" (*mashari 'saghira*). They were owned by "the youth" (*bitu 'el-shabab*). Other apartments and former workshops were redesignated for another new category in the neighborhood: "the returnees." An allocation for this target group of the Social Fund, consisting of Egyptians forced to return home from their jobs in the Arab Gulf during the first Gulf War in 1991, had been demanded by the Egyptian government as a price for its participation in the war. These various categories invented by state entities and IOs shaped the face of the neighborhood. By the early 1990s the craftsmen had 549 workshops, the "youth graduates" were assigned 296 "micro-enterprises" (many originally built as "workshops"), "returnees from the Gulf" had thirty-three workshops, and craftsmen evicted from workshops across from a building of the Foreign Ministry accounted for fourteen more.

Few of the craftsmen actually lived in el-Hirafiyeen. Some of the women married to workshop masters had refused to leave their friends and relatives in their own neighborhoods to move out into a geographic and social desert. It was not a far commute from Heliopolis or Nasr City, and many of the craftsmen had easy access to free transport—the cars on which they worked. While the craftsman was known to "like" living near his work, as the engineer put it, many preferred to be near their old homes. For them el-Hirafiyeen became a commuting town. Men and women often found better opportunities in trading, selling, or renting their apartments, or using them as warehouses or for other informal economic ventures. Many rented their flats to groups of child workers who came from towns too far away for them to go home more than one night a week.

Most of the craftsmen who lived and worked in town built up a new social world in el-Hirafiyeen; the mode of their operations and forms of social life gave vibrancy to a place that to many eyes seemed stark. But the youth entrepreneurs worked differently. Few had strong links to their colleagues, let alone to their neighbors. Most commuted to work as well. Among their wives (for the women were mainly partners on paper, added on to get funding for women's empowerment schemes), few had the social skills of the Cairene woman from the popular neighborhood, for whom creating and sustaining social networks was a habitus of daily life. These women complained bitterly about the impossibility of living in such a dead and empty town. Those who could persuaded their husbands to live elsewhere. To them el-Hirafiyeen was an empty place, a ghost town, from which they were eager to escape.

"El-Hirafiyeen is a terrible place," said Laila, partner in her brother's textile factory. "I love our home downtown, in Sakakeeni. People there live crowded into a few small rooms, but they don't mind, they just take life how it comes. They have no aspirations, they don't want to improve their lives." Laila agreed that she was ambitious, wanted to go somewhere, do something. She was taking a course downtown in an institute for management, trying to improve her skills in running the workshop. She and her sister-in-law—now pregnant with her first child—were just waiting for the day when conditions would get better and they could get out. "This place? We'll use it as a warehouse." Laila loved to walk on the streets of Cairo, to look at the shops, just to window-shop. But in el-Hirafiyeen, she said, there was nothing. Only workshops. There was nowhere to go: the greengrocer, the cafeteria, the factory. That's it. The emptiness seen by Laila and her sister-in-law Hanan when they peered onto the streets of el-Hirafiyeen was desolate indeed. Emptiness is not a comfortable sensation for many Cairenes, whose sensory world and movement through space are intensely social.

When I looked out from the apartment where I lived in el-Hirafiyeen toward the desert behind during my first weeks of work there, the sight of emptiness behind gave me ease. The sea of real estate had not yet overtaken the desert. I felt sadness at the thought that that view would soon be blocked as the buildings were going up. But what I saw as a welcome empty space with soft colors was something fearful, a place to avoid, in the eyes of my hosts. Such variations in the experience of space are not restricted to the divide between foreigner and local. They can also mark the line between the *sha'bi* and the *afrangi* Cairene. In el-Hirafiyeen, those variations marked the line between the craftsman and the graduate; between the women of the popular neighborhoods and the women married to microentrepreneurs. In contrast to the emptiness that Hanan saw on the streets of el-Hirafiyeen, women from workshop families saw a world full of life. That contrast between emptiness and fullness was one that reappeared over and over in my fieldwork.

Most of the Youth Graduates moved through the neighborhood as if they were in a desert, a place from which to escape, in which there was nothing but a loan to repay. But those same streets were vibrant for craftsmen whose production functions depended on a web of social interactions that shaped the way they walked down the street. That experience of space as social shaped the punctuated rhythm, marked by conversations and greetings, with which they walked down the street—as opposed to the steady stride of the Youth Graduates. It marked the way they bought and sold, with much face-to-face conversation, as opposed to the Graduates' anonymous search for "the market." It marked the intensity with which craftsmen's senses were attuned to the rhythms, smells, and sounds of labor emanating from their workshops and those of their neighbors.

The husbands and brothers of Laila and Hanan also saw el-Hirafiyeen as empty, as desolate, as a place from which to escape. The buildings in which they worked were just that, buildings. The apartments in which they were forced to sleep from time to time were little more than four walls, much as those walls marked their achievement of social adulthood. Life for these men moved between their places of work—the enterprises—and the house. They did not go to the coffeehouses. They were not involved in networks of social life within the community. They did not pray at the mosque. Because of the emptiness of their social relations within the community, they saw the streets as empty. In contrast, el-Hirafiyeen was a dense social fabric to the craftsmen and their families. The space was not more crowded, and the amenities were no better for the craftsmen. But the density of their social networks and daily life shaped a sensory landscape completely different from that experienced by the graduates and their families. When Hanan saw desolate space, the wife of a craftsman would draw out for me a spatial map of rich complexity, of friends and relations and enemies and social interactions and life.

In el-Hirafiyeen the starkest contrasts in the lived reality of bodies moving through space, in the experience of sound and sight, in the sensations of emptiness and fullness, lay at the cusp between craftsmen and microentrepreneurs. Those two groups walked the same streets but did not move through them in the same way. Their differing experience of their social and physical worlds was intimately tied to the kind of markets they built and the degree of success they could find. Only those who experienced their streets as full of life were able to create markets and succeed in their economic ventures. The different worlds of physical sensation created by these two groups were also expressed in the different subjectivities of the workshop master and the microentrepreneur. The fullness of space was expressed in the forms of value that craftsmen created in their workshops together with the commodities and services that they sold for a price. The emptiness of space that the microentrepreneurs lived in was another expression of the negative values that their enterprises produced.

Maneuvering the Market

If the creation of the town as a center for "workshop labor" and its subsequent designation as a site for "microenterprise" illustrate the power of the state and IOs, then the way the neighborhood evolved shows the limits to that power. The creation of the neighborhood was an experiment launched by petty state officials to clear up certain neighborhoods of Cairo and create a different mode of urban markets. Those moved into the neighborhood were the objects on which that experiment was carried out. Once launched, experiments take on their own parameters. That was certainly true of the building and transformation of el-Hirafiyeen. The state had no power—or it did not try to exercise power—to keep el-Hirafiyeen as planned: an urban space appropriate for workshops and craftsmen. The objects of the original experiment turned the categories around to their own effect. Those categories and parameters were shifted once again when the Social Fund adopted the neighborhood. Now the neighborhood became a home for "youth microenterprises." New categories of users were assigned. Social Fund money inaugurated two new social categories: "youth graduate entrepreneurs" and "return migrants from the Gulf." And as the dynamics of the secondary, informal real estate market appeared, so did other dynamics, far from the planned categories for this craftsmen's town.

Although those who had been given the apartments and workshops with long-term leases and minimal monthly mortgage-like payments were forbidden to sell until the mortgage was fully paid off, selling was common and acknowledged. Some workshop owners gave their rights to family members for whom they were responsible: a number of sisters and their husbands became renters and owners through such kinship relations. Others simply came for the relatively low prices: one factory worker commuted daily to southern Cairo but relished el-Hirafiyeen's clear air and the friendly atmosphere of a "popular neighborhood" where you could "leave your door open," unlike el-Salam nearby, built for "the workers." A husband and wife who were both schoolteachers worked nearby: as for many Cairenes, the drawbacks of living in this workshop town were slight compared to the time and expense of commuting in the megacity on salaries that covered little more than the costs of transport, which had been made to soar by structural adjustment plans (SAPS).

In the apartment block where I lived in town, flats built for craftsmen and their families were used for storage, for workers to sleep in, as offices, or as homes for "apprentices" and their families. One was occupied by a factory worker and his wife, who was related to a workshop journeyman. Another was owned by an unemployed factory worker selling goods on the street (in the "informal economy") and his wife, a secretary and sister of a workshop master who had granted her his rights to the apartment in an internal family transaction. One master used his apartment as a mini-factory staffed by women workers commuting from nearby areas. Another apartment was owned by a workshop "apprentice" acknowledged by all as a "master" but unable to open his own workshop, who worked most days until midnight if not later. He and his wife had managed to buy an apartment in town when they were still cheap. The walls were unpainted, the furniture purchased on installments that they barely made, and payments for social security or insurance were just a dream. But the house was theirs. Yet another apartment had become, informally, the office for a government employee who had opened up a marketing project for microenterprises. This state employee, the beneficiary of a program to wean youth from the state, was one of the partners of a closed-down microenterprise project, its debts the subject of legal battles. It had two desks, two telephones, and no business.

Much as this actual use of the town was a complete reversal of the plans set by the town's builders, the governorate itself had set into motion this informal system of building use. Workshop masters, not used to being told what to do in the first place, had rebelled at the thought of assigned workshops and apartments, and they had been "allowed to pick." Variation in the availability of resources such as money, relations to officials, and the quality of customers made a difference in outcomes.

From the beginning, internal social dynamics took sway over the planner's map, with all the algebras that go into the distribution of goods by the state coming into play. But when the graduate entrepreneurs and Gulf returnees arrived to take up the "extra" places, there was less choice. Even so, solutions were found. One man, a Gulf refugee and former railroad man, much beloved and much crossed with bad luck in his life, came to town to find his blacksmith's workshop on the second floor and all the apartments gone. He arranged a swap of his downtown apartment with that of his sister, who had been moved into el-Salam after the earthquakes.

In these new arrangements, the dynamics of a booming real estate market played a major role. Speculation in land and real estate, fueled by oil rents recycled into Egypt by migrants in the Gulf, was at the heart of the new wealth generated in Egypt between the 1970s and 1990s. According to analyses based on World Bank figures, the 1980s and early 1990s witnessed the birth of a new class in Egypt, made rich by the skyrocketing value of land and land-rent in Cairo, most of it in informal property relations linked to state public sector companies. By 1993 there were 20,540 millionaires in Egypt, measured in U.S. dollars, and twelve to fifteen billionaires, most of them having become rich through such means (Haykal 1996). This is particularly striking in a country where average yearly income in agriculture was $300, and in industry and mining about $400 (World Bank 1994, table 22).

New millionaires were not the only ones to benefit from the boom in the real estate market in the 1990s. Even the master of a workshop who had not migrated to the Gulf benefited from this trend (leaving aside the rise in wages of skilled workers over this period). The renter of a workshop in a wealthy neighborhood like Heliopolis could sell "key money" rights to a lease, according to which he paid perhaps 40 LE a month to the owner, for hundreds of thousands of Egyptian pounds, making craftsmen with long-standing leases wealthy regardless of the condition of their businesses. And once a new neighborhood was built, whatever the motivation, the dynamics of the real estate market took off and went to work on land that might have been "worthless" only a few years before. Those who were given a free workshop or apartment in the new desert town, for example, had only to hold on to it to see its value rise.

Between 1991 and 1994, according to our informants, apartments in el-

Hirafiyeen more than tripled in price. Men and women of the neighbor-hood could recite with great accuracy the worth of apartments in their own neighborhood and others, and how they had changed over time. (Those prices were the subject of daily discussion among my women informants.) In the words of one banker in the public sector bank that was an intermediary for Social Fund lending, this dynamic helped to make the youth microenterprise project a disaster, since like alchemy it turned a closed-down workshop into gold as long as one held on to it over time:

> When I first went down there, and saw the neighborhood for the first time, my impression was that the whole thing would fail. Why? The lack of harmony [*taganus*] among the partners. They were one-Muslim, one-Christian, one-woman companies. There was no harmony among the partners . . . one from the College of Arts, another from Social Work, another from Physical Education. . . . No backgrounds to complement each other. . . . None of the partners knew each other, they didn't have any shared language, any trust. Egyptians don't work "team work" well.[3] So they differed, argued, and split up the bequest. They put the shops in cold storage until the price of the workshop gets up to 70–80,000 LE. At first there was nothing out there, those places were worth nothing. Now, they just have to sit on them and the prices go up, and they make their money.

Craftsmen Don't Mind the Noise and Din

El-Hirafiyeen was organized around notions of "the craftsman" and how "he likes to live." Social scientists and engineers were central to creating this social space that I, the social scientist, would study in this research. Repeatedly my ethnographic research involved study of the categories that had shaped the production of life in el-Hirafiyeen. Since el-Hirafiyeen was not planned by professional urban planners but by engineers, the categories that shaped their thinking were less well the-orized than in larger urban planning projects in Cairo. And yet the social science categories that shaped their work were no less distinct.

The engineers who planned el-Hirafiyeen worked around distinct social categories which they associated with distinct forms of built space. Typologies of social class were at the center of their design decisions for the different "New Communities" that they were charged with building. My informants who built "New Communities" for the governorate described four social categories of users whom they served, and the architectural forms that they associated with each: worker, educated entrepreneur, government employee, and craftsman. Workshop and living arrangements in el-Hirafiyeen, for example, were designed in accordance with engineers' ideas of how "the craftsman of Egypt likes to live." Apartments were built right over workshops, since "the craftsman likes to live near his work." By living over his workshop the craftsman "saves the expense of transportation." Moreover, he "doesn't mind the noise and din . . . because it's his noise, he's not educated, he's from that world, and it doesn't bother him."

Workshops and apartments in el-Hirafiyeen were built like a series of courtyards, a planning decision explained in practical terms as a way to use the available space most economically. Workshops in Cairo use the street or sidewalk to carry out some of their work. This practice sometimes led to conflicts with residents of the street. (In Heliopolis those annoyed by such practices were often powerful and could land a workshop owner in jail.) With a public square set up for them in advance, craftsmen "wouldn't get in the way" of other residents. In the traditional "popular neighborhoods" of Cairo, people who worked in quite different trades had lived together on the same street; work and home were integrated into one neighborhood. Here an entire settlement was being constructed around "the craftsman's needs," with the idea that those practicing different categories of labor should be separated into different neighborhoods of the city.

The craftsman's needs stood in stark contrast to the needs of the "working class." Unlike the craftsman, the worker "liked" blocky uniform flats like those built in the "New Community" of el-Salam. Since it was assumed that the workers would commute to work in other parts of Cairo, transportation was ample in this settlement, unlike in el-Hirafiyeen. Life in el-Salam was more anonymous, something that "the worker" was supposed to prefer. But according to some of the factory workers who lived in el-Hirafiyeen, it was taken for granted that el-Hirafiyeen—despite the many problems with life there—was "better" than el-Salam, just because it was less anonymous, and its character was closer to that of a "popular neighborhood."

As I have said, the youth entrepreneurs were moved into el-Hirafiyeen after it had been built. The engineers were not happy that youth entrepreneurs had been housed in a settlement built for the craftsman and his mentality. The youth should "have their own town." Housing for the young, educated entrepreneur should be separated from the site of production, unlike housing for the "craftsman," who likes to have his housing and work sites integrated. And while the craftsman wasn't interested in community centers, the educated youth had ample need for them, which should be provided by the state planners. In the words of an engineer who worked on the original plans for el-Hirafiyeen:

> The craftsman likes to be near his workshop. Then, he's saved the expense of the transportation. He doesn't mind the noise and din of the workshop, because it's his noise. He's not educated, he's from that world, and it doesn't bother him—he can sleep in the middle of din and noise. We also made the neighboring area, Madinet el-Salam. . . . That area suits workers, the working class, versus the character of the craft worker, who likes to be right near his work. If I had my way, the Graduates would have their own City (and not live together with the craftsmen). They need different things than the workshop owner. The graduate is educated, he doesn't like noise. He needs more social services, like a Cultural Center, which the craftsman isn't interested in. The graduate [like the worker] likes to have his work in one place, then his home in another place, and needs cultural, educational activities. He should have his own city. If the idea had begun with the Youth Graduates, the planning of the city would have been different. If I planned for the Youth, for someone educated, I would have to include possibilities for expansion, because he won't make do just with a small shop. The educated person, a person who thinks, I have to provide to him calm.

Another Model for Life and Markets: Heliopolis

The idea of building a model community on the fringes of Cairo, constructed around notions of what built space was appropriate for a certain social category, was not a new one (cf. el-Kadi 1989). In fact some of the craftsmen moved into el-Hirafiyeen were the grandsons of men who had migrated into Cairo via Heliopolis, which was built as a model community and desert oasis at the beginning of the twentieth century.

Heliopolis is relevant to the story of el-Hirafiyeen in a number of ways. First, Heliopolis was the home of many of the craftsmen moved to el-Hirafiyeen. Most kept their apartment in Heliopolis and used their apartment in el-Hirafiyeen as a warehouse. Many of the workshop customers also lived in Heliopolis. Those workshops that specialized in imported cars maintained their customer base in Heliopolis after the move by providing transportation for customers who had dropped off their cars. And for those who couldn't afford any car, let alone a Mercedes, the only public bus line in el-Hirafiyeen went back and forth to Heliopolis (its last stop was in Roxy).

The two neighborhoods were linked in other ways as well. They were linked through the family histories of many of the craftsmen who were my informants in el-Hirafiyeen. Family history is an important resource for understanding shifts in the nature of power, economy, and markets without making the assumptions that underlie a structuralist orientation (Bertaux and Bertaux-Wiame 1981). At the same time, family history can give to ethnography a historical dimension, a window into broader transformations that a present-oriented ethnography can miss. In a context where the "familial ethos" is central to the organization of social and political life (Singerman 1995, 41–71; cf. Wikan 1996, Wikan 1995), moreover, family history takes on additional importance. In Cairo family histories are also a history of movement in space, owing to the vital importance of rural-urban migration in Egypt, and the equal importance of circular migration within the Arab and Muslim world. Likewise, the life-course of individuals, and their movements into Cairo and out to the Arab Gulf in circular migration, must always be understood in conjunction with broader family projects. Family history is a history of the spatial production of Cairo, and Egypt, as well.

El-Hirafiyeen and Heliopolis are fascinating in this regard. For family history across three generations in el-Hirafiyeen is also a history of two planned communities. Heliopolis and el-Hirafiyeen, moreover, represent two polar-opposite ways of thinking about markets, craftsmen, workers, and economy in Egypt. Heliopolis was built at a period of many utopian colonial urban plans, some of which were linked to the "garden city" movement in Europe and the United States.[4] The plans for the neighborhood reveal a common attempt of the time to end anti-modern practices, to transform traditional people (craftsmen, in this case) into "workers," and to separate the interwoven institutions of family, workshop, and community. In el-Hirafiyeen, by contrast, a postmodern ethos prevailed. The anti-modern practices of craftsmen, such as the blurring of boundaries between home and workplace and the tendency to let popular Egyptian Islam influence production as well as worship, were seen as something to preserve rather than destroy. And the "craftsman's mentality" was seen as something to respect, not override.

Family histories of craftsmen in el-Hirafiyeen reveal much of how the gap between these two approaches to the market was bridged. The grandparents and parents of many of the craftsmen who were moved into el-Hirafiyeen came from Heliopolis. Family and life histories of the craftsmen over three generations reveal more than personal history. Their life and work histories over three generations link the two projects in a revealing fashion. Grandchildren of men who moved into one planned urban project—Heliopolis—were moved into another planned urban project three generations later—el-Hirafiyeen—with distinctly different ideas about the appropriate place of workers and craftsmen in the urban structure of Cairo. The life histories of workshop masters in el-Hirafiyeen shed light on some of the ways that this shift from one ideology to another was effected. Those life histories also reveal some important dynamics underlying the construction of markets, and the crafting of neighborhoods, in Cairo.[5]

Heliopolis was the brainchild of Édouard Empain (later Baron Empain), the leader of a group of Belgian industrialists active in Egypt at the end of the nineteenth century.[6] An industrialist, banker, and financier, he established the Cairo Electric Railways and Heliopolis Oases Company in 1906 together with his local counterpart, Boghos Nubar. This holding company carried out many projects in Egypt and held the controlling shares in other companies, including the Société Égyptienne d'Électricité, which built and operated the original Shubra power station (Vitalis 1995, 36, citing Levi 1952, 314). The Empain group built and operated a light railway in the eastern delta of Egypt, near Alexandria, and near Port Said, as well as building and operating electric tramway lines in Cairo (Vitalis 1995, 35). With the participation of banks in Paris, Brussels, and Holland, the Heliopolis Company bought 2,500 hectares of land from the Egyptian government outside the northern reaches of Cairo, with a seven-year option to buy 5,000 more contiguous acres (Besançon 1958, 129). The company undertook the development of this desert land, its provision with water, and its linking to the city of Cairo by means of its electric tramway lines, for which it had a monopoly.

Heliopolis was planned as a luxury settlement out in the middle of the desert: it was to be an oasis, built by man, to serve the most luxurious tastes of Europe's upper classes. Empain named his planned desert oasis after the ancient capital of the thirteenth district of Lower Egypt, On (named Heliopolis by the Greeks). Empain was an amateur Egyptologist and ordered an archaeological excavation of his new Heliopolis before the engineers began to lay the infrastructure of the desert town in 1905 (Ilbert 1981, 9). While the town turned out differently, much of the original vision did come to fruition. The largest luxury hotel in the world was built in Heliopolis; it was graced with one of the world's first Luna Parks, a racetrack, a sporting club, and architecture presenting the exotic East in a more familiar guise, complete with modern plumbing and forms of transport. But the financial crisis that wiped out the value of much of Cairo's stock exchange and real estate markets in 1907 put an end to the future of Heliopolis as an exclusive desert oasis playground for Europe's adventurous wealthy.[7] Land became difficult to sell: by 1909 only 335,000 square meters had changed hands (Besançon 1958, 132). Empain was wealthy enough to be able to bide his time and take advantage of the changing circumstances, such as those afforded by the intersection of the financial crisis with the "first modern housing crisis" of Egypt (Ilbert 1989). His company was able to get new land from the government at greatly reduced prices by undertaking to build a certain number of units of housing for state functionaries, in what was originally planned to be a separate "Oasis #2."

The idea for Oasis #2 was eventually abandoned. In its place housing for functionaries was built near the mosque in the northern end of one united town. Another challenge came with the Second World War, when British troops were stationed in Cairo, some in Heliopolis; again a potential disaster was turned to advantage when many of the officers stayed around after the war. A cotton boom in 1918–19 further increased land sales already revived by British officers (Ilbert 1989, 133). By the 1920s Cairo was once again a favorite holiday destination of the European rich and famous: its famous hotels like the Shepard hosted royalty and millionaires, and the Heliopolis Palace joined the ranks of world-class hotels.

Heliopolis was a fully planned town. Its architecture was designed for specific categories of users identified by its French urban planners.[8] Retaining a strong architectural unity throughout, the city also encompassed a distinct and highly planned spatial and architectural hierarchy. The area of villas built for wealthy Europeans (which some wealthy Egyptians ended up buying as well) was separated from that of the workers. But the process of spatial separation and categorization went further. Workers' areas themselves were built according to categories; the cultural and housing needs of each were determined by fieldwork studies. For while "workers" were clearly and simply opposed to the wealthy users for whom the oasis had originally been planned, differences among those workers came to predominate in the planners' thinking.

At the time when Heliopolis was being planned, Cairo was full of European workers, Italian and Greek in particular, who dominated skilled sectors of the building trades. With the Egyptian economy booming and cheap steamship service available around the Mediterranean, it was relatively easy for workers from different countries of Europe to seek a better life in Egypt (Beinin and Lockman 1987, 35). In 1907 there were 147,000 Europeans resident in Egypt, in addition to 34,000 immigrants for geographical Syria (35). In 1899 alone, when the British were building the Aswan Dam, so many thousands of Italians descended on the port city of Alexandria in search of work that many had to be sent back—deported, to use today's language (Ilbert 1989, 267, citing *La Bourse égyptienne*, 6 October 1899). Peasants forced off of the land after the cotton crisis of 1865–66 (which began during the American Civil War), those recruited by the state for corvée labor before the 1880s, and peasants recruited through indirect means that took the place of corvée (Lockman 1994, 83) sometimes stayed in Cairo when their contracts expired, together with streams of newly landless peasants ready to work for low wages (83–84). While workers seen as European were signed on as "workers" by the company alongside Egyptian peasants, and the two groups were deemed fit to work together, it was not expected that they would want or be able to live together.[9] Each was seen as having different housing needs.

"Needs-assessment studies" were made, and according to the results planned proletarian blocks of flats were partially scrapped. Free-standing houses were added, with internal courtyards where newly urbanized peasants could raise their chickens and provide their own food.[10] But needs assessments for suitable architectural forms went further. Each type of building had a title, and a marked denomination of its intended users. The large buildings in an "L" shape carried the initials MUS (for *musulmans*, one assumes), and the workers' city was subdivided into areas marked for *Maisons pour ouvriers européens* and *maisons indigènes*. The "garden cities" (that had, however, no gardens) were destined for either *petits employés européens* or *petits employés indigènes*. All these documents and plans set up a structured opposition between the categories of "indigène" and "other" (Ilbert 1981, 115–16).

Two things are striking in this structured pair. "Indigène" was merged with "musulman" and the two were used synonymously. At the same time, Egypt's native Coptic Christians, Armenian Christians, and Jews were evicted from the category of indigenous, and sent out to a nebulous zone where they were not quite European either.[11] Category confusion did not stop there. For example, where should the local "Levantine" population, such as the long-resident communities from Greater Syria or Anatolia, be placed? What about the Maronite Christians (Ilbert 1981, 16) and those called "Greek" (who had usually never seen Greece)? What about those long resident in Egypt, originally from Italy or the Balkans, whose cultural practice seemed "non-European" to the French (120)?

The focus of this early-twentieth-century model town project was on residence, not labor. It was for the design of housing that these typologies of class, ethnicity, and religion were mobilized, and spatial division and internal homogenization were planned.[12] Hygiene for the Europeans and those locals whose cultural practice made them seem quasi-European was ensured not only by modern plumbing but by the distance of their neighborhoods from the "germ-infested" neighborhoods of Cairo. Contact with workers, outside that necessitated by work of servants in the home, for example, was minimized as much as possible. The movement of the indigène workers outside their living area after working hours was regulated by the company's monopoly over the means of transport through the desert: A separate tramcar line led to their neighborhoods, and its hours of operation were restricted to those necessary to get low-level state functionaries to and from work in Cairo. Tramlines into the other neighborhood of Heliopolis, on the other hand, operated far into the night (Ilbert 1989, 276).

In contrast to the elaborate system of categories devised for housing, matters were simpler when it came to labor. Labor was not categorized along cultural lines and no appropriate architectural structures were designed for its performance. Heliopolis was designed as a residential town; labor was not high on the planners' agenda. But it inevitably slipped in the back door. Heliopolis had become home to low-level state functionaries, and they were workers of a sort. In any case, even an oasis had to be operated and maintained. The relevant issue, however, goes beyond the obvious fact that Heliopolis was first planned as a residential city. While residence was a locus where people were differentiated and spatially homogenized, the labor process was treated as a site of unification. That different groups, according to typologies of class and pseudo-ethnicity, would mix in the labor process was, it seems, taken for granted, and did not pose a problem. Where and how those living in the more élite section of town—foreigners, local Christians, or local Muslims— would work does not seem to have been the subject of discussion. As things developed, many of the inhabitants of Heliopolis, both European and Egyptian, came to be members of the "free professions": doctors, lawyers, pharmacists, and high functionaries of the British-Egyptian regime (Ilbert 1981, 119).

Among the workers of Heliopolis things were bit more complex. After all, when it came to workers, a variety of subcategories were involved. The northern section of Heliopolis was built (once the plans for a separate Oasis #2 had been scrapped) for two main groups of workers. The first consisted of "functionaries" of the British-Egyptian regime, for whom the company had specially built housing. These workers commuted daily into Cairo by trolley. The second group consisted of employees of the Heliopolis Company itself. They operated the trolley lines, and maintained all the buildings and infrastructure of the town that we would today assume to be under the jurisdiction of the city government.[13] Both groups lived and worked in Heliopolis.

Most interesting for my purposes were the artisans needed to keep the complex machinery of Heliopolis in working order (demands for the Luna Park alone must have been quite high), and to build and maintain the structures of its complete urban order. Quite striking here are the absences and silences. In Heliopolis, at least in its first decades, the notion of "the artisan" was markedly absent as a recognized form of labor. Rather, artisans were incorporated where necessary into company projects as a subcategory of "workers." If based in one of the shops leased from the company, they could fit into the category of "shopkeepers." (Stores might include workshops, since the workshop is also a site of selling.)

The best available material on the types of labor carried out by license in the town of Heliopolis relates to the types of its shops, workshops, and factories. An enumeration of the types of stores present in Heliopolis in 1912 is illuminating. In 1912 there were about 2,500 permanent residents in Heliopolis. Most of the stores catered to European consumption styles, like the bakery, pastry shop, and dairy shop. There were also two "Arab bakeries" and, close to the workers' neighborhood near the Avenue of the Mosque, some other small shops catering to "indigenous" taste. In 1917, according to Ilbert, there were about a hundred shops in Heliopolis altogether. Although there is no extant list of just what those shops were for, we do know that some were designated as artisanal workshops. Those workshops were, however, strictly regulated and confined to designated streets (Ilbert 1981, 51); in 1920 there were only a few carpentry and mechanics' workshops licensed by the company to operate in all of Heliopolis (56).

Official maps of the town include those small factories run by the company in its "industrial zone," off to the east of the *cité indigène*. While the presence of artisans was highly regulated, the company's need for them in all but name was intense. It maintained works for making bricks and compressed fuel briquettes, and workshops for servicing the company's transport systems, water, and electricity (Ilbert 1981, 56). Close by the works in this company industrial zone (and in a pattern typical of Egyptian industry to this day, where workshops set themselves up close by larger "formal" factories and serve their needs) were two carpentry workshops, one blacksmith or ironworker, and one lampmaker. The company also maintained fields for growing seeds, beans, corn, and barley. Two feddans were reserved for cultivating cotton. The growth of crops was intended both to reduce company expenditures and to give incentive to some of the employees to stay and live in the company town (56).

In short, planned industrial activities in Heliopolis were reduced to those for which the company had a direct need. Where possible, this type of labor took place not in independent workshops but in larger, more "modern" *usines* with the craftsman transformed into a company worker. While in their place of residence those deemed "European" or "other" were to live apart from those deemed *indigènes musulmans* and in different types of buildings, these groups mixed together in the usines of the company town. The desert oasis and model town did not encompass that part of Egypt's indigenous economy known as the "workshop." Where local artisans were employed, they were largely transformed into "workers"; the few who seem to have retained their identity as artisans in this period were regulated in their access to company stores and workshops.

Once again, as in any project undertaken by the state or an "international" organization of any form—be it the Empain group or the World Bank—practice reshapes even the most elaborate of plans. The point is not only that we should be more precise about what kind of organizations we are looking at. Plans are not sovereign. If the workshop disappeared in the plan, it did not in practice. It took less than forty years for workshops to reemerge there as a dominant form of economic practice noted by scholars. Here I can only highlight a few relevant factors. When the British Army took up residence in Heliopolis during the Second World War, new kinds of workshops—those of mechanics, garage men, and body workers, and lubricating works—opened to serve its needs and stayed on after the war was over (Besançon 1958, 145). By 1958 the neighborhood had a reputation as a center for workshops specializing in work on cars, imported cars in particular. Car agencies began to open in the neighborhood after the war, often doing better than their downtown main branches (145). What Besançon calls the "urban neo-artisan" became characteristic of a neighborhood unconstrained by the tourist trade, in medieval Cairo where the craft guilds had been centered.

In the 1970s and 1980s new services flourished in Heliopolis to cater to the new classes' conspicuous consumption. This meant the growth not only of boutiques inside the heart of Heliopolis but also of industrial service shops. These workshops could turn out spare parts not yet available in Egypt or too expensive. They would repair televisions and paint cars or make them over altogether. The money flowing into Egypt under Anwar Sadat had a multiplier effect on this second level of workshops that served those with the money to enjoy new consumer goods. As the money of these craftsmen grew and multiplied, their workshops grew in size as well. But those élites who were the primary beneficiaries of Sadat's economic liberalization did not relish its secondary effects, like the spread of noisy workshops. The presence of messy, noisy workshops on their streets was a blow to the prestige of the neighborhood and also disturbed the modern feel of the streets of Heliopolis. The neat spaces of Heliopolis, where the artisan had been remodeled as a company worker, came unraveled at the edges. Life histories of the children and grandchildren of those company workers tell the story of this evolution. One of those grandchildren, who was moved into el-Hirafiyeen, was Khaled, a machinist born in 1955.

From Indigène Worker to Workshop Master

Khaled's grandfather migrated to Cairo from Sohag in the early 1930s. His family moved directly into Heliopolis, where his grandfather, and then his father, worked for one of the companies set up by the builder of Heliopolis, Baron Empain: the Heliopolis Company for Housing and Construction. Like other Egyptians who moved into Cairo with artisanal skills, his grandfather settled into a flat designed for "indigenous workers" in Heliopolis and became one of those labeled indigène workers. Good housing and access to agricultural plots were two incentives offered by the Heliopolis Company to attract and keep good workers. Khaled's father took advantage of another company benefit: access to industrial training courses for the children of workers. When Khaled turned twelve his father sent him to a course in industrial studies.

Khaled's family lived in a house that bordered the "informal" part of town near the street of Geser el-Sawais, which had been built as a boundary between Heliopolis and its more rural neighbor al-Zaitoun. Khaled's youth coincided with one of the early waves of rural-to-urban migration into Cairo. New migrants into Cairo settled into these fringe areas of Heliopolis, blurring in the process the boundaries between the different neighborhoods that would soon collapse altogether. In a pattern typical of the "informal neighborhoods" of Cairo, craftsmen reproduced the integrated pattern of residence and work that marked the older popular neighborhoods of Cairo. Such happened in the street where Khaled lived as a boy. A neighbor opened a workshop in the ground floor of the building where they lived. That workshop was where, in his words, he really "began to learn."[14]

Being the son of an employee of the Heliopolis Company who also had worked since childhood in a neighborhood workshop, Khaled was well positioned to enter the labor market. Khaled went to work in what is called today the "formal industrial sector" of Cairo, in a machine shop of fifteen workers in the industrial neighborhood of Shubra. There similar workshops provided many of the goods and repairs needed to keep the large factories of the public sector running. In this shop Khaled improved his skills and confidence, and reached the stage where he thought he could run his own workshop. To open his workshop, however, he went back to his own neighborhood, back in Heliopolis, where he knew people and was rooted in networks that could help him succeed. He married a neighborhood girl whose father owned a workshop that soon enough became his own.[15] That the workshop was in Heliopolis, home to many of Egypt's army officers, made it easy to arrange the conduct of his army service in Cairo—the key to reasonably comfortable survival during grueling army service that paid, in the 1990s, the equivalent of about $3 a month.

After his army service Khaled opened his own workshop together with his brother, who had similarly strong training in both workshop and company-based industrial skills. Conflicts between their wives led the two to separate. The job of providing for the family's future shifted from the extended to the nuclear family, and Khaled's brother moved out to one of the industrial "New Cities" built in the desert after the Six-Day War with Israel of 1973. Back in Heliopolis, Khaled's business boomed in what he called the "good old days" of economic liberalization under Sadat, when foreign companies moved into Egypt and "were all ordering all kinds of parts" from him. The 1990s, as for most of the workshops, brought recession. The move to el-Hirafiyeen hit Khaled's business badly, but by 1994 he had built up relations outside the specialization marked on his business card, installing car air conditioners, into making diverse spare parts for Egyptian and foreign-owned companies in the northern industrial district around el-Hirafiyeen. His business was doing well, and a crisis in his marriage had resolved itself when his wife finally followed advice to leave her family and friends in Heliopolis and come to el-Hirafiyeen, where she could keep a closer eye on her husband's movements. He recreated a market, and his wife recreated their home. Their life remained tied to their friends and family in Heliopolis, the neighborhood in which they had such deep roots dating back to his indigène worker grandfather.

Khaled's family history was deeply marked by interventions of organizational power: the Heliopolis Company's creation of Heliopolis in the desert, the Egyptian state's closing down of Khaled's workshop, and the World Bank's creation of the Social Fund are just some of the most obvious examples. Those interventions were in part social science experiments organized around categories such as the indigène, the worker, and the craftsman, and notions of their rightful place in urban life. Those categories were conceived on a level different from the high-theory level of the gift and the market that I analyzed in chapter 1. The engineers who discussed the different needs of craftsmen and educated microentrepreneurs, and the bankers who discussed the nature of craftsmen's markets, were less eloquent than Adam Smith or Marcel Mauss. The categories that they mobilized were not worked out as theoretical concepts. But their endeavors are as much a part of social science as textbooks of macroeconomics and the theory of the gift (following Callon 1998).

The very presence of both the craftsmen and the microentrepreneurs in el-Hirafiyeen was the outcome of social science experiments. The craftsmen who were moved from Heliopolis to el-Hirafiyeen had lived through many such experiments since their grandfathers' days. Across those ninety years they continued to practice their crafts, to move into new fields of work, and to build their markets. Those markets were not constructed from the top down thanks to theories of the market. Instead the craftsmen constructed what we can call a market of practice, or a market of habitus (Bourdieu 1977). As such, it was also a market of experience, touch, and taste.[16] This kind of market contrasted greatly with that of the microentrepreneurs. They learned of the market through the lessons they had been taught in Cairo University, in training sessions of microenterprise, and Social Fund pamphlets. They spoke of the market a great deal: their talk was sprinkled with references to GATT, the internet, and competition. But with important exceptions (see chapter 7), they could not find the market. The space they moved through in el-Hirafiyeen was empty and stark. They moved through the streets like a deputy going through a ghost town in an old western: poised, waiting, worrying, alone. The craftsmen and their families, by way of contrast, experienced space as full. Their movement down the street was punctuated with stops and starts, with side trips into and out of neighbors' workshops, and into the coffeehouse where so much of social and market life went on. Their working lives were shaped by smells and sounds, which told them whether the work was proceeding well, and what their neighbors were doing. For some, their paths through town moved out into higher geographies of power. Their market life moved as well into the offices of the local government and through the organization of the NGO.

3. Mappings of Power

Informal Economy and Hybrid States

The Problem of Ahmed Sa'id

Ahmed Sa'id was secretary of his neighborhood NGO and a member of a joint government-NGO committee. He was also a successful owner-operator, or master (*usta*), of a workshop (*wirsha*). He owned a body shop that checked the alignment of cars with computerized equipment. He had paid 120,000 LE (about US $36,000) for that equipment—produced in Italy to his specifications—with money he had saved as a migrant worker in Germany, Turkey, and Italy. Sa'id's equipment gleamed in the center of his workshop. To the left stood his desk, which attested to the business function of a workshop master, and his special status as secretary of the NGO and member of the joint committee. Under the glass of his desk lay a display of the business cards of some of his most valued customers—mainly army officers.

Sa'id had entered the NGO after development had become the main referent for public pronouncements about the association's work. When he spoke about his work for the association, it was in terms of his service to "the public interest" (*el-maslaha el-'ama*), of which he was extremely proud. There were things in town that made him angry, things that were not right. Like the fence near his workshop, which should not have been there. To accommodate that fence, the builders had short-changed Sa'id and his neighbors of valuable working space. The land behind the fence was illegally occupied and, he often repeated, the state should do something about it. Although the land behind the fence was on paper owned by the governorate, someone else had long been using it. Such squatting is both illegal and an everyday practice in Cairo, and in many other cities of the world. When practices that violate laws are accepted as the norm, and have a legitimacy that is not the state's, they are often called "informal practices." In this case, the squatter on state land was another part of the state—the army, or rather a poultry farm owned and run by the army.[1] Sa'id went on a hunt for an official map of the neighborhood to find out where things had gone wrong. He thought that having the official state map of the neighborhood, with the boundaries clearly drawn to show what land belonged to whom, would help him prove that the poultry farm was illegally squatting on state land. And once that point was proven with the map, he thought, he would be able to force the poultry farm to move the fence and get off those square meters of land that were rightfully his. He never found that map. Neither did we.

Essam Fawzi and I started our search for the official accounting of property relations in el-Hirafiyeen in the offices of the Governorate of Cairo, which had built the neighborhood in the first place. But the relevant information had recently "died" along with an official responsible for the neighborhood's overall planning, to use the language, only half in jest, of an official of the governorate. Officials and staff were happy to learn that we were conducting research in a neighborhood they had built, which had become so important to the progress of the Social Fund—itself an institution of great importance in Egypt. Given the paucity of information on hand, officials were pleased at the chance to contribute to the research and hoped to gather information for their own use as well.

Planners in Egyptian ministries produce maps for reports and state planning projects, often in cooperation with visiting French experts. But the governorate is a ministry without professional planners, although it has the power to build on state land allocated to the governorate. When I visited the Ministry of Planning, professional planners, Egyptian and French, were engaged in different stages of planning projects. All such plans, of course, entailed the drawing and redrawing of maps laying out the contours of envisaged, and completed, planning projects. This was not the case with the governorate, although it also is a builder of state projects on state land. Of course there were planners in Egypt, and in the governorate; but according to one of the engineers who planned some of the "New Communities" built by the state in the 1980s and 1990s, those working in the governorate were not trained planners but engineers who took on planning projects as a way to save the governorate the expense of hiring outside consultants.

And as noted above, the project lacked not only professional planners but an official map. After many inquiries and investigations through various routes during my fieldwork led to no results, I concluded that there was no official map of the neighborhood at all: clerks in the governorate still had only a preliminary sketch of its bare outlines. Other drawings were with the firm that had subcontracted the building project. I was also given, by the end of my study, a map of the area that had been drawn and used by the army. Officials in the governorate were kind enough to provide that map for my research even though it had not been drawn for civilian use. There were no maps at all of el-Hirafiyeen in the offices of state agencies responsible for planning in Cairo, including the office that makes maps available to the public and researchers, since el-Hirafiyeen was "the governorate's" responsibility and not theirs. Nor was Ahmed Sa'id able to find a map. He could find no official representation of how property was supposed to be allocated, and where the lines were supposed to lie between el-Hirafiyeen and the poultry farm. The obvious conclusion—as he often repeated—was that the map was being withheld from him. His enemies in the NGO and local government officials were conspiring to keep the map out of his hands. Without the map, he said, he could not prove his case against the poultry farm and force it to move off of the land that was rightfully his. Such a situation could not have arisen by accident. How could the state have no official map of its own land and property rights?

Accounting for the Map

To think about that question, it is useful to first consider the gap that often exists between official accountings or maps on the one hand and actual relations of power and property on the other. Throughout Cairo and many other cities of the world, what is on the ground is often quite different from what is on the map. Land in Cairo is rarely empty, but its users may not be seen by the official eye of the state. There are many reasons why a state might choose not to see what is obviously there. Informal housing often exhibits a situation of "ambiguous persistence," to use Smart's term for illegal activity that has a "significant degree of social legitimacy" and is "usually tolerated, or only occasionally and situationally repressed" (Smart 1999, 104). Smart's formulation of the problem has its limitations, but it is useful in its emphasis on the political and fluid nature of state decisions whether to "see" or "repress" social situations where informality or illegality prevails. It creates analytical space for thinking about situations in which some things are "seen" and others "overlooked" at one and the same time.[2] A very different explanation of the discrepancy between official accounts of property relations and day-to-day realities is provided by Hernando de Soto in his book *The Mystery of Capital*. De Soto argues for the revival of Marxist categories in a fashion endorsed by Margaret Thatcher. His argument is important, if for no other reason than because of his influential role as a "public intellectual" whose research has a direct impact on development policy. According to de Soto, official property rights are but a "bell jar" of privilege floating in a veritable sea of disenfranchised entrepreneurs (2000). Leaving aside for a moment the many problems with de Soto's book, the extent to which informality prevails in Egypt seems to support his stance.

In many ways, the arguments of Smart and de Soto could not be more different. But they share one important feature: an assumption that the state is in one place and informality is in another. And yet, I will maintain, the state cannot always be so neatly located outside informality. The small story with which I opened this chapter, about a fence that moved, a state that squatted on its own land, and a map that could not be found, lays out in a nutshell some of the problems surrounding the issue of informality in Egypt, and elsewhere as well. The issue is of great importance in and of itself, and it is one that states are grappling with throughout the world. I am more interested, however, in informality as a diagnostic tool that sheds light on some of the obstacles faced by researchers who want to investigate transformations in the nature of the market and the relationship of "the state," "international organizations," and "NGOs." I will pursue that interest by laying out the contours of the story recounted above in more detail, including its broader context. But first I would like to provide an overview of how the issue of informality developed in Egypt—as an empirical phenomenon, a research issue, and an organizing concept for development intervention.

States of Informality

The problem of informality in Cairo was in front of everyone's eyes by the 1980s. It emerged as a question of housing or, in other terms, changing forms of the production of space. According to a leading authority on informal housing in Cairo, 84 percent of the building in the city in 1975–90 was done without authorization from the responsible government agencies, did not conform to building regulations, and was not included in official government statistics and publications of the period on urbanization (el-Kadi 1994, 31).When new maps of the city were drawn up in 1990, entire "informal neighborhoods," built through such methods, took up about 40 percent of the land mass of Greater Cairo (31).

We cannot attribute the complex phenomenon of informal housing in Cairo to one factor like circular migration across state boundaries, although the connection between the two is clearly more than casual.[3] However, assessing the degree of causal relation between the two is not my concern. Instead I am interested in a complex process, one without unilateral causality, through which new social spaces emerged in Egypt where sovereignty of the state did not hold sway. I am also concerned with why some of those spaces were perceived as a security threat and others were not (or, in Smart's terms, why some were situationally repressed and others were not). Finally, and most centrally, I want to elucidate the diverse levels of power that operate in those social spaces, and especially the interactions among the forms of power that we call the state, international organizations, and NGOs.

Much of the housing built informally during the 1970s and 1980s was funded by millions of individual Egyptians who worked in the Arab Gulf states and moved their savings to Egypt through financial networks that remained outside the official banking system and that by and large bypassed state financial institutions. These transfers can be characterized (depending on one's definition of the term) as part of the informal economy. Once inside the sovereign territory of Egypt, moreover, little of this money was deposited into the banking system of Egypt. With the banking system weak and distrusted, and interest rates low, informal alternatives were very attractive. One significant part of migrants' savings was invested in Islamic Investment Companies (IICs), which pooled small and large sums (both from inside Egypt and from migrants still in the Gulf) to invest in the money markets of London and New York.[4]

The IICs built on informal networks created by Egyptian migrant workers in the Gulf to move their money into Egypt and back to their families. With an investment structure resembling that of mutual funds, and yet organized along specifically Islamic lines so that profit, not interest, was paid to depositors, the companies gained the trust of many Egyptian workers in the Gulf. The debates surrounding them echoed other concerns of the time among bank regulators worldwide, regarding new possibilities for unregulated financial transfers enhanced by the new computer technology of the 1970s. These involved what were then called the Euromarkets, and they have been more recently debated in terms of offshore banking.[5] The "crowning flower of the hidden economy" (Sadowski 1991, 232), the IICs brought migrant savings networks in the 1980s together with important money center banks and investment houses in the United States. They also practiced the kind of currency speculation that was then still regarded as being part of the black market.[6] By the end of the 1980s the three largest IICs claimed more than $1.3 billion in deposits belonging to more than 254,000 investors (231). Officials were of two minds about these leaders of the "hidden economy." Even as efforts to suppress this source of competition to the official banking system were under way, in 1988 the IICs were a source of liquidity for the state when it was faced with a severe food crisis (238). But later that year Law 146 was passed, which created a new set of regulations that forced most of the companies into bankruptcy or reorganization. A large number of Egyptians, many of them former migrants, lost all their savings.

Migrants who turned their cash into real estate assets had better luck. Some of the remittances that had been transferred across borders without recourse to the official banking system were invested in real estate through various forms of informal property relations. This money also stayed outside the national economy when migrants or their relatives bought land and helped create new or transformed neighborhoods, whose contours were shaped without regard to state law. Some gained unprecedented windfalls in the 1980s from an astronomical rise in real estate prices that continued through the 1990s. Again, the investment of remittances in housing assets was not the sole cause of this real estate boom, but it was clearly an important factor. Others were massive military investment in the new neighborhoods of Cairo and state subsidies of speculative investment in real estate (Mitchell 2002, 274–75). In this period real estate replaced agriculture as the country's fourth-largest investment sector, after oil, manufacturing, and tourism.[7] By the early 1990s, a complex set of factors had created a veritable real estate investment bubble in Cairo.[8] Between December 1993 and April 1994 alone, the price of land for building in most neighborhoods of Cairo rose by 50 percent (*el-Ahali*, 21 April 1994, 3).

Much of this phenomenal rise in real estate prices occurred through various systems that were technically illegal, but were normalized social facts. In the "informal neighborhoods," for example, individuals invested large or small sums of money saved over a lifetime in land owned by the state, or in land zoned for agriculture that was gradually being incorporated into Greater Cairo. Surrounding villages were absorbed into the capital city. Previously uninhabited land owned on paper by the state became the de facto private property of others in fully developed land markets, with the state receiving no compensation in the process.[9] The city grew at an unprecedented pace, though little of the growth went on according to the rule of law. Since there were no criminal statutes against squatting on state land in Egypt, there were few legal instruments to put a stop to such forms of building once they were facts on the ground, beyond ineffective fines and threats of razing buildings.

Such informal "squatting" had transformed the face of most large third world cities in this period. In the thinking of many development theorists of the time, squatting, and the ability of the poor to produce solutions to their own housing crises, were a positive thing. There was hope that the poor might provide some of the answers that development had failed to supply. De Soto's *The Other Path* (1989) was the strongest and most influential statement of the view that informal neighborhoods of squatters were not the problem—the state was.

But not everyone agreed. Much as it was tolerated on the whole, informal housing also became the object of direct attacks by the security apparatus of the Egyptian state, especially when neighborhoods became conflated in official discourse with "Islamic fundamentalism." When some informal neighborhoods associated with Islamist organizations were attacked by security forces, the notion that "informality" was in itself linked with "terrorism" became common. Informal neighborhoods in Cairo were often portrayed in official state discourse as a cancer on the social and political body. When the Egyptian government laid siege to the informal neighborhood of Imbaba, the semantic association in Egyptian Arabic of informal neighborhoods ('*ashwaiyyat*: random, disordered) with disorder was extended to an association to terrorism.[10] Here I would like to point out the extent to which state discourse echoes the assumption made by both Smart and de Soto: the state is in one place, informality in another.

And yet, I would maintain, "the state" and informality cannot be so neatly separated. Given that informality was defined in terms of an opposition to the state, such a conclusion raises a number of questions.[11] Cross-border circular migrations, pervasive unregulated financial networks across borders, and a growing share of territory in the capital city that seemed immune from state regulation were all too central in this period to be relegated to a sphere of negative phenomena—the "not formal." "Informal housing" was associated by the state with specific "problem neighborhoods" such as Imbaba, I have said, but informality as a mode of technically illegal activities with a high degree of social legitimacy was extremely widespread by the 1990s. Nor was informality characteristic of the poor alone, as is often assumed in discussions of the Middle East.[12] Informal property relations had become a crucial generator of wealth and power in society at large. Indeed, the state itself was not isolated from these dynamics.

The issue of widespread squatting on state land by the wealthy and state officials in Egypt, for example, such as was evident in el-Hirafiyeen over the course of my fieldwork, became the subject of debate in official public space by the Islamist press in the 1990s, exposed as part of a wider campaign to publicize alleged instances of government corruption and malfeasance. The government acknowledged that there was little it could do to stop the squatting, even by official agencies of the state, in the absence of criminal (as opposed to civil) laws against it. In some cases military orders were issued to enforce the rights of the state against its own agencies in the land it legally owned. Informality, it seems, had become part of the state itself.[13] That is, making sense of the "informal"—be it informal housing or informal economy—is impossible without a parallel story of the state. And, I would add, without a parallel story of international organizations as well.

What Is Mapped and Who Is Counting?

Informal housing in Egypt, I have said, became regarded by the state as a security threat associated with Islamic fundamentalism and terrorism. But when applied to the economy, the term "informal" assumed

73

positive attributes: the informal economy was an agenda item that IOs and the state alike could adopt as their own, and informality gained new prominence and official sanction.

When structural adjustment programs (SAPs) enforced by the World Bank and the International Monetary Fund in the 1980s and 1990s became official state policy in Egypt (on paper if not always enforced), the issue of informal economy acquired new policy implications. IOs supervising the state's retreat from the economy realized that the practices through which the poor in Egypt had always managed to survive were a good thing, and could become the basis of a "safety net" for those who might fall through the holes made by SAPs. In other words, they undertook to develop the informal economy. But before IOs could do this, they had to gain a better knowledge of just what that economy was.

To intervene in any given social reality, an institutional power first has to map it. That is true of IOs as well as states. With informal neighborhoods identified with "terrorism" and "Islamic fundamentalism," as I have said, the security dimension was paramount. But with the informal economy, security of the state did not emerge as a key motivation for deciding to see, and to map. Rather, security of the global order under conditions of widespread unemployment and structural adjustment was on the agenda of international agencies around the world. Here it is significant that informality was cast as an economic issue at a time when definitions of just what the economy is were the subject of widespread debate within and outside the profession of economics.[14] Recast as economy, informality became an issue solvable by economic means. Specifically, to understand the development of the informal economy under the sponsorship of IOs, a statistical mapping of the massive informal economy was needed. But informal activity by definition is not included in state statistics, so mapping it was no easy matter. Doing so required rewriting some of the basic categories around which statistics are gathered on both national and international scales.[15] Such a project was sponsored by IOs in different parts of the world. Once the contours of the informal economy were mapped out, it became possible for IOs and others to begin funding this thing which they had helped to define.

I have made a shift here, of course, from literal maps to the more metaphorical notion of mapping. Not all maps are images of roads in space, or engineers' plans. The statistical summaries that we call "national income accounts," for example, give a numerical mapping of "national economy." We can read off those tables of value added an image of a country at work, of laboring bodies within the bounds of a distinct national economy. Once we speak of "national economy," moreover, the state is an implicit unit of analysis as well. National income accounts, like gross domestic product, are mappings made by the state of the officially recognized national economy. If such mappings are accounts of the present, they are also plans for the future (Scott 1998). As such, they are also instruments in the deployment of power. This is true of other kinds of accounts and mappings as well. The account, David Stark reminds us, is a term that "simultaneously connotes bookkeeping and narration" (1998, 133). Any accounting, he says, draws on and reproduces social orders (133). This point could not be clearer in the United States in the wake of the accounting scandals of 2002: what goes into accounts is highly contestable. And so, too, what goes into the map.

In the words of an engineer in Cairo who built el-Hirafiyeen: "there is no state decision without the map." The engineer was speaking about Decision #242, to move workshops from neighborhoods of northern Cairo to el-Hirafiyeen. His pragmatic statement captured something broader, however, including the fact that sometimes decisions about what goes into the map, and what stays out, are not so simple. Maps and accounts of the state reflect the official story of the state, how resources will be deployed in plans for the future. Decisions about what goes into this story involve contests for power among different groups. And in circumstances where the official rules of the game often do not prevail, conflicts over mapping take on special significance.

Mapping is also about power exercised through property in land. The question of what goes into the map—the official accounting—involves contests for power among different groups attempting to assert control over land. As such it is useful to think of property in these contexts as a "bundle of rights" or a "bundle of powers" (Verdery 1998) over which contestation is never-ending and rampant.[16] In the situation encountered by Ahmed Sa'id, I suggest, contestation over the bundle of rights in this one parcel of state-owned property resulted in a negative outcome— the official map was not drawn.[17]

Maps were absent in other arenas as well. I have outlined above some of the spheres of economic exchange in Egypt that were not captured by the official state accounts of the economy in the 1970s and 1980s, and the extent to which this "informal sector" was growing. Moreover, in a parallel development, questions were being raised about the adequacy of dominant definitions of economy within the economics profession as well. The need for new maps of economy was becoming clear. Redrawing the maps involved extensive projects of counting, and a rethinking of what to count and how. Most of those projects were sponsored not by the state, which had counted, taxed, and managed the "national economy." Instead, most new contests over what went into the map, and efforts to include that which had remained outside, originated this time in IOs.

The redrawing of maps of the economy is part of the shifting relations between states on the one hand and IOs on the other. Projects sponsored by IOs to generate research and statistics independent of state institutions and state statistics are simultaneously a deployment of power in that changing relationship. We should remember that since Bretton Woods, IOs have been given the authority to oversee not only relations between states but the conditions of life of their citizens as well (Escobar 1995, 39). This aspect of IOs' work was reinforced when mandated concern for human rights was added to earlier humanitarian concerns of alleviating poverty.[18] With this switch, the person being counted became no longer a citizen of a nation-state but an individual in a universal humanity.

By the 1970s, when it had become clear that a significant portion of the people living and working in third world cities did not appear in government statistics and were ignored by the appropriate authorities (Tripp 1997, 22), this aspect of the IOs' agenda became extremely significant. If so many people did not appear in government statistics, then the IOs would have to generate an alternative set of statistics. To exercise their mandated responsibility for the citizens of member states, the IOs had to know more about their life conditions, but again, they were now counted as individuals, not as national citizens.

The statistical agencies of nation-states were deemed insufficient for such a task. First of all, they lacked statistics about the informal economy. But this was not the only shortcoming. Statistical systems for tracking the economy in the third world were often transferred wholesale from industrialized societies, and assumptions embedded in the numbers were often incompatible with local economic conditions. Furthermore, a breakdown of the social science tradition and state educational institutions in the 1970s and 1980s in Egypt and elsewhere around the world under the pressure of SAPs reduced the state's capacity to track its own economy (Fergany 1991, 27). Planning and statistical agencies in the "third world," it should be remembered, were often set up in the capitals of the imperial powers. Development lenders continued the imperial tradition, linking their aid to the implementation of alternative systems of information gathering (Cooper and Stoler 1989; Cooper and Packard 1998; Gardner and Lewis 1996, 8; Mosley 1987, 21; Robertson 1984, 16). From the time of its first loans in the 1940s, in fact, the World Bank had borrower states sign a statement of commitment to provide the bank with any information it requested, stipulating as well the right of bank officials to freedom of movement in all the territory under the sovereignty of the state (Escobar 1995, 231). Gathering detailed information about borrowing countries was an integral part of the work of World Bank "missions" sent to third world countries (231–32).

Informal Economy: A Brief History of a Concept

By the end of the twentieth century the assumption that the nation-state was the appropriate unit of analysis for the study of economy and society—an assumption inherited from nineteenth-century social theory—was no longer tenable. Academic debate about this problem in sociology began with the study of the "new social movements" in the early 1980s (Touraine 1980; Touraine 1985; Cohen 1985). Anthropologists started from another perspective, usually inside the boundaries of the nation-state but among marginalized populations who would later become identified with informality.

Two theoretical approaches dominated early debate about informal economy in Egypt and elsewhere.[19] The first was related to modernization theory and the issue of rural-to-urban migration. Under this approach the informal economy was seen as a resting place on the way to integration into the modern economy of the city, and residence in a shantytown was a sufficient marker of informal economy. This approach was linked to the debate about "squatting" that I referred to above. It was also linked to anthropological and sociological accounts of the culture of poverty and dual "traditional" versus "modern" markets (Boeke 1953; Geertz 1963a; Geertz 1963b). Another early strand in the informal-economy debate had roots in the Marxist tradition. In this view actors in the informal economy were seen as a lumpen proletariat outside the direct social relations of capital, engaged in petty commodity production and articulating capitalist and precapitalist social relations.

Among economists the issue of informal economy was approached from still another standpoint. Corporations in the United States and Europe learned during the 1970s that subcontracting work out to small workshops was often cheaper than having workers on staff full time, even when wages and benefits, where they existed at all, were as low as in Egypt. While the term "informal economy" was not important in these debates, this form of downsizing or informalization as a response to working-class struggles in the 1960s and economic stagnation in the 1970s laid important groundwork for the rise of the informal economy paradigm. Neo-Marxian research emphasized the political implications of this informalization: subcontracting to firms employing unprotected workers in the third world was a strategy amounting to job flight, declining wages, and the end of stable labor contracts for pools of unionized workers in the North (Beneria 1989; Castells and Portes 1989; Portes and Sassen-Koob 1987; Meagher 1995; Wilson 1993).[20] By the 1980s, and even more in the 1990s, it became possible to argue that the flexible structure of small businesses in the informal economy was more fully developed than the economy of the first world, which was meanwhile coming to resemble the third world in employment conditions and the production structures of key sectors of the economy. Economists began to argue that small business had great potential in a globalizing economy for economic growth in a traditional sense.[21]

These debates were not restricted to the academy. IOs that had been granted the power to oversee the living conditions of citizens neglected by their state also needed to gain a better picture of the informal economy. For this task, fieldwork at the margins of national economies and nation-states would not be sufficient. In the late 1980s, therefore, the International Labor Organization (ILO) assumed a coordinating role in research on the informal economy and began to assist the statistical agencies of its member states in gathering standardized information on the "informal sector." In 1993 a "Resolution concerning statistics of employment in the informal sector" was adopted by the fifteenth International Conference of Labor Statisticians (Hussmanns 1996, 18). The new ILO definitions subsumed the "informal enterprise" within the already established category of "household enterprise," and recommended household-based (rather than enterprise-based) surveys to ascertain the extent of activity in the informal sector (20).

Given the thrust of ILO work to make the "hidden economy" visible so as to produce new data about the state of the global labor market in its broadest definition, the concept of informal economy now acquired a more technical meaning. In the new definitions of informality rooted in economy and not culture, the concerns of statisticians became paramount, and the informal became what was hard for the statistician to see. As a first pass, this meant activity not included in national income accounts and estimates of gross domestic product. Practically, it turned out that most economic activity missing in national accounts was carried out in small production units: workshops employing fewer than ten people, and shops using simple tools of labor or having a low capital base.

While the new approach to the informal was technical and reflected statisticians' concerns, there was an implicit connection between informality and the state on two levels. First, because informal economic activity was not counted in state-generated statistics of national income and gross domestic product, it was effectively omitted from accounts of the national economy (in the sense that the economy consisted of economic activity carried out or registered within the sovereign territory of the state). Second, the "informal economy" or "informal sector" was an economic space where state law regarding economic activity, be it labor regulations or tax law, was effectively void. The new definition of informality facilitated a purely technical approach. Once informal activity was associated ex post facto by statisticians with small-scale economic activity, an association became a definition. With this change initiated by the ILO, informal economy was transformed from a negative concept—establishments of labor not recorded in state statistics—to a term usable by statisticians. Even this was not a uniform criterion. What was small in the United States could be considered large in Egypt, as my informants repeatedly reminded me.

In Egypt the first attempts to carry out macrostudies of informality had little choice but to rely on national surveys using previous databases and other definitions. Microsurveys had confirmed that informality was statistically correlated with small size. And thus it was a logical and quite acceptable approximation, given the available data, to take size-of-enterprise data, which were available, as a proxy for informality (Fergany 1991; Handoussa 1991; Lubell 1991). The next step, however, was to see informality as an issue related not to registration or legal status but only to size and technical criteria, and therefore as applicable only to small and microenterprises.

Research into informal economy had begun with an anthropological edge focused on the marginalized from modern society—either in the third world or on the outskirts of first-world developed cities. Fieldwork, long the disciplinary trademark of anthropology, had become popular as a way to study social movements and informal economy alike. But fieldwork projects were not sufficient to understand a broad issue like informal economy on a global scale. The concept would have to be statistically relevant as well. Through the efforts of international agencies under the UN umbrella, informal economy was transformed into a term usable by statisticians. The concept was now applicable to establishments employing fewer than ten workers (for microenterprises) or fifteen (for small enterprises).[22] While informal economy as "that which was not measured by the state" had only a shadow existence, informal economy as small enterprises could be tracked only by either massive census-like efforts, or by generalizing from microscale anthropological studies characterized by depth, not breadth.

Articles published in Egypt and articles about Egypt gathered together these existing studies in frustrated attempts to draw general conclusions (Kharoufi 1991; Rizq 1991; El Mahdy 1995). While some argued for further and "more sensitive" field research that would help reveal the contours of the informal economy and the role of culture in the "Egyptian miracle" of surviving extreme poverty (Kharoufi 1991, 17), others inside and outside Egypt were clearly trying to lay the groundwork for a more effective large-scale statistical survey strategy (Fergany 1991; Charmes 1990; Hussmanns 1996). It was then discovered by the World Bank that the informal economy—small workshops employing small numbers of people, and not always complying with the law—constituted the bulk of the productive private sector economy in Egypt. How did this discovery come to be made?

Competing Maps, Converging Practices

The U.S. development agency, AID, was part of the story. AID has long been involved in setting up small businesses for the poor in Egypt, and small business has been identified as the site of the private sector in Egypt since larger businesses alone were nationalized under the Free Officer's Regime in the 1960s. One banker, responsible for managing a large part of the money directed to microenterprise by the Social Fund through the banks, pointed out that his bank had instituted a separate administrative unit for small enterprise because of conditions set by the World Bank for soft loans after Sadat's economic opening. Donors had set as a condition that 70 percent of their loans must go to small industries under a separate administrative unit.

Research sponsored by AID had long concluded that strengthening small business and traditional crafts was central to both growth of the private sector and avoidance of widespread unemployment and social unrest in Egypt. AID Egypt was instrumental in setting up NGOS to distribute bank loans to microentrepreneurs of the "informal economy" and to voice the interests of the private sector.[23] While the ideological orientation of these projects, which stressed the free market as the path to democracy, was originally quite different from that of other government donor agencies and NGOS interested in self-empowerment of the poor and disenfranchised, by the end of the 1980s the two trends came together in projects oriented to the informal economy. Free enterprise merged with the language of self-empowerment, and the different strands of the NGO and IO development community and the state united around an informal economy and microenterprise agenda.

Studies advanced by AID years ago targeting crafts and small business as a means to jobs and democracy gained new currency, and follow-up studies appeared. Other NGOS with quite different agendas reached conclusions similar to those of AID (Community Economics Corporation 1993; Tinker 1993; Jones 1988). NGOS that had been sponsoring income-generating projects for the poor, with a special focus on women, sponsored evaluation studies of previously existing projects. Drawing on these conclusions, new research and new projects were funded that shifted the focus from generating income to building small, sustainable—profitable—small businesses. One consequence was the creation of NGOS to provide credit to small borrowers that the formal banks would not touch.

Once IOs had mapped out the rough contours of "the informal economy," it became possible to begin funding that something that they had helped to invent.[24] NGOS (or "foundations") of "civil society" sponsored by AID began providing loans to small and medium-sized businesses in

81

1990 (Stallard, Bagchi, and El Agouz 1995, 18), first in Alexandria with the Alexandria Businessmen's Association, another organization that AID had been instrumental in setting up, and then in Cairo. A program established in 1989 in the National Bank for Development, a private bank that offered credit to microenterprises in el-Minia with support from the Ford Foundation, and in Dumiat and Sharqiyya with AID funding (Community Economics Corporation 1993, 15), soon gained funding to expand its operations into Cairo. (This program provided one of my points of entry into el-Hirafiyeen.) By 1995 programs for microenterprise in Egypt ranged from (to name a few) the Women's Initiative Fund funded by the Canadian International Development Agency (CIDA), the Rural Women Project funded by UNICEF and the Egyptian Ministry of Social Affairs, and the Youth Entrepreneurs Society funded by the Social Fund for Development and the Egyptian Ministry for International Cooperation (Stallard, Bagchi, and El Agouz, 1995, 8)—in addition to programs that I have already mentioned such as the Social Fund, the AID foundations and NGOS, and the National Bank for Development program.

But there was a problem. States were unlikely to welcome the prospect of IOs running rampant to promote informality—which by definition negates the role of the state. To enact projects that would develop the informal economy in real time and space, states had to sign on as well. The new technical definition of informal economy based on size—not legality—helped solve this problem. If informal economy is defined as consisting of enterprises with only a very small number of employees, then they can be called "microenterprises." That term does not have the same whiff of extralegality as informal economy does. Microenterprise also has quite different ideological connotations: it stresses individuals and their entrepreneurial qualities over the community and its genius for survival.

This was no mere discursive switch job, and not an abstract exercise. When the World Bank and other large IOs decided that microenterprise could become a "safety net" for the collateral damage of SAPs, they had to work out that strategy with real states, in real programs, in real time. Without the involvement of state institutions, it would be difficult to carry out the broad statistical surveys so much sought after by the World Bank and other IOs. For there is still no mechanism in place for IOs to directly survey populations that enjoy the nominal label of "citizens" in relation to the state. Such alternative surveys and statistical mappings have been carried out with funding from IOs and under their direction, from within the institutions of the state. In Egypt establishment of the Social Fund helped to make such efforts possible.

SAPS in the 1980s did not yield the expected results that macro-economic theorists had predicted, and short-term disequilibrium between the forces of supply and demand began to look like long-term equilibrium. Reformists within the bank (who acquired great weight with the appointment of James Wolfensohn as its president), enforcing these programs of financial discipline, began to voice doubt in the economic doctrine that they preached.[25] It had been expected that massive layoffs by the state and public enterprises, and the withdrawal of state subsidies on food, would be temporary, but as they began to look permanent, new development programs were devised to relieve the suffering of those groups negatively affected by structural adjustment. In a number of countries where SAPS were being enforced, the World Bank established Social Funds as the "social safety net" of choice. These experiments were carried out in the Caribbean, Latin America, and Africa (Graham 1994).

In Egypt the Social Fund was set up in 1991 as a World Bank project with $572 million from fifteen donor countries, the European Union, the United Nations Development Program, and the Arab Fund. It was established as a new agency, inside and outside the state, created especially for this purpose (World Bank 1991a). What does it mean for an agency to be both inside and outside the state? For all intents and purposes, the Social Fund was an institution established in Egypt by the World Bank, organized as an autonomous agency and funded by sources outside the state budget. In the words of its 1994 Annual Report, the Social Fund was a "semi-autonomous apex agency, under the chairmanship of the Prime Minister" (Government of Egypt 1995). Its semi-incorporation into the state, however, gave the regime access to crucial levers of power, such as chairmanship of its board of directors (reserved for the prime minister), the right to choose the managing director, and a say in the distribution of funds, as long as the funding guidelines of the donor agencies were respected. Target groups of the Social Fund (women, graduates, those laid off from public enterprises, those with low income), which were not determined by the Egyptian state, also included migrant workers forced back to Egypt during the first Gulf War.

The Egyptian Social Fund began funding microenterprise soon after its founding. With the appointment of Prime Minister Ghanzouri after the parliamentary elections of 1995, the new government stated three objectives: increasing investment and production, improving the chances of productive labor, and raising income for the average Egyptian. Microenterprise seemed tailor-made to meet these goals, and statements about its importance became commonplace. One headline went so far as to state that "expansion of microenterprises was the goal of economic reform."[26] In other words, the Egyptian state had adopted as its own an agenda that had begun as a way to bypass and overcome the corrupt essence of the third world state. Informal economy had come full circle. It was being reabsorbed, through microenterprise, into its supposed inverse—the state. With informality neutralized, moreover, the state could insert itself into the new flows of money coming into Egypt, even if the money had been intended to reduce reliance on state institutions now condemned as repressive and inefficient. Access was opened to a new source (reputedly worth millions of dollars annually)[27] of grants and low-interest loans to the Egyptian government. Microenterprise became a means through which access to flows of funds could be privatized by individuals as well.

Microenterprise and the Social Fund provided a means through which the informal economy could be reabsorbed into the state. They also provided a means for absorbing informal information networks. Assaad, Zhou, and Razzaz have argued that the main function of informal networks is to "facilitate the flow of information when formal channels of information dissemination are weak or ineffective" (1997, 3). IOs like the World Bank are well aware of the importance of such informal networks for generating information that the state cannot be trusted to provide. Efforts were thus under way in the 1990s by the World Bank and other IOs to establish continuing, alternative information-gathering systems from within the Egyptian national institute for statistics and planning, known by its English acronym CAPMAS.[28]

CAPMAS has long lent its name to researchers who bring it funding (author's interviews with staff and researchers), but formalizing a nonstate information-gathering capacity within the buildings of the state itself was something else again. Information gathering was seen as a central part of the Social Fund's mission from the start. As an agency that was both inside and outside the state, it had a new capacity to undertake research without being condemned by local public opinion as an out-sider's imperialist venture. At the same time, the Social Fund became a framework through which the World Bank and other agencies could gather information nationwide without having to rely on the discredited state statistics. In that context, the Social Fund project entailed the devel-opment of new databases within CAPMAS itself. Data deemed necessary for the Social Fund's needs were to be collected and analyzed through surveys and studies. As a government agency, CAPMAS was to act as a "steering committee" for these surveys to ensure broad government par-ticipation (World Bank 1991a, 23). In line with the approach to informal economy advocated by the ILO, these were to be household surveys. Such an approach was no departure for Egypt, where household-expenditure surveys had long been conducted, but this time the surveys were the basis for generating information about "the economy," not about "household expenditure" or consumption. With informal economy relocated by the World Bank to the center of its notions of "the economy," the surveys were a logical way to proceed, since they are generally known to render better data about informal economic activities than do surveys of eco-nomic enterprises traditionally defined.

In the meantime, the rewriting of informal economy as microenter-prise facilitated the use of existing data to rewrite the contours of the economy in Egypt. Economic activity once outside the accountings of the economy that mattered now merged into the broader statistical map-ping of "the Egyptian economy." Workshops that had often been seen (with the caveats above) as backwards and a block to development were now the essence of the market economy that the World Bank and other development institutions should help to promote. A new map of Egypt had emerged.

This is well illustrated in a World Bank report issued in 1994, written for a public-private sector conference about the future of the Egyptian economy.[29] In this report, the micro and small enterprise sector in Egypt, defined as privately owned shops employing fewer than ten workers, was found to constitute 99 percent of private sector units (World Bank 1994, 3), to produce 80 percent of private value added (8), and to employ 76 percent of nonagricultural labor (25). Microenterprise was seen as the key to increased employment, and as central to economic growth as a whole (26). Overregulation by the state—of health, safety, the environment, and labor—was said to be an important constraint on the growth of microenterprises and small enterprises into larger firms (13).

The approach advanced in this World Bank report echoed that of Hernando de Soto in *The Other Path*, which identified unwieldy and irrational state regulation as the main cause of informality. In this view, the so-called informal economy was the private sector, it was the economy, and it was merely up to the state, with prodding from the IOs, to wake up and recognize this. Rendered formal and licit, informality became microenterprise and the star of the private sector in the global age.[30] De Soto and the network of researchers around the world that he drew on provided extensive documentation of the tangle of regulations and laws on the books, in Peru and Egypt in particular, governing the establishment of economic enterprises. The solution that de Soto offered was a retreat of the state, one that would render informality (noncompliance) formal by eliminating state regulation of labor and the workplace. In de Soto's later book, *The Mystery of Capital* (2000), microenterprise emerged as the vanguard of a new democratic world order, and microentrepreneurs as a new global army that had nothing to lose but the chains of the state.

The Fence and the Map Revisited

When I first visited el-Hirafiyeen in 1993, a mood of both despair and heightened expectations pervaded. Many of the craftsmen who had been moved from their old neighborhoods had closed down their workshops. Some had opened new kinds of businesses, in a new line of work. A master carpenter opened an unlicensed coffeehouse—an essential part of workshop life that had been overlooked by the neighborhood's planners. Others sold their workshops and apartments to new kinds of users, although by law they had been forbidden to sell. Buyers included government clerks glad to find low prices and fresh air, a factory worker with a job nearby, and a sister whose unemployed husband, downsized under the terms of saps, could never afford to buy a flat for his family. None of these were users for whom the neighborhood had been built. But although the sales were technically illegal they had complete social legitimacy and were de facto accepted by the state as well. In other words one could say, if one were attached to the term, that the craftsmen and users of the neighborhood changed the nature of their businesses and residences "informally."[31]

Many craftsmen were full of resentment toward their neighbors, the "youth microentrepreneurs," whom they saw as spoiled, ignorant "students" carrying briefcases to play the role of businessmen. They minded that the banners over town and elsewhere celebrated the students, and not themselves—those who really worked. Only a few of the craftsmen attempted to benefit from the new microenterprise and NGO funding, while most looked on with grim amusement at best. The air of resentment was fed by a steady stream of funders who made field trips to el-Hirafiyeen and other Cairo neighborhoods and found them marvelously authentic and down-to-earth. The megastars of IOs came when they were in Cairo for their international meetings. For example, the president of the World Bank, James Wolfensohn, visited the project of the Social Fund that his organization had started, and the president of the European Union was there as well. The semi-official newspaper *al-Ahram* was full of his accolades for microenterprise in Egypt.

When Sa'id took up his posts as secretary to the NGO and to the joint committee, he was sure that he would be able to turn matters around in the neighborhood: he would abolish the illegal workshops outside the bounds of el-Hirafiyeen that had no licenses to operate and competed unfairly; would get the fence of the Army poultry farm moved so that he and his neighbors could get their rightful allotment of working space; and would force state officials who had squatted on state land near the access road to move out. As I have said, Sa'id was sure that a "correct" map of el-Hirafiyeen existed. This map would show that all these informal acts of the state were wrong. He believed that the map had gone missing, deliberately, in a conspiracy against his efforts to put things right. Some readers of my work have suggested that the map was rather being kept from me, for different reasons, by loyal Egyptian nationalist clerks and officials who did not want me, a foreigner, to see what was none of my business. Personally I think neither Sa'id nor I was important enough to inspire such bureaucratic conspiracies, and I find it far more plausible that the complex forces acting on the production of space in Cairo had simply prevented an authoritative official map from being drawn up.[32] This explanation seemed still more plausible to me after Sa'id, Essam, and I attended a local government meeting in late 1994.

The Oversight Committee and Hybrid States

One day Sa'id invited Essam Fawzi and me to attend a meeting of the Committee for the Oversight of the Affairs of Medinet el-Hirafiyeen. He brought us in as witnesses—one a foreigner at that—in an effort to embarrass his opponents in the NGO and the state into heeding what he interpreted as the law.[33] He thought that in front of us, the outsiders, the Committee would be forced to admit the legality and justice of his claims to the public good, and to support his petitions to force the army-owned poultry farm to move off his land, and his efforts to close down competing workshops that had informally opened outside the boundaries allotted to the workshop neighborhood of el-Hirafiyeen. The meeting that day, 19 November 1994, was held in a large hall of the local government of the sister neighborhood to el-Hirafiyeen, el-Salam City. The meeting was open to the public, and various constituents with grievances—almost all having to do with different problems of "informality"—were in atten-dance. The first item on the agenda was the need to expand the access streets into el-Hirafiyeen, which included the street on which Sa'id had his workshop. Despite the picture of confrontation drawn by Sa'id, all were in agreement that this expansion of the street, and thus of the work-shop's de facto working space as well, was necessary. The only question was what to do about the informally constructed buildings in the way. Up for debate was whether houses that had been built without permission on state land should be demolished to expand the access roads.

Meanwhile, the issue that had so incensed Sa'id and led him to suspect a conspiracy against him had been settled. It was announced in the meeting that a deal had been made with those running the army poultry farm to buy out some of the land they had made theirs by occupation. In other words, this state-owned land that had been the subject of contro-versy between two state agencies was settled by a third state agency mediating the details of financial compensation. Since the issue had been settled it did not come up for debate (whether the settlement was en-forced is another issue, one that I cannot answer here). Rather, the discussion that occupied us for some thirty minutes concerned houses that had been built along another of the access roads on another part of state-owned land. It was said (although not openly) that some of the builders were state bureaucrats.

The president of the locality of el-Salam explained his predicament:

He had in front of him two conflicting orders from state ministries. The first told him to enforce the law and demolish buildings that had been built without permission on state-owned land. But he had also been told to enforce Law #25, under which any building that had been finished, and provided with services before 1992, should be formalized and accorded legal status. He presented a sophisticated overview of the problem of informal housing in Cairo. This included a comparative analysis of how things proceeded in other neighborhoods, ranging from the élite Nasser City to Manshiet Nasser. The latter had been completely informal and was gradually being formalized, a process mediated by NGOs established with support from IOs and development agencies (Assaad 1996).

As he spoke, the president of the council expounded his theory of informality. Informal housing, he explained, was housing for which the state provided no services—water, electricity, roads, or lighting. People who built in such conditions enjoyed lower prices in exchange for doing without these services. Those who lived in informal settlements had to provide for themselves, until they were well established enough that the state had to recognize them, as had happened in Manshiet Nasser. They had the right to build, he explained, but not to demand anything from the state. Therefore, he went on, it was unclear whether the state had the right to take back the state land on which these people had built. In the end a compromise was found: an engineer would be sent to survey the houses on that stretch of state land, to estimate the value of the land, and to see if the residents were willing to pay compensation to the state for the occupied land. If they were so willing, then they would be accorded full property rights. The compromise turned state law into a generator of revenue, with mediation worthy of the most advanced jurisprudence in the United States, that sought to reduce the costs of litigation (Mnookin, Peppet, and Tulumello 2000).

Also on the agenda that day was the problem of lighting for the public streets of el-Hirafiyeen. Who was responsible for this? Workshop owners had long complained that the lighting was inadequate. Many of their customers came at nightfall, after work, driving in their cars for minor repairs. The craftsmen expressed their fear that female customers in particular would not bring their business to unlit streets. They claimed, as citizens, that the state should light public streets. But the state representatives refused to accept the responsibility to allocate social services to the craftsmen as citizens. State responsibility, they said, was restricted to the main public square of the neighborhood, where, it so happened, the buildings of the state stood. Around its periphery were the public sector bank, the post office, a public sector bus station, and the official mosque. Space where the state was symbolically and effectually sovereign (although no one put matters in these terms) was the only section of the neighborhood for which the state would provide lighting. Further inside the neighborhood, in the spaces shared by the craftsmen and micro-entrepreneurs for their work and home life, it was up to the users to provide their own lighting.

Searching for the State

In his book *Seeing like a State*, James Scott presents a picture of an all-powerful state that uses maps to deploy its power in projects to reshape society. Maps, as he puts it, have the "apparent power . . . to transform as well as merely to summarize the facts that they portray." And, he adds, this "transformative power resides not in the map, of course, but rather in the power possessed by those who deploy the perspective of that particular map" (Scott 1998, 87). Scott shows how the high-modernist state has used maps to impose its visions of the future on society.

But what happens when the state is not the dominant institution drawing maps within its own sovereign territory? What if the state refuses to shed light on the back streets of its own sovereign territory? What if the state reveals itself to be a far less coherent force than that portrayed by Scott? What if, as with Sa'id and many others whom I could cite, maps are less an instrument of a sovereign state than another ground on which competing visions of reality and contests for power are played out? And what if they are played out inside the state itself?

The conflicting users in this corner of Cairo were all part of the state: the governorate that legally owned the land, the army poultry farm that squatted on the land, and the government officials who built their homes on the land, also as squatters. The opposite seems to have been true regarding the project to map the informal economy. It was not the Egyptian state that set new definitions of economy. It was not the state that initiated surveys to decipher just what was that new economy within which the informal economy was now subsumed. Instead it was IOs that set the new definitions and supplied the funding and expertise to carry out the statistical surveys.

The modern state imposes power, according to Foucault, through the gaze that sees (1980, 146–65). If seeing, counting, and mapping the activities of citizens have moved, at least in part, to the level of IOs, then there are implications for state sovereignty. That is only part of the story. Efforts to map out and develop the informal economy were, as I have said, eventually incorporated into the Egyptian state. If the gaze that sees has its nerves in institutional settings other than the state, and yet functions as part of the state, then the implications are many. Lurking inside the formidable offices of the state can be a complex range of forces competing for power, or forging new ways to work together, and perhaps to create a new (even if informal) institutional entity altogether. The lines between the state, international organizations, and the civil society that is assumed to lie outside the state are far fuzzier than we often realize. A more hybrid state seems to be emerging that bears further analysis.

Like the informal economy, IOs and NGOs are defined in opposition to the state. The two can seem to be in stark opposition, but practices have evolved across their boundaries, as the state can absorb informality, and IOs can enter the state. The all-powerful state portrayed by Scott and others, which can confidently count, map, and measure the activities of its citizens to better control them, was in question in Egypt by 2000.

Governmentality and the Ethnography of Power

How to approach this problem as an ethnographer conducting research at the point where the state, IOs, and informality intersect? Three possible approaches come to mind. One is deconstructive in nature and argues that "the state" is a problematic state in the first place. Such an approach has been useful in making clear that "the state" might never have been unitary in the fashion portrayed by much social theory.[34] The second approach focuses more on historical changes, under the idea that something has "really" changed out there. Such inquiries might explore the changing nature of state sovereignty or explore the nature of globalization as a whole.[35]

A third approach to the study of evolving forms of power that cross state boundaries is that inspired by Foucault's concept of governmentality. In his essay of that name, Foucault writes with great prescience of the context that many anthropologists and other social scientists are trying to grapple with only now. Writing at the close of the era marked by 1968, Foucault notes that there is a tendency in the literature of "overvaluing the problem of the state" (1991, 103). By the beginning of the eighteenth century, he writes, it was no longer sovereignty over territory, but rather population of a certain volume and density, that was the object of government: "Population now represents more the end of government than the power of the sovereign; the population is the subject of needs, of aspirations, but it is also the object in the hands of the government, aware, vis-à-vis the government, of what it wants, but ignorant of what is being done to it" (100).

Governmentality, in turn, is defined by Foucault as "the ensemble formed by the institutions, procedures, analyses and reflections, the calculations and tactics that allow the exercise of this very specific albeit complex form of power, which has as its target population, as its principal form of knowledge political economy, and as its essential technical means apparatuses of security" (102). In the history put forward by Foucault, the modern state appears as but one moment in a longer historical process of the evolution of forms of governmentality, and ceases to figure as the sole, or even most important, container of power. An approach drawing on Foucault's formulations of governmentality is an appealing solution to the dilemma of the missing map and the intersecting agencies that I have addressed in this paper. Those targeted by IOs or states as part of the informal economy or as microentrepreneurs are not of interest as citizens of a sovereign state. Population—not citizenry—is the object of programs of intervention that were initiated by IOs to "alleviate poverty" or to help the poor help themselves. The object of these acts of governing is clearly not to increase the sovereignty of the state. (And without the state, it makes little sense to talk about citizenry.)

At the end of the 1960s Foucault's opinion that the problem of the state was being overvalued must have seemed strange. But not by 2001. In political protest actions at the turn of the millennium such as the antiglobalization movement, it is often not the state but rather the World Trade Organization and the World Bank—international or global organizations—that may be "overvalued" (Elyachar 2001b, Elyachar 2002). The state often disappears from view as the object of political protest. Likewise, when world leaders of states and business gathered in Okinawa in July 2000 to discuss the most pressing problems of the global era, they too called for new forms of "global governance—new, cooperative, though as yet largely unspecified ways of running world affairs in response to the massive changes wrought by globalization and rapid technological change."[36] The state per se was not an object of concern; practices of governance—governmentality—were. The concept of governmentality is easily amenable to a discussion of new forms of "running world affairs."

But the use of Foucault's concept of governmentality to examine the complex relations of states, IOs, NGOS, and informality is also problematic. As a concept, governmentality defines away the state as an object of analysis. This, although Foucault was theorizing the nature of power within the territory of the state when he developed his concept. In the notion of governmentality, the move to transnationality—like the move to micropower—is already subsumed into the theoretical perspective, rather than problematized as an issue for analysis. For once the object of disciplinary measures is defined as a "population" rather than a citizenry, the move to a global scale is already implicit. Populations are universal; they refer not to political identity but rather to human identity as a category outside of political divisions (Malkki 1994, Mastnak 1996). If this is so, then the adoption of the concept of "transnational governmentality," as recently proposed by Ferguson and Gupta, may not solve the dilemma (2002).

The concept of governmentality is appealing in a world where the World Bank has at least as much power to govern as many states in the world do (whether with "good governance" or not is another question), but I would argue that it can obscure some of the issues that we need to focus on. Perhaps we need to start approaching "governmentality" itself as a practice rather than a concept. From being a concept developed by Foucault at a historical moment when it still seemed strange to say that the state was overvalued, "governmentality" (or "governance") has now become the daily practice of "world leaders," such as those who met in Okinawa. As a theoretical notion, it is not crucial if a governmentality is located in the state, or in the World Bank, or in an NGO. But I would suggest that it matters very much where practices of governmentality are located. We need to take note of changes in the locations, and meanings, of practices in specific institutional settings. This point was made by Coronil in his analysis of the state in Venezuela (1997). There, he critiques the Foucauldian approach of seeing the state "as the structural effect of dispersed disciplinary formations" (Coronil 1997, 63 n. 22). From such a perspective, he suggests, power is not located in specific structures or institutions; rather it is diffused throughout society, and thus dissolves as a specific form of power. Coronil argues as well for the importance of locating "power in historically constituted structural relations."[37]

Thus despite the importance of the analyses of the state inspired by Foucault, perhaps we should not shift our level of analysis too quickly away from the state as imagined (Gupta 1995), or as an effect of dispersed disciplinary practices (Mitchell 1991). Likewise, it may be a mistake to extol the virtues of "economic citizenry" in the global age,[38] or membership in "global civil society," as a viable substitute for political citizenry. I suggest that we first spend more time observing the transformations under way in historically constituted fields of institutionalized power. In such a project, ethnography becomes crucial, for unlike other modes of research, ethnographic research can look at seemingly fixed institutional entities such as the state to reveal the processes of change occurring within them and across them (Ashraf Ghani, personal communication, 2000). At its best, ethnography is located between structure and process, and can help to illuminate complex processes of change at particular historical conjunctures. Ethnography is essential for any project that aims to analyze the changes taking place in historically constituted forms of power in hybrid states like Egypt.

In the face of such a complex configuration of power, ethnography can in itself be a theoretical undertaking (Moore 1987, Ghani 1992, Wolf 2001). At such a moment, it might be more productive for us to set aside some of the usual arguments about "the state." For example, throughout much of this chapter I have written of "the state" in a manner that some will surely find unsatisfactory. There is no doubt that the state is changing, and that our categories have benefited from deconstruction. But rather than try to definitively resolve ongoing debates about "the state," I suggest a slightly different direction: more research on the forms of power that are emerging at the interstices of the state, IOs, and NGOs. The hybrid forms that we find there require much more analysis, as do the processes that defy many of our assumptions about the state, and about related binary oppositions such as "global and local," "state and global," and "state and NGO."[39] In these inquiries, problems like informality can be of crucial importance, as what Sally Moore has called "diagnostic events" (Moore 1987), but I would call them diagnostic points of analysis. Ethnography must itself be strategic, and tactical, in its nature, choosing those nodal points of research where the state appears "fuzzy" and categories are blurred. In a context where all institutionalized forms of power—whether the state, IOs, or NGOs—are attempting to cope with unplanned dynamics outside their control, and to devise programs to fit those dynamics into a planned future, we need to rethink both our categories and our ethnographic methods.[40] All of that is urgent for anyone trying to understand the nature of the market, power, and forms of dispossession in the twenty-first century.

4. MASTERY, POWER, AND MODEL WORKSHOP MARKETS

In this chapter I turn to some of the unplanned dynamics of workshop market life with which planners attempting to intervene in the informal economy, and to benefit from the values that it produced, had to contend.

Workshop markets are a good starting point to support my statement that markets are not made by the invisible hand. How are those markets made? This chapter will be more ethnographically dense than those that came before. The detail is necessary to substantiate my claim that relationality is central to the making of workshop markets, that social capital is not an adequate concept for understanding those markets, and that the lionization of workshop markets as social capital is congruent with a broader process of dispossession in neoliberalism. I will show how workshop markets are historically constituted through family and work histories. Those histories, I argue, create a resource of mastery transmitted across the generations of the popular classes of Egypt.

Mastery is a form of embodied power. It is a habitus performed by masters daily in a network of relations with workers, family members, customers, and officials. Once we understand the nature of mastery, it is possible to turn to the workshop, and to grasp what distinguishes the workshop from the microenterprise. Here too I analyze the workshop as a form of practice rather than as a physical place. Workshop markets are concrete and embodied. The master is not a discrete subject in one place, with the market in another. Rather, master and market are mutually constituted. It is more useful, I argue, to understand market life in Cairo by employing an approach grounded in this insight than it would be to map out an abstract space where supply and demand curves meet at a price, or to understand these relations as social capital. I will not claim that the markets I found among craftsmen in Egypt are paradigmatic of the market in general—for one thing there is no such thing as "the market." But I will argue that those markets are far from marginal, and that their lessons are of general import.

Model Markets in Cairo

Economists usually draw models of the market to grasp how it works. Ethnographers, on the other hand, often trace detailed pictures of specific processes of exchange. In my own fieldwork I was struck by how often my informants themselves mobilized particular models of the market. In a neighborhood like el-Hirafiyeen that was built to serve the market, people who had planned the neighborhood, or who worked and lived there, had a lot to say on the subject of markets. One opinion was expressed by Ashraf, the college-educated son of a craftsman, who only reluctantly worked with his father in a shop that repaired and installed exhaust systems in cars. His father was addressed with the honorific *el-hag*. He often dressed in white, a sartorial statement that he had performed the *hag*, or pilgrimage to Mecca that is a religious obligation of all Muslims who are able. White also claimed his status as a master, one who did not get his hands dirty in the workshop. His son also set himself apart from the workers through his choice of dress: he wore clean-pressed polo shirts and khaki pants ironed to a firm and efficient crease. Ashraf made his statement to me about how markets "the craftsman's way" were supposed to be on one of my early visits to his shop:

> Things are organized badly in el-Hirafiyeen. They put people who practice the same craft together, next to each other. . . . They should have put a guy who works with wood next to me with the exhaust systems. Then I could bring him customers, and he could bring me. Here, there's no cooperation. . . . People here compete over workers—the guy across the street, he tried to take my good workers. And customers also. The way it's supposed to work is that you watch out for each other, respect each other's customers and workers. But here, no. If I'm closed for a few minutes and my customer comes, the guy across the street will try to take him, tell him I'm not there or something, rather than that I'm on my way back. And they envy you, put the evil eye on you. They sit there, look at you, watch what you're doing, see how well you're doing. They want your

business if you have it. If you're doing well and they're not, they look at you with envy. They also do things like spread around bad rumors about you. Talk about you in the market in a bad way. This isn't supposed to happen. In the real craftsman's world (al-'alam al-hirafi al-haqiqi), this doesn't happen.

This is a statement about model markets in Cairo. It describes how the market is "supposed to be." Such statements tend to present official images, pictures of how things are supposed to be, and how an informant wants to be seen. It is, in Bourdieu's terms, an officializing strategy elicited by the ethnographer's questions (Bourdieu 1977). In his statements Ashraf clearly drew the distance between how (he thought) things worked in el-Hirafiyeen and how they had been—or how he wanted to think they had been—in the past. Ashraf's words, that is, were suffused with nostalgia. "The true craftsman's world" that he refers to is an idealized, nostalgic view of the market. It is a market of nostalgia or, as Herzfeld put it, "structural nostalgia," in which a "static image of an unspoiled and irrecoverable past often plays an important part in present actions." (Herzfeld 1997, 109). Structural nostalgia was an important part of life among the craftsmen. Since their lives were so deeply shaped, often negatively, by the move of their workshops into el-Hirafiyeen from other established neighborhoods of northern Cairo, nostalgia for the "old neighborhood" was understandable and predictable.

The idealized picture presented by Ashraf of "how things used to be" might suggest that he was a master craftsman of the old school, one who had lived the experience of "the craftsman's way." But in fact he was a recent college graduate who had not "taken his father's trade." His father was the one who was a master, who knew his work from the inside out: whose knowledge was integrated into the cells of his body in addition to being stored as information in his brain. I soon came to know that for Ashraf, like others in the neighborhood who were struggling or had problems with their neighbors, complaints about the present always had reference to the past, to the way things were supposed to be.

Other images of how the market should be were conveyed to me in el-Hirafiyeen. In stark opposition to the nostalgic model market of craftsmen was the model market typical of college-educated youth. Their model was closer to the classic pictures that one might find in a textbook for Economics 101, such as Ashraf might have read when he studied business at Cairo University. The youths, particularly those who had received microloans from the Social Fund and had no family members who were craftsmen, saw the market as an impersonal force in abstract space where supply and demand met and resolved into a price.

Yet a third model of the market was presented to me by another informant, Ahmed, a consultant who had worked in the private banking industry in Cairo for over thirty years, specializing in small and micro-enterprises. He had a second career as a consultant to development agencies such as AID and local NGOs that promoted microenterprise. Ahmed's model market had yet a third focus, on technical relations of production. Here as well an ideal was presented, of how things should be, as a way of complaining about what had gone wrong. "It would be better [in el-Hirafiyeen] if you had blocks, with 3–4 groups of similar activities grouped together, integrated into a larger factory. Those engineers of the governorate, and lots of people, when they speak of microenter-prise, they don't have any idea of the fine elements of what goes into the makeup of the Egyptian artisan. Microenterprise is not a workshop [*mish wirsha*], it's not the physical place. Artisans also need a place to go, and room to grow into."

Ahmed knew a great deal about *hirafiyeen*, craftsmen, in Cairo. And yet his view of production and the needs of the craftsmen was purely tech-nical. Despite his long acquaintance with craftsmen in Cairo, he gave no more weight to craftsmen's concerns about "being seen" and about the evil eye than did the youth graduates funded by the Social Fund. Perhaps that was because he was talking to me, a foreigner. Or perhaps as an *afrangi* Egyptian he did not identify with *sha'bi* culture and the evil eye, even though he deemed himself an expert on the world of the craftsmen.[1] But I think the matter different. Rather, I am sure, he put economics in one place and concerns about the evil eye and neighbors in another.

In Ahmed's view, and in sharp contrast with Ashraf, workshops *should* be placed next to each other. The reason was clear. Proximity would allow an increased division of labor. Like the workers in the pin factory in the famous passage from *The Wealth of Nations*, craftsmen in the same trade who worked in close proximity could specialize, each in one subsection of their trade, and gain from an increased division of labor.[2] Ahmed's Adam Smith was that of *The Wealth of Nations*. Ashraf's

Adam Smith, by contrast, was that of *The Theory of Moral Sentiments*, which reflects concerns about the invisible spectator and the ethics of market society.

How can we reconcile these three notions of the market? Of what a market should be? How could a model market, in which the impersonal forces of supply and demand are the dominant arbiter of price and competition, have anything to do with neighborly relations? Why shouldn't a competitor in the same field of work be located on the same block? And what, moreover, does a superstition like the evil eye have to do with markets? Each of these models of the market was associated with the interventions and mobilizations of power on the part of different "partial spectators" (Smith 1976a) in the neighborhood of el-Hirafiyeen: the Governorate of Cairo that had built the neighborhood "for the craftsmen"; the Social Fund and its IO donors who had adopted the neighborhood as a home for microenterprises; and the bankers who had given loans to its residents and wanted to improve their productive capacities and their ability to repay outstanding loans. Those models of the market were all linked to social science experiments launched in the name of the market on residents of el-Hirafiyeen. It is important to identify the market models that lie behind mobilizations of power on the part of different kinds of organizations and institutions such as the state, NGOS, and IOs like the World Bank. But none of those idealized market models is an adequate picture of the production and market practices of the craftsmen of el-Hirafiyeen. Nor do they provide space for understanding the specific modalities of power in the workshops of Cairo and the communities in which they are located.

Markets, Mastery, and Memory

To understand more about the markets that craftsmen make, it is useful to turn away from these idealized models to practice. I draw on Bourdieu here to analyze the form of practice that I call mastery. Mastery is a process of inculcated, embodied learning acquired over a lifetime. It can be thought of as a *habitus*, a set of dispositions that are inculcated in the body itself. The ability to create markets is one aspect of mastery. Mastery is a quality of the workshop master.

I use the word master in a dual sense. It is first a loose translation of *usta*, an Arabic word with Ottoman origins used in many areas of the former Ottoman Empire.[3] But I also use it to refer to the issue of power that the word master implies. According to *Webster's New Twentieth Century Dictionary*, a "master" is "a man who rules others or has control, authority, or power over something." It is also a "person very skilled and able in some work." A master in Cairo owns and runs a small workshop with the assistance of workers over whom he exercises authority through multiple means. There is no master without a workshop, and no workshop without a master. The two must be defined, and understood, in relation to each other. Lying behind both are relations of power. Power is central to what makes one a master. I will argue that mastery is a specific form of power generated in workshops of Cairo, that mastery is embodied social power within a specific cultural setting, and that mastery is essential to the markets made by craftsmen.

Mastery means mastery of the workshop and of the home. Paternal authority is inscribed in the very labor process of workshops (cf. Adams 1993, 212). There is an isomorphism between the "I" of the workshop master, the workshop, and the house. When a master uses the word "I," he could be referring to his person or to the workshop. This is parallel to discourse in patriarchal family relations in Egypt, in which the terms "father," "the house," and "the family" can sometimes be used as synonyms. This discourse and modality of power in workshops in Egypt draws on a legacy of craft workshops in Egypt, which provided a particular legal code for the submission of the apprentice to the master, and the master's obligation to the apprentice's father. Since workshops are embedded in patriarchal power relations that prevail in the sphere of the family and home, they can easily become invisible to the eyes of the state (Wilson 1993) and become part of the "informal economy."

In the absence of a legal code regulating the relation of master to apprentice, mastery is a historically constituted practice embodied in the person of the workshop master, and in his relations with his apprentices and family members. The master begins to gain his mastery as a child worker (*sabi*) becomes a man, in the biological, social, and professional senses of the word. Mastery is also formed over a chain of lifetimes. It is embedded in a historical trajectory or lineage (*nasab*) of master-teachers. People linked through a *nasab* of mastery are sometimes kin, sometimes neighbors, and sometimes connected only through labor relations in the workshop.

The transmission of knowledge from master to master is shaped by broader historical and structural events. For my informants, relevant sociostructural determinations shaping their life history (Bertaux and Bertaux-Wiame 1997, 76) would include the Revolution of 1952, Abdel-Nasser's nationalization of industry in Egypt in 1963, and the oil boom in the Gulf of the 1970s. Such structural changes in Egyptian history directly shaped craftsmen's lives in intimate ways. A young apprentice who worked for a *khawaga* (meaning, among other things, an Egyptian national whose heritage or cultural practice was "foreign"), for example, had an open path to mastery when his employer and master decided to leave Egypt after Abdel-Nasser's nationalizations of industry in 1963.[4] At such moments, when large forces of history intersect with an individual's life course, one man might become a master without mastery, while another might become a master without power.

Another relevant form of history in the formation of mastery is embodied knowledge passed on from master to master. If, as the Egyptian sociologist Sayyid 'Uways has argued ('Uways 1989), Egyptian popular religion is a storehouse of history in which practices of today refer to all the religions of Egypt back to Pharaonic times, then the same might be said of craftsmen in Egypt. This does not mean that practices today are a carbon copy of practices in the past. Things in the past were not perfect in the way presented by Ashraf and others. The "way we do things" referred to by many of the craftsmen has continuously changed over the past hundred years, let alone over millennia. But it is equally ridiculous to think that we can make sense of "economy" among the small workshops of Cairo, which the World Bank has estimated make up 99 percent of the private sector economy of the city (World Bank 1994, 3), without reference to history.

Mastery is a social construction and a social resource. It is a quality of the individual master, but it is not individually constructed. Nor is it constructed inside the nuclear family. Bertaux and Bertaux-Wiame have argued that the most important capital passed on from generation to generation in craftsmen's families in France is not know-how but rather goodwill (Bertaux and Bertaux-Wiame 1997, 79). They note that specific know-how is not necessarily the most important resource passed on across the generations in craft families. Since structural conditions change over time, the son of a baker might not benefit most from knowledge of his father's trade. The customers might shift to buying bread from a large supplier, for example. In conditions of structural uncertainty, the most important resource that the son of a baker gains from his father might be the goodwill that his father built up in a community over his working life. The son might best mobilize that resource by becoming a miller who supplies the flour ground from the wheat of his father's former customers to a larger-scale bakery.

In Egypt generational transmission of mastery is not necessarily within the individual family. The apprenticeship system provided a broader social structure than the family structure of France for transmitting mastery and goodwill. Transmission of mastery in Egypt creates a re-source shared across a broad sector of the population called *sha'bi*, the popular classes of urban Egypt. Transmission of the different elements of mastery across the generations in Egypt entails a lineage of practice that is itself a storehouse of history. Family history is often inscribed in a vast geographic scale, even while remaining firmly rooted in Egypt. Migra-tions are part of the living history of almost every craftsman whom I interviewed. The recounting of family history over as little as two genera-tions always included migrations: from the countryside to Cairo; from Cairo to the Gulf in circular migration; and within Cairo from one neighborhood to another, as the traditional stability of urban life in Cairo broke down. Looking with hindsight over the individual's life-course and work history, we can see in those stories the moments when apparently random decisions took on greater implications for the unfolding of the life-course. Similarly, we can see how structural transformations in the region shaped individual choices. Let me now turn to some individual masters to shed light on how mastery is a specific form of power generated in the workshops of Cairo, how that form of power is enmeshed in broader constellations of power in Egypt and the Arab world, and what about mastery is so essential to the model markets of craftsmen.

Masters without Craft, Apprentices without Masters

Ibrahim was a master in all senses of the word. He was only thirty years old, but in the time-and-authority scale of the craft workshop he was an elder. While he was younger in biological terms than his "Youth Microenterprise" neighbors, who had been given loans from the Social Fund for Development and whom everyone did call "the youth," no one in town would ever call this young man young but rather addressed him as "*el-Hag*." Ibrahim had not gained the right to this term because of the religious character he had acquired rather late in his short and successful career but because of his undisputed status as a master of the trade, and a wealthy one at that. He could diagnose and solve any problem with the expensive cars of Cairo's wealthy—BMWs and Mercedes were his specialty—sent to him from miles around. He could sit upstairs in the loft he had constructed for an office (informally, without a license), in his clean polo shirts and pressed sports pants with an American label subcontracted inside Egypt, and know exactly what was happening on the workshop floor below. His clothes were never dirty or wrinkled, but he was the master of all that went on in his workshop.

Mohammed was another master. Another who knew his trade as well as anyone in the business. He could bang a car back into shape, and make a car that would be trashed in a richer country or by a richer clientele look just like new—almost. With long experience, a dedication to serving the customer, and stubborn skills, he saved his clients the expense of buying new imported parts for their cars. He was the best. No one dared say a word to him or intervene in his labor process. His assistant was trained at his hand, and his hand alone. And yet his status in the workshop was that of an *apprentice*. The profits from his work, and the favors with customers that it generated, were accumulated in the hands of his former friend and partner, now his master. His work and life history had not graced him with the attributes of mastery besides "master of the trade" that could have allowed him to become master of a workshop and master of his life.

Malak was a third man called master, but he knew nothing of his trade—turning on the lathe. When masters complained that anyone could call himself an usta these days, it was people like Malak they were talking about. Malak had been to college, worked as an accountant in the Arab Gulf, and put his savings from migrant labor into a number of ventures. His latest venture was a shop selling the acid-based chemicals used by workshop children for cleaning machinery and floors. While he had stood at the machine when he first bought a workshop, it was the master skills of his brother Hassan that made the workshop go. And yet Hassan could be called an apprentice in the workshop. A true craftsman, Hassan scoffed at his brother's way of getting into businesses that he knew nothing about. The craftsman's way, as they would all say in the face of these new workshops opened up by outsiders, was different. You only open up a business in something you know. And for the true craftsman, knowing is something not just of the intellect: it extends into every sinew and cell of the body as well. They would have been better off, he said, if Malak had used his money to expand the lathe workshop, which was doing very well tooling spare parts for companies in the area. But his older brother had been motivated by other concerns. "I didn't like my brothers knowing what my income was. If I opened up another shop they had nothing to do with, they wouldn't know my business, and couldn't ask." While not a master of the trade, he was the master of authority in that workshop. And lose money he might, but his authority would not be threatened.

The stories of these three men—the twists and turns of their work history, and how and why they ended up where they did, as a master, a master without a workshop, and a master without a trade—tell us something about the nature of markets and power in Cairo. It will become clear that rather than "mastery of the trade" alone, it was also mastery over real estate, and over regular flows of kin labor, that allowed (or made it impossible for) men like these to consolidate their mastery of a workshop over the course of long work histories and vast changes in the political order and social structure in Egypt between the 1960s and the 1990s.

Properties of Mastery

Let me return to the story of the master craftsman Ibrahim. Despite his young years, Ibrahim's mastery extended far beyond the immediate scope of his physical presence. All masters of the trade extend their sensory perception out from the body into space, and know whether the work is going well or not even when they are outside the workshop. Some report that it is the sound of the instrument on metal or wood, others the sight of finished materials piling up, that lets them know exactly how the work is progressing. But Ibrahim seemed to have extrasensory perception. Even while giving extended interviews about his life and work history, his presence on the floor flagged for not a moment. Workers (sanay'iya) in grease-stained overalls trudged up the stairs with questions or to retrieve a tool from time to time. His interventions were rapid, his diagnoses of problems unhesitating, and his reprimands sharp. He moved around town quite a bit, given his religious and political obligations as a prominent member of the craftsmen's NGO, but work in the workshop was completely under his control. Three of his workers were his brothers, one of them an older brother—someone to whom authority relations of the family would demand the display of respect. But inside the workshop, he said, authority structures of the family were subsumed to those of the workshop. One of his brothers was a sabi, the lowest rank in the apprenticeship chain of the workshop. In a conflict between this brother and a worker in the middle rank, he "would take the assistant apprentice's side if he were in the right." If his brother came late to work, he said, "I might fine him for being late. Inside the workshop, our relations are between the owner and a worker. I apply the rules of the workplace to my older brother."

Having successfully translated the wealth he had garnered from repairing the cars of the rich into social prestige by marrying the educated daughter of a wealthy trader from Heliopolis, and having become a publicly religious man and then the only craftsman involved in local NGO politics who was not thought a crook, Ibrahim saw that his mastery was strong and secure. On religious holidays he extended the aural scope of his presence into the shared public space of the street. Against the constant banging and clanging characteristic of the workshop neighborhood, punctuated by the sharp sounds of metal on metal close at hand, and the softer sounds of cars zooming in and out, customers chatting with the master, and the calls back and forth between the apprentices, the sounds of the recitation of the Koran—heard and yet not heard, so familiar are they—marked out space as sacred and as his. His mastery of the trade was undisputed, but it was not the sole source of his mastery in town.

Things were different with Malak. While the workshop was his, not he but his little brother was the master craftsman. Departures—from institutions tied to the state, from Egypt to the Gulf and back, and from this world to the next—were central moments shaping many Egyptian families' life-courses between 1963 and 1993. This family is a good example. The boys' father had died young, and the pension given to his widow was small. Malak went out to work when he was thirteen years old to feed his mother and brothers and sisters, taking over the leadership of the family. When his little brother dropped out of school, he sent him out to work in a mechanic's shop, thinking that the hard work would send him back. But once in the workshop, the brother didn't want to return. So he stayed in the craft world, where he would be joined by two brothers.

When he had a bit of experience, he went to work for his uncle's brother-in-law (*akhu marat 'amu*). This man was a successful craftsman with a solid reputation in the industrial neighborhood of Shubra. Workshops in such a neighborhood had good business with the factories of the Egyptian public and private sectors. Rather than buy spare parts, which were far more expensive and hard to find in Cairo than cheap skilled labor, the factories put out the work of maintaining and fixing their machines to the craftsmen who, "standing at the machine" in a small workshop, were and are an integral part of Egyptian factory production.

Malak's father had worked for the national telephone company in Cairo. He had been clever with his hands and skilled with machines, and made money on the side by selling small inventions he had made. (In those days this was not called "microenterprise," and he was not encouraged to leave his state job and work on his own.) He had been able to buy a house in the neighborhood of Shubra, and a house in Dokki as well. His young son sold the house in Dokki, with the mistaken thought in the early 1970s that more could be gained from workshop production than from simply holding on to land and doing nothing but waiting. If he had kept that villa, he would have been a millionaire, in dollars, by the 1990s. But instead he moved his brother and his skills into a workshop, bought whole from a craftsman who had ruined its reputation. He brought in his little brother to stand by his side, teach him the trade, and invest in building a name for their workshop.

Another uncle (*khal*) brought in the first customers. This uncle worked for one of those companies that depended on a steady and reliable working relation with a lathe craftsman. The uncle could decide where this work would be sent—and he sent it to these nephews who had been left without a father. Still learning the craft in its details, they worked around the clock, day and night shifts, servicing the factory of this company. One thing led to another. This was the boom period for workshops: it was right after the *infitah*, or opening of Egypt's political boundaries, to global flows of capital in 1973, when foreign investment started to pour into Egypt and skilled laborers to migrate out to the Gulf. The money was good, very good. Another brother was brought into the shop, to quickly "take the trade." The brothers soon became rich, or what felt like it.

But the inflows of money and outflows of workers that had already changed their lives even as they sat on the same street soon swept along two of the brothers directly. Out one night in 1978 with some Saudis on a regular visit to Cairo to sign on Egyptians for work in Saudi Arabia, arrange their papers, take their money for the service, and fly them out to their jobs, Malak himself was offered a job, one paying twenty times what he earned in Cairo. He was not the only one to go. Jobs like these in the 1970s took millions of Egyptian men away from their jobs and streets and families in Cairo, to build streets and buildings and institutions in Saudi Arabia. After he spent six years abroad his brother took his place in the migration chain, heading up a large lathe workshop in Saudi, where he also earned far more than he could earn in Cairo, even at the height of the migration boom.

But when physical absence was seen as more destructive to the family than the presence of new money, both brothers dropped their high-paying jobs to return home. Here as well, in the stories of departing and absence, the authority structures of the family and workshop were maintained: Malak returned home when he feared that his investment in the workshop and his little brothers were threatened by their newfound wealth and their bad habit of drinking up the profits with army and police officers of the neighborhood. And Hassan returned home when his big brother took ill from the strain of standing at the machine himself, rather than supervising his little, more skilled brother.

In and out of the elder brother's workshop, Malak preserved his authority. Using an expression heard from the master toward the apprentice and the father toward his sons, he explained that he held the authority in the family and workshop: "I would punish my brothers and provide for them economically." Hassan, master of the trade inside the workshop, addressed his older brother, the owner and master of the property and wealth, as el-Hag Malak. Ibrahim, thirty years old, was called el-Hag by other craftsmen, his biological elders; the craftless master Malak was called it by his own kin.

Mastery without Power

Mohammed, the third name I mentioned above, was a master of the trade but master of little else in his life. He too had acquired his skills in childhood, after taking the first step into the workshop hierarchy by dropping out of school. In this new "school," unregulated by the state, he might also be hit in order to learn, but along with sustaining blows he would bring home some money to his family and some coins for his own pocket.[5] The first steps on his work path were auspicious. His first master worked down the street from his house and was well known to his family. And the bad luck of his second master was his good fortune. This master had been disabled from a work injury that left him unable to carry out many tasks in the workshop himself. This gave scope to a boy like Mohammed to learn all aspects of the trade. In those days when formal schooling by the state, and the jobs in the bureaucracy that it could lead to, were still the aspiration of many craftsmen for their sons, this master had sent his sons to school rather than keep them with him in the shop. In the absence of his biological sons, he took in Mohammed to learn the trade instead. For a master without a son in the shop, the passing on of the trade, in which the trade is spoken of as a kind of charisma passed on from one biological person to another, from one generation to another, can be diverted to an apprentice who is not his son. "I became like a son to him," Mohammed said, "God bless his soul, he taught me everything he knew."

As the eight years that Mohammed spent in the workshop went by, he became a "full apprentice" (*sanay'i kamil*). When his boss died, he "stood in his place." The ability to "stand at the machine" is the statement of mastery—mastery here means the ability to physically stand at the machine, the tools of labor in hand, and direct the workshop and the labor process. He who "stands at the machine" is in this sense master of the workshop. Only a master can "stand at the machine" with no one to oversee his labor. And yet, this mastery, this ability to fill the presence of the departed boss, was not enough. For there is another lineage of power in the workshop, besides that one stretching from master to apprentice. And this is the lineage of property—from father to son. With the father gone, the sons reappeared and asserted their authority over this workshop as their property. To this new authority of the new master owner Mohammed could not submit. He would not submit to the authority of property possessed by someone who was not a master of the trade. It was time to move on.

Mohammed headed for the Libyan border, staying on the Egyptian side of the "Western Desert," where the Bedouin were the masters of long-distance trade across the border in legal and illegal items, often sold informally out of workshops like that which Mohammed opened in the then empty border town of Marsah Matrouh. That he moved not to the

Arab Gulf but to the border with Libya was another determining step in his work history and his ability, or lack of it, to consolidate "mastery" over his future. The money earned by workers in Libya or at its borders in the 1970s and 1980s came nowhere near that of skilled workers in the Gulf. The resources with which Mohammed returned to Cairo were enough to buy presents for his mother and sisters, the tea that was still a rationed item in Cairo, and little else. He moved with his family upon his return to a new, so-called informal neighborhood (*mantiqa 'ashwaiyya*), where holding a formal lease or having complete property rights in space was not a precondition for "opening a workshop." Here a workshop could be opened on the sidewalk. These spaces also are regulated, and access to them is bought and sold in markets. Sometimes the state generates revenues by asserting its rights in the property relations of the "informal economy." Regular fines paid to the municipality for this "illegal" purchase of space are usually seen as a necessary if annoying expense of production in a Cairo flooding with cars in need of repair. This is how it was for Mohammed.

Mohammed did quite well on the low end of the market that was his specialty. His customers were many, his work relations stable. He worked together with a partner who painted the cars whose bodies he fixed. But when the decision came through to close down the workshops and move them elsewhere, the different degree of rights in private property that the two enjoyed set one up as master and the other as apprentice. The partner who had a lease for the shop in the back—painting cars needs a larger space than bodywork, which can be done on the street—got a free workshop space from the state as compensation for having his workshop closed down. For the rights that he had purchased in open "workshop" space out on the sidewalk, without the benefit of four walls, Mohammed got nothing. And after a time, Mohammed went to work for his former partner. Master he had been—but now he was a worker, "apprenticed" to a former partner who did not interfere in his work but did take the profits and, equally important, cultivated relations and favors with the many officers and bureaucrats who frequented the workshop. The state invalidated the property rights that Mohammed had acquired in "the informal economy," and stripped him as well of the social power that this form of property accorded. He was also blocked from access to another form of power in the political economy of the workshop. Here I refer to the power that accrues to workshop masters in regular exchange relations with officials of the state (a topic to which I will return). Unable to establish control over flows of labor or property in land, Mohammed was sent back to the status of a skilled apprentice (*sanay'i*). Unable to open a workshop anywhere other than the open air of the street, he had nothing left but his labor to sell, once again. Mohammed was recognized by all as an usta, and no one, not even his boss, dared interfere in his work. But he was not a master.

Saved from the State by the State

Ibrahim's work history had also moved on and off "the pavement." But the street that he that grew up in, and worked on, was a whole different world from that of Mohammed. His grandfather had migrated into Cairo, like the father of Mohammed and all but a very small minority of the city's residents today, from the countryside of Egypt. But he had moved into the new model town of Heliopolis, built at the beginning of the twentieth century by Baron Empain as a private enterprise for profit and for realizing his utopian dreams of a new city in the desert where Muslims, Christians, and Jews, Levantine workers of European origin and native Egyptians, would live together in an urban environment built to match their religious beliefs and social status (see chapter 2). Peasants from all parts of Egypt who found their way into this neighborhood in the early waves of rural-to-urban migration opened little trading ventures and small shops in the corners and hidden pockets of this most modern venture.

Many of the skilled laborers and masters in Heliopolis were *khawagat*, Italians in particular. Some of those Italians were Egyptian born and had never seen Italy. These khawagat left Cairo en masse in the early 1960s, in the period when President Abdel-Nasser nationalized large industry and made those called "foreigners" fearful for their future. Their departure opened a new place in the workshop hierarchy for the sons and grandsons of those peasants who had brought their families to the great city of Cairo. Those boys of the neighborhood who had found their way into the workshops of khawaga Antoin or khawaga Georgi in the early 1960s found a rapid way up the ladder of the workshop hierarchy. Now not the sons but the masters were absent, and their skills became irrelevant as an index of social status in a state changing its terms of who was, and who was not, accorded political and economic rights in Egyptian society.

So when Ibrahim went to work and found a master who "treated him like a son," like Mohammed he had the luck to benefit from accidents. But these accidents were not the master's loss of his motor skills in the accidents common to workshop life. The accidents he benefited from were rather the accidents of history and changing social structure. As a center for foreigners and a favorite location for embassies and the foreign companies in Egypt, Heliopolis was home as well to the imported cars that the employees of embassies liked to drive and the companies to sell. And with spare parts for these cars out of reach, it fell to the khawaga masters, with whom the foreigners might have felt more "at home," for a word or two of French or Italian and the knowledge that the god they worshiped was Christian, to dominate all aspects of the repair business for the foreigner crowd. The children and young men apprenticing in these workshops came often from the pockets of rural migrant families around its fringes. A clever boy like Ibrahim could learn quite some skills in a specialized sector of the car business. And when the place of the master at the machine stood empty—through not biological death but political transformation—there were no sons to appear and assert their claim on the workshop as property rights over the rights of craft lineage.

The path of Ibrahim's work history was shaped by such abrupt transformations in the political and social structure of Egypt. He started out in a car repair workshop next to his father's fruit stand on a central street of Heliopolis—a good place for a child to start, in a shop close to and known by his family. His second job was in the workshop of the khawaga Usta Antoin, an Egyptian-Italian who specialized in foreign cars and automatic transmission. He started out with Usta Antoin in the mid-1970s, when the waves of migration to the Gulf began and skilled workers were in a strong position to assert their rights as workers, rather than apprentices. When workers in the shop walked out in protest against the wages and working hours, he stayed on. He explained his decision to stay on by noting his origins in upper Egypt, as a Sa'idi man who couldn't leave an old man helpless. When the workers came back, they didn't want to work again with this young man so loyal to the boss Usta Antoin. They "made problems for me," Ibrahim recounted, until he walked out.

In the new workshop Ibrahim got himself hired as a "senior apprentice." And the knowledge of specialized automatic cars that he had gained at Khawaga Antoin's workshop gave him a good chance to work on the foreign cars that few others knew. He improved his skills and worked on developing independent relations with the customers. When he thought his work strong enough, he quit. For the only way up in the workshop hierarchy, as he put it, was to quit and take work in a new workshop: an unskilled apprentice remains an unskilled apprentice forever if he stays in the same workshop under the same master. Horizontal movement is the necessary step for ascension.

The death of a master gave him his next chance in 1978. At the garage of Isma'il el-Sunni on a neighboring street, the name of the man remained on the front of the workshop, but his body had departed for the next world. The brother who appeared on the scene to assume control of his property had not "taken the trade" from his father and could not "stand at the machine." Ibrahim stepped in. Since the brother was from outside the workshop world, he didn't know, as anyone else from the inside would have known, what Ibrahim had been earning. So when Ibrahim reported his wages as 2 LE higher than they really were, he got the raise, in money and thus in status. "That's the only way you ever get a raise," he said, by getting a new usta to pay you more than the last one. And in the free market workshop, where there is no legal order or craft order to regulate wages and status, it is wage increases that mark the movement of the young man who is not kin up the workshop hierarchy.

In this workshop Ibrahim "made his name," an important step in becoming an usta that depends not only on mastery of skill but also on crafting a steady customer base, and maintaining relations with those officials who can make work possible or impossible. The Egyptian workers in the foreign embassies and companies of Heliopolis who brought in the cars for repair, Ibrahim recalled, "asked for me by name." His time with Khawaga Antoin paid off, when the obscure skills he had gained working on automatic transmissions and expensive foreign cars came into high demand with the growing presence of foreign capital and its foreign overseers on the streets of some Cairo neighborhoods.

Ibrahim told the story of his next move, out from the authority of a master to the free market public space of the street, as a struggle for control and authority over his junior in the workshop hierarchy, the sabi, or boy worker, of the workshop world. Ibrahim had trained this boy at his own hand, and as his skills and renown grew, he attempted to assert direct control over the boy's labor. One day, when the master tried to use the boy to clean the entire workshop, Ibrahim protested. The boy was only to clean his section, the section where Ibrahim was sovereign over the labor process, if not the property or profit created in it. When the dispute became an overt conflict, Ibrahim walked out—together with "his sabi," and finally opened his first workshop, out on the pavement.

Like Mohammed, Ibrahim purchased legitimate rights to occupy this bit of space on the street from the owner or lessor—in this case a friend who sold Coca-Cola from a little stand. For the sum of 5 LE a day he purchased the right to sole occupancy of the pavement in front of his friend's stand, and the use of his friend's workshop to lock up his tools each night. Without a master to take the profits of his labor, he "was blessed by God with success." He soon persuaded his friend to shift from soft drinks to a spare parts shop. And, Ibrahim recounted, "as things got big with me, he did well just the same." The money was soon good enough to purchase a store on another street of the same neighborhood. He bought it outright as full private property, completely in the letter of the law. But despite its legality, Ibrahim could not consolidate his mastery over this space.

Things had changed in Heliopolis. By the 1970s no area was left to workers alone. Real estate values were high, and the neighborhood was popular among the state-army élite. A general lived above Ibrahim's first legally registered workshop and was able to block his legal right to exercise his trade and his rights in private property. Summonses to stop his legal work rained down on him, until he was forced by this high state official back "onto the street," into the informal sector. But there was no peace for him on the street either. Now another general made life hell for him. He was saved only when the state closed down the workshop and he was moved with the others out to the new desert model town of el-Hirafiyeen. The state had saved him from the state. "Finally [after working for others and on the street], I was able to buy a shop and register it. Then I found General ———— living upstairs. He threatened me with prison. Whenever I opened up my shop, he sent me a summons for working on the street! So I locked up the shop and went back to working on the street. My mother-in-law lived on Ramsis Street, a dark shaded street. I took the cars to work on them there. But living there was a head inspector for the Eastern Region of Cairo. He threatened to put me in jail. I asked him, would you really imprison someone like your own son? [The head inspector was friends with Ibrahim's father-in-law.] He told me, 'I'd put my own father in jail if he was bothering me.' He put me into jail for a day or two, and gave me another summons. This was in 1989. Then the decision came down to move the workshops."

What Makes a Workshop; What Makes a Master?

What made Mohammed a master at some points in his worklife, while an apprentice in others? How did Ibrahim become a master and el-Hag even though he was younger than the youth microentrepreneurs funded by the World Bank and the Social Fund? And what made Malak a master without mastery? And how did everyone know which were the workshops in el-Hirafiyeen and which were the microenterprises, when from the outside they looked exactly alike, and the activities under way in many of the workshops had nothing craftlike about them in the least?

The workshops in which Mohammed, Ibrahim, and Malak labored were made of exactly the same four walls and ceilings, with the same specifications, as the microenterprises of youth graduates funded by the Social Fund. The two rooms in two buildings were identical. But they were at the same time completely different. If the workshop is not a room in a building, then what is it? I approach the workshop as a form of practice through which distinct relations of power are consolidated and expressed. The small physical space of the workshop can usefully be seen as a spatial condensation of relations among masters, workers, other masters, and households, and as an indivisible part of larger networks characterized by regularized patterns of exchange, cooperation, and competition, with symbolic as well as material content.[6]

The workshop operates with rules of the game invisible to outsiders and instinctual as a habitus (Bourdieu 1977) to insiders. When outsiders first step into a workshop in Cairo, they see a small, isolated, individual physical space. But complex patterns of exchange form a web of workshops, their customers, households, and officials of the state. In what follows, I will look at this set of patterned relationships and how those relationships intersect in the physical space of the workshop. I will start at the pinnacle of the workshop, with the master, whose workshop relations extend in four directions: to his workers, to his wife and family, to customers, and to other masters.

The master is the focal point of this nexus of relations within the workshop, among workshops, and between the workshop and the home. The workshop is the spatial expression of this nexus, of which the master is the primary beneficiary; in his person the network comes together as one and faces out to the world. What, then, makes the master a master? How does he consolidate his power? In the workshops I studied from 1993 to 1996, four factors were decisive: mastery of the trade; enforceable claims to property in land or housing; networks of contacts that directly or indirectly provided a market; and the ability to mobilize labor in the household and across kin relations. While not all the owner-masters displayed these characteristics, if more than one was lacking the master was vulnerable to the fate of many of his neighbors: going back to selling his labor as a skilled worker, or moving into the "informal sector" by working on the sidewalk or in an unregistered workshop.

Master of the Trade

The usta is, first of all, a master of his trade. He is a man (definitively a man) who came up in the workshop system from the bottom, starting as a boy worker when he was a child.[7] For the master, the craft has been practiced so many times since childhood that it is engraved in the nerves and muscles of his body and, as with the dancer, can be performed in the illusion of effortlessness. It is a habitus, the ability to spontaneously produce a set of practices that while performed by the individual body are part of a social process as well.[8]

Mastery can reach so deeply into the body/mind that the physical body can be presented as being above labor. Ibrahim could often be found sitting at his desk in his well-pressed clothes far from the site of labor. Greasy skilled workers would climb up to ask him a question about the work. He could know from the few words communicated to him what the problem was: his eyes had seen and his body worked on so many of these cars that he didn't have to use his organs of sight and sense to diagnose and solve a problem: The information was in his brain. Ibrahim demonstrated the master's ability to jump back into the labor process below without being there—in crafts as different as carpentry, mechanic shops, and machinist shops. Craftsmen expressed this integration of intellectual and physical knowledge in a number of ways. Another master spoke about the dual location of his knowledge, in his head and in his arm, and said that his craft knowledge (*san'a*) couldn't be lost. A carpenter reported knowing what was going on in the workshop, even while sitting upstairs in his separate office, by the sounds of the instruments on wood.[9]

This mastery gives the usta a particular form of authority and thus power. What he says is followed not only because he is the boss (*sahib al-'amal*) but also because his skills are, at least ideally, better than anyone else's in the workshop. He cannot be "tricked" by his skilled workers, since he is a master who knows the games even better. The journeyman is less likely to attempt to trick or cheat a master of the trade than a boss who does not have this embodied knowledge. That knowledge is gained through "situated learning" (Lave and Wenger 1991) in apprenticeship relations of child labor. An owner who doesn't know the business is exactly that: an owner or an employer, rather than a master. Those masters who had bought their workshops as outsiders, and learned the trade as owners rather than through situated learning as children, reported that they suffered many losses in the workshop during their first years, not least because their workers continually "cheated" them—that is, took advantage of the master's lack of mastery to subvert the labor process to their own advantage.

In some trades, like installing car exhaust systems, skill was less a prerequisite for asserting authority in running the shop. This was so for Ashraf, with whom I opened this chapter. Ashraf had only reluctantly taken on this job, standing in for his father, who had been a master craftsman in another field, when he could not use his college education to get a job. However, even in this trade so easy to "master," he was not able to physically leave the space of the workshop for more than a few moments. Lacking the skills of the master craftsman (including his cultural capital of knowing how to deal with the workers), Ashraf attempted to assert his authority through his direct bodily occupation of space in a way that left no room for ambiguity: he planted his chair right in the middle of the workshop floor. As he put it: "I have to be there to make sure they work. They get paid whether they work or not, so someone has to sit there to make sure they work, and work right."

This integration of brain and body, and inscription of knowledge in the body and senses, broadens the spatial scope of the master's authority. The master knows what is going on in the workshop even if he is up in his second-story office. Wealthier owners in town often built a separate office, sometimes "informally" in an apartment that they had been given by the governorate to live in, or bought out in an informal property transfer from a failed craftsman or youth entrepreneur. Some, without access to another apartment, lowered the ceiling of their workshop to create a small office space. Informal chats with the anthropologist, as with casual customers, took place on the workshop floor. But longer, more serious interviews were often conducted "in the office," interspersed with constant interruptions by boy workers passing on messages, or by skilled workers coming to consult the master about a problem in the labor process. In itself displaying the master's ability to be distant from the labor process, the office was also a stage for the display of mastery.

The greater that mastery, the freer is the master to move in space. The more the master's senses are deepened and heightened, the less his body has to physically occupy the workshop to dominate and direct its proceedings. With the carpenter able to "hear" the work from a distance, and the metal worker to "see" the sound of an instrument on metal in the finished objects of labor, the body can physically leave while the master remains. Achieving this level of mastery is a necessary, but not a sufficient, precondition for the craftsman to accumulate other forms of power as well. With the separation of different aspects of the labor process between "office" and "workshop," the master also creates a division between mental and manual labor in the body, the integration of which is central both to the so-called crafts and to the arts.[10] At the same time, the master submits more of the space around him to his domination, relying on patriarchal forms of labor in which those working under him are tied to another aspect of his body, his "blood" in kin relations, or in "as-if" kin relations.

Master of Space and Property

Through his ability to extend his senses and authority beyond the immediate scope of his physical body, the master inherently has the potential to dominate space in his immediate community. Such forms of mastery of space cannot be transferred outside the sphere of the workshop, however, and thus are not sufficient to consolidate control over space as property—something that becomes clear in contests between master apprentices and master owners. Be that as it may, it remains true that inside the walls of the workshop, allowing the skilled worker to exercise too high a degree of control over "his space," or "his worker," can challenge the craftsman's control over his workshop. Successful tactical moves in contested space can help transform authority over others into defended control of space.

The apprentice, for example, might be conceded authority over the space in which he carried out his labor, and over the labor of a child worker whom he had trained as "his." This was the case with Mohammed, the reader may recall. Mohammed used to run a workshop with a friend, but he never possessed formal property rights in that workshop, and in el-Hirafiyeen he was forced to go to work for his former partner as an "apprentice," even though he was acknowledged to be a master of the trade. No one dared go near Mohammed when he was working, enter his workspace without his permission, or call on "his" boy worker to carry out tasks for anyone other than him. Ibrahim, for his part, took the decisive step toward opening his own workshop—informally, on the street—when the master whom he then worked for ordered Ibrahim's boy worker to clean up the entire workshop. "He cleans only our part of the workshop," Ibrahim retorted, and ordered "his" boy worker to refuse the orders of their master. When the master wouldn't back down, the mechanic apprentice-becoming-master Ibrahim took the boy worker with him, and left for good.

The master in his workshop attempts to gain control over as much space as possible. There are many ways of asserting such control, and many forms of claims, some more permanent and more transformable into money and other kinds of social power than others. One man who grew up in the neighborhood of Old Cairo, a master of the trade but not master of a workshop, told how he had learned his craft from a master he had worked under for eight years, from whom he had "learned everything, God rest his soul." His master had been disabled by a work accident, just as happened to Mohammed's first master, and none of his sons had taken on the trade. In the absence of sons inside the workshop, he handed on his mastery of the trade to his long-time assistant, to whom he ceded authority over the space of the workshop as well. But upon the death of the master, the man—who was "like a son," much as Mohammed had been—discovered the limits to workshop kinship. Although he was standing in the place (wa'if makanu) of the deceased master—had become the usta, or master craftsman, of the workshop over which he was sovereign—when the sons reappeared and asserted their rights to the workshop as property, the limits to other forms of mastery appeared as well. The sons, outsiders to the craft, became owner-masters.

Mastering a Market

The master must also be master of a "market." Equally crucial to the achievement of "mastery" is the crafting of a network of relations through which flow regular exchanges of money for services—that is, the crafting of a market. Creating a market is one of the essential steps to ensuring the success of a workshop. In workshop masters' recounting of their moves toward "opening up a workshop," the key assessment was that their customer base would follow them into their own, new workshops. The customer base revolves around the personality and embodied skills of each master craftsman; it is neither abstract nor transferable to another, except through the transmission of mastery to an apprentice. Such a market is, literally, crafted; my use of the word is not gratuitous.

The gap could not be greater between how workshop masters made and talked about their markets and how the model market was discussed in the training manuals of NGOs and banks that supported the informal economy or microenterprises in Egypt. I sat through innumerable discussions over the course of my fieldwork, in bank and NGO training sessions, and with development experts in NGOs and IOs, about the "importance of markets" for the success of microenterprise and informal economy in Egypt. This great discovery that markets did matter marked the second phase of the Social Fund and other informal economy and microenterprise programs in Egypt, which had originally operated on the assumption that providing loans to individual entrepreneurs would automatically solve all ills. Microenterprise pundits had thought that all commodities found their market. It didn't take a Marx to discover that Say's Law was a poor joke: the scores of failed projects and missed loan payments made the point. (Nor, it was found, did distributed loans necessarily lead to even unsold commodities.) When the importance of creating markets was finally discovered in the microenterprise lending programs, the model market the administrators had in mind was an abstract "free market," in which buying and selling proceed according to the signals of supply and demand among anonymous players with complete information. It was the market of Economics 101. Many of the young people taking part in training sessions for microenterprise that I attended in Cairo in 1994–95 really believed in the market. They wanted to be taught how to find it. Finding the market, they believed, entailed gaining access to the internet, learning about advertising, and taking marketing classes in school. Granted, many of those who took part in the training courses were cynical, and were attending simply because they were paid to do so. This church of the market was one that helped its believers: sums of about 50 LE (about $15 U.S. at the time—a large sum of money in Egypt) were often given to microentrepreneurs who attended training sessions. Disappointment and disbelief among those who really believed in this model market and could not find it were palpable among my informants.

Belief in the market often went along with the conviction that access to computer technologies, faxes, and the internet would solve marketing problems by providing endless possibilities of communication. The notion was pervasive that the market was someplace else. Those who tried to reach an abstract market never found it. But one machinist who was also a retired army colonel and an engineer was more successful. His search for a better market built on his network of fellow retired army officers who had, like him, opened small machine shops. He hoped that buying a fax machine to communicate directly with his customers in distant parts of Cairo would create vast possibilities for expansion. Training sessions of a BONGO (business-oriented NGO) led by a professor of a technical university and missionary for NGOs and SMEs (small and microenterprises) in Egypt, however, which revolved around the promise of the internet for "opening up markets," offered no ideas of how to translate this ideal market of infinite possibilities into something from which a newly starting-up graduate in Egypt with no experience in production could benefit.

In contrast to this idealized picture of "the market" in capitalism, the market for the workshops was a highly personalized matter, demanding much attention from the master. This was true whether the workshop was selling services or commodities. And given the personalized nature of the workshop market—as captured in the notion that the most important "capital" of the workshop is the master's "name"—dealing with the customer is perhaps the most sensitive part of workshop operations. Even the master who has the authority and knowledge to follow the labor process from a distance likes to be close by to deal with the customer. The master can delegate authority to another for dealing with customers and taking money from them, but that authority is something awarded by him alone, and under his conditions—and usually only when he is so far from the workshop that he cannot be easily summoned by one of the boy workers running like lightning across the shared public square.

If the master is absent, the skilled worker has the right, indeed the obligation, to make a deal with any customer who comes along. For in the workshop market, gaining the customer for a long-term relationship is more important than gaining or losing in an immediate transaction. Even if a little money is lost in a deal made by the worker, "when the deal is closed by him I won't open it again." Not paying enough attention to getting the deal from the customer can be grounds for the skilled worker to be expelled from the workshop. Explaining why a skilled worker had been fired, one master cited as his most serious mistake: the worker had told a potential customer that an item he tooled in the workshop was available on the market for a good price. Such an act of sending away a customer could even be seen as an act of insurrection against the master, and the grounds for firing an apprentice. Making "the market" is such an important part of workshop mastery that subverting an opportunity to build the market is also a subversion of the master's authority.

The skilled worker given regular authority to make deals or take money is the most trusted employee in the workshop. In the workshops of el-Hirafiyeen, where relatives often held the keys to the money and books, a younger brother, brother-in-law, son, or sister's son tended to be in charge. Kin working under the master are already in a position of subordination according to patriarchal authority systems. The wife's brother, a younger brother, or sister's son—categories of affinal and agnatic kin found working in workshops—already have a subordinate relation to the craftsman in kinship status hierarchies. In workshops the potential split between the master's different kinds of mastery, and between mental and manual labor, is embodied in kin relations, as the trusted relative takes on the "white collar" mental labor of the master.

In a competitive market, in which the customer is free to go to any other workshop practicing the same craft, and social ties with a stable community have been broken, the craftsman works hard to build up and maintain his customer base. The removal of workshops in el-Hirafiyeen from their old neighborhood had stripped them of most of their customers. The need to recreate a customer base brought about a crisis for the craftsmen from the time they were moved from their old locations through the end of my fieldwork in 1996. Many workshops, such as carpentry shops that produced goods for houses and apartments, went out of business altogether. The owners and operators of workshops specializing in small jobs for individual customers complained that they had lost their customers to former workers who started working in Heliopolis informally "on the pavement."

For those who survived, new ways had to be found of acquiring and keeping customers despite the geographic distance of the workshops. Being close to new formally zoned industrial neighborhoods worked to the advantage of some machinists, who were able to forge new links with companies in the immediate area through auctions, visits to factories, and word of mouth. All those working on cars, which became the dominant business in the town after the shakeout of crafts engaged in production for the home, had to devise new strategies to acquire or keep customers. One man who painted cars in a factory-like "oven" sent one of his sons to pick up, deliver, and return customers' cars: the surplus of trusted kin in his workshop gave him the means to maintain customers. Top mechanics and others who worked on expensive cars maintained their customers' loyalty: the problem was greatest for the lower strata of workshops that served customers with cheaper cars. These customers' needs were met by informal workshops on the pavement in front of the craftsmen's old locations, even if the work was of lower quality.

But maintaining a customer base demands more than such strategies: it also involves psychology—the art of sizing up customers, knowing what they will pay, and what will make them feel safe. Craftsmen are known in popular culture as cheaters and tricksters. A rich tradition of using language and the brain to outwit rulers in Egyptian and broader Arab culture is often thought of as an art among the craftsmen, or hirafiyeen. Dealing with the individual customer, the craftsman must create an air of trust. As mentioned above, the wise craftsman, according to the accepted rules of the game, will not try to get as much money as possible out of a customer, nor charge so little as to hurt his neighbor: He will "take the job in the middle."

Informants told many stories about buyers-in who did not understand this principle of valuing relationships over short-term gain or vicious competition. They soon went out of business. Historical sources about craft workshops and guilds in Ottoman Egypt refer to a band of maximum and minimum prices fixed by the state and enforced by the market inspector.[11] Among the craftsmen during my fieldwork, instead of formal regulation there was a shared notion of what was the "smart thing to do," or simply "what we do" to keep everyone in business. Focus on short-term gain, or undercutting neighbors—two things once banned in mechanisms of the craft orders—remained "taboo." In conversations craftsmen usually cited the market itself as the regulator of this popular wisdom. This market was a form of embodied practice. It was not the market as the abstract meeting point between supply and demand. When the market showed its wisdom, it was through the action of networks of people. The failures of the graduates and microenterprises, for example, were usually traced by craftsmen and others to their lack of "a market." While instructors at NGO and bank training sessions talked endlessly about the "importance of markets," in practice newcomers in el-Hirafiyeen who made it were those who brought with them a built-in "market" through kinship relations and connections to people working in organizations of the state or large companies.

If workshop markets are personalized, their maintenance demands different kinds of skills, depending on the type and structural location of the customer. Skills in maintaining the "market" vary, depending on whether the customer is an individual, an individual with status in the state, a small company, or a large capitalist firm.

Networking Companies, Networking the State

Even when the workshop's customer is a capitalist or state-owned firm, the cultivation of networks is crucial. Sometimes contracts are won in public auctions, which may be settled through various informal means. But generally they are won through connections. One retired army colonel mobilized a network of officers who had retired young and opened businesses to create markets for his products. A master whose brother was employed by a large company got access to company contracts that his brother was responsible for farming out.

Many large companies in Egypt get their spare parts and service machinery through subcontracting, rather than keep people on permanent staff inside the company or pay full price for imported spare parts.[12] And since subcontracting takes a high degree of personal contact and social skills, an employee may spend much of his time farming out work to small workshops and others, which also gives him opportunities for extracting rents. These forms of passing work from company to workshop through connections of kinship or "friendship" are examples of what are called business relations ('*ilaqat biznis*), but from an anthropological point of view they might be better translated as "relations where the exchange of money for providing access to work is open and direct." In such instances a commission ('*umula*) may be paid for getting the work contract, even if it is was kin who initiated the contact. Where the customer is a person with a position in the state, as is often true in particular with the business of car repairs in a neighborhood like Heliopolis— home to many officers of the army and police—yet other dynamics beyond abstract pure market exchanges need to be managed. Apart from the previously mentioned rule that building relationships over time is more important than immediate financial gain, additional skills are needed, and a different, nonfinancial calculus comes into play.

The time expended on cultivating these relations has no direct economic value on the market. It is priceless. In anthropology, these kinds of exchanges are usually discussed in terms of gift exchange, although the exchange of money and commodities may be involved as well, as it is here. Such exchanges are not simultaneous in time, return is not guaranteed, return must be in a form other than that which was given, and the exchange is conducted in modalities of sociability. Such relations allow the master to acquire "rights" to services inside the institutions of the state itself through a personal connection, based on face-to-face interactions in the workplace or workshop, friendship, or kinship relations.

The benefits of a customer base that includes army officers and others with positions in state institutions are immense—for the master. The accumulation of "goodwill" in the exchange of favors between the workshop and the customer accrues to the master of the workshop, no matter who carries out the actual work. The master takes the blame for bad work in his workshop and accumulates the goodwill resulting from good work; the workshop is synonymous with his "name." Mohammed, for example, complained bitterly about this form of "exploitation" by his boss and former equal. When his former partner took on work from a customer with a position inside the state, he offered the work at a lower price, doing the customer the "favor" that calls forth another kind of "favor" in the future. When the master has his workers perform labor at a lower price for a person who can make things move within state bureaucracies, the action is named with a term that invokes notions of generosity central to systems of honor and prestige in Arab culture (*ka-ram*), or with a word that literally means doing favors (*mugamlat*) but also invokes the entire system of gift exchange binding together networks of individuals in survival strategies. Being generous is a highly valued attribute in all Arab cultures, and as in any system of honor and gift exchange the person who gives generously acquires a kind of power over the person to whom he gives.

That the goodwill does not necessarily accrue to the man who does the work becomes quite clear when a workshop is shared by two masters with different specializations (here bodywork and paint jobs), and when a relation of master and apprentice has developed solely because of who consolidated rights to property rather than skills alone. Even when the boss-master has ceded to the apprentice-master the right to control his own working space and his own apprentice (as discussed earlier), a more decisive level of their power relations emerges in exchanges with "the state." For it is only the master-boss who accumulates both money profits and goodwill with the many army officers among his customers. When the price is reduced as a "favor" to the officer, a master worker paid according to the money profit on the job loses out twice. Mohammed put this dilemma in the following terms: "There are problems between me and the boss [sahib el-'amal] about the work. He's a paint job man, and I'm in bodywork. There are things he doesn't know anything about in my work, and he starts interfering in things he doesn't understand. We do our business, he and I, by the day, not by the job. And I work really long hours. Our deal is that we split the profit on the work that I do, but this arrangement isn't a good one. He does lots of work for some officers, and he's the one to benefit from these favors [mugamlat]."

Some favors that accrue to the master are visible inside the workshop. When a workshop owner casually mentions that his son will be doing his army service in Cairo, and able to come to work in the shop every day, it is clear that connections with officers in Heliopolis brought about this important service for the survival of the family.[13] Connections to other states can be forged as well: the impossible dream of a visa to America was easily arranged by this family for another son, at a price, they said, of 2,000 LE. That the family had such connections inside the embassy, and mentioned so casually the opening of this gateway to America, is even more striking here than the sum, which is surprisingly low and affordable.[14]

Master of Kin and Household

MALE KIN LABOR—AND ITS ABSENCE—IN THE WORKSHOP

Even when there is no kin labor working in the workshop, the master is still the possessor of patriarchal authority over his subordinates. "He is the father, the patriarch." Such metaphors of kin and household are surely part of the reason why workshops are so easily rendered "invisible" to the state, like women's labor in the home.[15] By virtue of controlling a workshop, moreover, the master is positioned to mobilize the labor power of his male affinal and agnatic kin. A profitable workshop will attract the male labor of men related to him by kinship or marriage, in addition of course to the master's own boys. This is particularly true in tight labor markets such as those that characterized workshops in the 1990s. Having access to trustworthy labor can be important for the success of a workshop, particularly in times of crisis when the existence or lack of solid networks takes on visible consequences. In some crises only the closest of networks, those of kin, can be counted on to help. And only a craftsman with sons or younger brothers in the shop can trust that work will go on during his long-term absence as if he were still there.

When one workshop master had a serious accident and was in the hospital and out sick for weeks, for example, his income from the workshop dropped over 50 percent. He had no male kin inside the workshop whom he could count on to keep things going in a correct way. While this master had come up in a popular neighborhood and been trained in a craft from a young age, like a true craftsman, he had acquired his workshop in el-Hirafiyeen as one of the "returnees from the Gulf," after being forced home and separated from his savings by the second Gulf War. While he had fulfilled the Social Fund's condition of "employing three" for every workshop that it supports (allowing the fund to publish impressive statistics about the benefits of microenterprise for reducing unemployment), this man, like many others, had partners on paper only. And even though they were his relatives, they were not relatives under his authority. He had spent many years abroad; meanwhile, his younger male relatives had become heads of their own families with their own workshops to maintain. Likewise, although he was a well-liked man, and thus many came to visit him in the hospital, no colleague would leave his own workshop and economic interests to look after those of another man. Having only the paid labor of strangers to rely on in a crisis, he saw the income from his workshop cut in half while he was in the hospital: "One journeyman and one boy worker work regularly in the workshop. When I was out sick, the journeyman ran everything. He would come to see me every ten days or so, and bring me the take of the workshop. Income went down over 50 percent while I was out. I didn't say anything to him about it, because the issue was obvious, and he understood by himself. It was for him to open up the subject. He said only that the market was dead. He told me to bring one of my relatives to oversee the workshop while I was out. I told him: there's no one to look over you but God and your conscience" (see chapter 5, note 22).

The line between the authority that flows from the workshop and that which flows from the family can become quite blurred when a son assumes the role of head of the family, as well as head of a workshop. If the eldest son not only assumes responsibility for the family but also provides it with income by opening a workshop, the younger brothers may work for their older brother and call him el-Hag, as happened with Ibrahim. Ibrahim's status as the provider of income to his older brothers made him an "as-if" older brother. His comments about the contradictions created by the different lines of authority are worth repeating: "I'm the center of the leadership of the family since the death of my father, even though my brother is older than me. I give my mother a monthly salary of 400 LE, and give my sister who doesn't work 100 LE a month. . . . If my brother came late to work, I might fine him for being late. Inside the workshop our relations are between the boss and an employee. I apply all the rules of the workplace to my older brother."

Authority and Discipline of Boy Workers in the Workshop

In the "guild order" that once organized workshops in Egypt (see chapter 4, note 11), the authority of the master over his workers was explicit and regulated. The father handed his son over to the master, and the boy had to submit to and respect the master in all he said ('Abd al-Halim 'Amr 1993, 36–38). In turn, the workshop master was subject to the authority of the head of the craft order, who could intervene when the master was seen to act inappropriately or unfairly toward the child. In the workshop of the 1990s the child still had to submit directly to the authority of the master, but he had no resort if the master treated him unfairly or abused him. The state agencies supposedly responsible for children's welfare were largely absent or ineffective, faced with an estimated two million children in the labor force working to support their families (Abdel-Latif 1995). And of all the agencies I studied during my fieldwork that gave loans and succor to the informal economy and microenterprise—IOs, NGOS, and bilateral development agencies—I was unable to find any that took steps to protect the health and interests of these child workers. Invisible behind the label of the individual "entrepreneur," or under the patriarchal structures of discourse used in the workshop, the children were simply not an object of interest.[16]

The master's right to hit the boy worker "in order that he will learn" was stated by masters and journeymen and by children as well. Journeymen have the right to hit child workers for the same purpose of teaching. The subject was neither hidden nor embarrassing to talk about or to allow an outsider to view. All the men would condemn the use of unreasonable physical violence on a child, but as a moral issue the use of force was left to the master—or father in the home—to determine.

Attempts to assert authority in the workshop—not only over space, as discussed above, but over the labor of children as well—are seen as something that must be defended. The right to control the labor of the boy worker and the right to discipline him are an area of contestation, and even the boy worker has ways of resisting the control of those whose authority he does not recognize. In one workshop where an assistant was deaf, a constant game could be seen between the boy worker and the assistant. When the assistant tried to tell the boy what to do, the boy would start acting "like a child" and refuse to meet the assistant's glance or let himself be touched. In other words, he didn't recognize the assistant's authority as a man working above him. Similarly, the deaf man, socially considered less than a full man, tried to assert his manhood by controlling the boy worker, particularly in the presence of outsiders like us.

Flows of Money between Workshop and Household

Although a worker, the boy worker does not "possess" authority over his own person, or over the money he earns. According to historical accounts, fathers once brought their sons to the workshop master themselves. When most of the masters in el-Hirafiyeen started in the trade, their fathers knew their masters from the neighborhood. As adults, these men often agreed that they should meet the fathers of the children they hired, and some claimed that they always did. But for others, doing so was both unnecessary and impractical, since the boys sometimes came from other cities and found their way to the workshop on their own. If the father had made the work arrangements with the master, however, the child's weekly salary might be paid directly to the father, with the child receiving only daily money for food. In such an arrangement, the boy is socially recognized as a man when he becomes a journeyman or skilled worker. That status as a journeyman is marked in turn when the boy receives his own salary. This system is given a succinct formulation by Mohammed: "My father had gotten the old usta to give me no more than 2 LE, while he would take 30 LE a week. My first wage in al-Manial was 8 LE a day. My father didn't take my wages anymore, because now I had become a journeyman."

Even after becoming a full-fledged skilled worker, the unmarried young man does not have full authority to decide where his money will go: family obligations are paramount. Refusing to participate in the financial obligations of the house would be tantamount to "leaving home," as a couple of the skilled workers in town had done. Many of the young men interviewed gave a good part of their money to general household expenses (literally to "the house," *lil-beit*), or to their sisters as money or presents. A father's demand for money from his son, moreover, is difficult to refuse. One young skilled worker explained that he didn't want to take out a loan from a microenterprise program to open a workshop because of his inability to designate the money as his rather than as family income over which the father had rights: "If I got a big amount of money like that my father would want it for something and I wouldn't be able to refuse my father. The money would be gone and I wouldn't have anything to show for it."

Where boundaries are not sharp and resources are shared among a wide number of claimants, contestation over resources of labor, time, services, and money can be intense. Women are far from passive in the ensuing negotiations, including those about money. Outright confrontation, however, is avoided where possible.[17] One girl responsible for the family budget gave detailed examples of her techniques for appropriating small sums to buy cosmetics and other items essential for presenting herself to the world. Women who negotiate in the household about the flow of workshop resources often invoke the needs of their children, since creating better chances for the next generation is a cherished value of the family- and child-centered Egyptian culture.[18]

Obviously men have different priorities in balancing the needs of the family they were born into with those of their own household. Likewise, the finances of the master are more complex than those of the skilled worker. For the skilled worker, a common issue of contestation is how much the man earns (many do not tell their wives), and what share of his wages goes towards maintaining the household. The financial books of the workshop (and of the "microenterprise" of most graduate entrepreneurs, for that matter) are not strictly separated from the household budget. The terms in which one craftsman discussed the fungibility of the two were striking: "The budget of the house is open. If there's work, then I bring home the monthly allowance. If not, then I take from the reserve of the workshop."

A person with authority does not necessarily want those whom he supports to know how much money he has. Women often have no idea what their husbands earn: "my father raised us that way," one man simply stated. Blocking access to such information closes off the possibility of pressure and negotiation about how money should be spent. Men "don't like women's talk," as a number of them put it. Too much passing of information among women increases each woman's possibilities of negotiation with her husband, and her chances of finding out information about his finances or movements that he might prefer to keep hidden. From the man's point of view, "trouble starts when women start gossiping with each other."

The lengths to which a man might go to maintain his authority over decision making about family resources are illustrated by an older brother who became the head of his family and employed his brothers to help run his workshop. While his position as "boss" and head of the family made him the "master," it was his younger brother who was master of the trade and really made the workshop go. The elder brother's wish to maintain patriarchal authority over brothers more skilled than he took precedence over "rational" decisions about profit and accumulation. While expanding his profitable machinist's workshop would have made good economic sense, the elder brother chose to enter, against the advice of his master-of-the-trade little brother, into a risky venture of a shop in a trade that he knew nothing about, with a partner who ended up cheating him out of money. But with his brother's authority in the workshop as master of craft and customer relations growing, the elder brother had been eager to block threats to his authority over his and his family's money: "I made another project rather than expanding the workshop for family reasons. I didn't like my brothers knowing what my income was. If I opened up another shop, they would have nothing to do with it, wouldn't know about my business, and couldn't ask."

Women's and Children's Labor Services in the Workshop

The workshop is related to the household in important ways other than the workshop's system of power relations just discussed. There are also direct and indirect contributions of the unpaid labor of women and children. In fact, household and workshop can be so closely integrated that they might be conceptualized as one entity. At the same time, this high level of integration is expressed in a bipolar gendering of space between the two. The relation of workshop to household was historically expressed in spatial terms of integration and separation. When the home is near the workshop, as it was in the old neighborhood in a structure that integrates the workshop into the social life of the local neighborhood (*hara*) and street, there are close, direct links of labor and services between workshop and home space. In the popular neighborhoods that the workshops were moved from, craftsmen usually lived with their families upstairs from the workshop or nearby. The master's wife usually cooked hot meals for him every day. In earlier times the wife prepared and served food that the master contracted to provide to his apprentices as well.

When the home is near the workshop, the wife also benefits from services of the workshop in her role as maintainer of the household. The dependence of workshop on household is inverted when the wife uses the facilities of the workshop to ease her household chores. A wife often sends the boy workers of her husband's workshop on errands of various kinds; the wife of a machinist might send the household knives down to the workshop for sharpening. Usually it is the boy workers of the workshop who perform the intermediation between the workshop and the home—as between the workshop and so many other kinds of spaces. At the same time, women clean the clothes and care for not only their husband-master but their children-workers as well. In return for these services, women enjoy the sociability of their family's presence. The proximity of workshop to home facilitates the integration of sociability and rest with work. During workdays that can go long into the night, those with close access to domestic space often rest after meals before returning to work.

When home and workshop are separated, the master suffers from the lack of free services that the home provides: a clean place to relax during the long day in which social interaction and labor are not fully separated, and food "of the home," which in Egypt is widely preferred to food "of the street." One man whose wife had refused to move to el-Hirafiyeen complained bitterly about having to eat outside the house, and said that he suffered from stomach problems he had never known before. In such conditions of spatial separation between workshop and home, the complex exchanges of services between home and workshop can be reduced on the one hand to the reproduction of labor power in the home and on the other to the generation of money in the workshop to guarantee the reproduction of the family over time. Stripped of the emotional sustenance given by the presence of her sons and husband in the house, the wife is revealed as a provider of services to her husband and children in a workshop that provides her with the necessary income to run the home.

Analyzing the family and household in terms of structured exchanges —particularly among workshop families in conditions of distance—is also relevant for understanding the structure of the household under conditions of more distant migration. In conditions where the husband sold his labor power in the Gulf states to provide a higher level of resources for his family, for example, the spatial distance between workshop and household became extreme. No longer maneuvering daily to capture a larger portion of income, the woman left behind became the manager of relatively large sums. Women became freer to manage household money and use their time as they saw fit. Household relations to income and labor then needed to be renegotiated when the husband returned.

One woman, who moved with her children back to the old neighborhood after only a week in el-Hirafiyeen, complained that now she had only the ghosts of her husband and children—their dirty clothes to wash at the end of the day—rather than the sociability of their presence. And without free household services, the workshop came to rely more on commoditized inputs to the reproduction of labor power. At the same time, apartments built for workshop families by the engineers of the governorate to allow masters to live close to their work were turned to other purposes. Some skilled workers were allowed to use the empty apartments of their bosses to rest during the day, and others informally bought out or sublet the apartments so that they and their working-class families would have access to domestic space and a place to relax during the working day.

But distance from the home gives the craftsman some benefits as well. Distance lessens the possibility that his wife will know about his movements, his income, his spending on illicit goods like beer and hashish, and his relations with other women. These benefits for the men were drawbacks for the women, some of whom chose to move with their husbands into a neighborhood that for them was a wasteland, devoid of the dense social relations that characterized their life in the old neighborhood. Most men commuted to work; despite the best efforts of the planners, few left their old neighborhoods. When the wife did move to town with her family, there were clear reasons for the move (which of course emerged only over time and the course of research). In one instance the master had had an affair with a woman from a family of renters, a woman known to be a "professional," and was spending too much money on her. Faced with this situation, the wife followed the advice of a family friend and colleague of her husband, who said that the affair was her fault. By moving to town, she would block the possibility of affairs by simply making her presence felt. In another case, a successful young master wanted his wife near him, to get away from the powerful presence of her family and to increase his prestige by having a woman sitting at home, showing the world that his wife did not need to work. For another family, the apartment in el-Hirafiyeen afforded the first opportunity to live outside the apartment of the husband's mother; to this family an apartment in the middle of the din and desert was a joy and an unexpected blessing.

The labor of girls in the family is absorbed in the home; the labor of boys tends to be absorbed in the workshop. Male children of craftsmen in el-Hirafiyeen went to work for their fathers at a young age. Some dropped out of school to begin work—something of which their fathers disapproved, but apparently not strongly. Given the relatively high wages that their sons would earn in the workshop, and the generally perceived uselessness of most school degrees in the 1990s, fathers had little reason

134

to fear for the future of their sons who left school. Some of the boys worked only after school.

Reflecting the dual nature of the workshop master as "master" of the craft and owner of property, two stances toward treatment of the son were expressed. On the one hand the boy was to be a "worker like any other, so he'll learn." But on the other hand, some argued that because the boy was a future owner himself, "it wouldn't be right for him to get a wage." In other shops, the son received a wage ("he buys his own clothes and enters his own saving circles for clothes"), but not as much as he would have earned "outside," in another workshop or a "Center." Sometimes all the sons of the family could be found working in the workshop. In a craft like carpentry or machine work, however, the master would make clear that only some sons had "taken the craft." A man with a number of sons who took the craft and either stayed in his workshop or opened their own workshops nearby had a particular source of power in his community. This was true of one workshop master, Samir (see chapter 5).

The mastery of workshop masters in el-Hirafiyeen had been acquired over a lifetime in lineages of workshop and family life. Mastery of the trade in itself, however, was not sufficient for masters to consolidate their mastery. Mastery in the sense that I have analyzed in this chapter was far more complex. The master of a successful workshop in Heliopolis or el-Hirafiyeen was a node in networks of ongoing exchange relations with state officials, company suppliers, individual customers, neighboring workshops, and sometimes NGO officials. Mastery entailed a master's ability to reproduce himself at the center, from his point of view, of a constantly shifting network of relations. Sometimes that meant negotiating complex relations of power, as we saw most clearly with Ibrahim.

Ibrahim, the reader may recall, was stymied in his pursuit of a market in Heliopolis by state officials who could use state power for their own ends. His attempts to work legally did not protect him from the state, since its power could be captured by those who worked in its name. Only the state's apparently random decision to close down his workshop, to save the president from the sight of eyesores like workshops (a decision carried out in the name of social science principles of good urban planning), saved him from the state in the person of his officer neighbors. He could not fully consolidate his mastery until he was relocated to a setting where his pursuit of powerful customers who owned expensive Mercedes and BMW automobiles would not so clearly demonstrate the limits to his mastery.

Likewise, a master had to consolidate his power over his workshop as property. The greatest master of the trade could end up working as an apprentice if he was not able to consolidate his hold on property over time. Mohammed's life story made this clear. The fluidity of property relations among workshop owners in el-Hirafiyeen underlines the old anthropological point that property is not a thing but a relation. Workshops owned by masters in Heliopolis were rendered worthless when the state exercised its organizational power under the tutelage of IOs like the World Bank. At the same time, those interventions opened up new pathways for some to consolidate power through property relations in the new setting of el-Hirafiyeen. This was so even though in both places the workshop masters had owned their workshops as private property.

The workshop owned by Mohammed on the pavement of Heliopolis was as much private property as was his neighbor's workshop in the back that had been registered in a fashion recognized by the state. I do not say this to emphasize the need for the state to recognize informal property relations, as argued by de Soto (1989). El-Hirafiyeen itself was one outcome of the social science research of scholars like de Soto into the importance of the informal economy and microenterprise. Without the championing of the informal economy propounded by de Soto, Mohammed's workshop on the street might never have been closed down. My point is rather that maintaining property relations demanded the constant attention and labor of workshop masters. The labor of maintaining property relations, like the labor of maintaining markets, was central to a master's constitution as a master. How he went about consolidating that mastery gave him a particular kind of reputation in el-Hirafiyeen. It is to the question of a master's reputation, and his production of value in workshop life, that I will now turn.

5. Value, the Evil Eye, and Economic Subjectivities

I have argued in this book that extension of the free market to absorb the cultural practices of the poor as a source of social capital and profit is one of the most influential developments of our times. In this chapter, I continue my analysis of what is being absorbed by the market's expansion, by turning to the production of value in workshop life.

I have suggested that the anthropology of value gives an important vantage point from which to analyze the process of market expansion in Cairo. In Cairo, I have said, much of social life revolves around the cultivation of relationships through ongoing exchanges of things, money, sociability, and emotion. I characterized this in terms of what I called relationality. The dynamics of relationality characteristic of workshop life can be analyzed in terms of relational value. This value has become an important resource for the process of market expansion that I claim is under way. I will begin my discussion of value by looking at notions of generosity and manliness in workshop life.

The Value of Generosity

A Dictionary of Egyptian Arabic defines the Egyptian term *gada'* as follows: "1. One possessed of one or more of the following groups of characteristics: nobility of character and integrity; intelligence and application; manly toughness and courage; or 2. fellow, young man" (Badawi and Hinds 1986, 151). The gada' is a person from the popular classes (*sha'bi*) who has the characteristics of "manhood" (*rugula*)—another word that has more than one level of meaning. Both words condense a set of characteristics: one who can take it, who watches out for those near to him, and who can bear a lot without complaining. It also implies a man who doesn't swindle or cheat, isn't treacherous, and generally acts within the moral universe of the Egyptian popular masses. He has the qualities of decency and gallantry (*shahama*). To say that someone interacts with gad'ana is to say that he watches out for others in his community.

Historically the gada' was one who watched out for the *hitta*, the local neighborhood within the larger community of the hara.[1] He was a guardian of community honor who protected his community from the outsider. A gada' does not look at (*ma yabusish 'ala*) his neighbors with an envious glance of the evil eye (*'ain el-hasoud*), or at women with a desiring eye. Within the workshop, an exchange *bil-gada'ana* implies much more than the absence of money.

Samir was known as gada'. He was the master of a duko shop, a workshop that painted used cars. The cars he worked on had just undergone bodywork, often in the neighborhood.[2] Samir cultivated relationships with a range of his neighbors and associates. He was known as a man who always offered help to those around him when they were in need. While his workshop looked poor, and his means of production meager, he had other sources of strength in the community. Many of his former apprentices had workshops in el-Hirafiyeen, and he had many siblings and relatives in the community as well. He did not run after money, and scoffed at the NGO. He was popular (*mahboub*) and generous with his time and money.

While Samir was gada', he did not relate to all masters bil-gada'ana. He regularly shared customers with a number of body shops, but used different systems of exchange, some with commission and some without: "There are two or three body shops I deal with regularly. There are those I deal with for a commission and those I deal with without money."[3] When differences in social status and cultural practice precluded close relations bil-gada'ana, Samir's courtesy toward his neighbor drew on, and reproduced, the value of neighborly relations.[4] This was true of his interactions with a machinist who worked nearby. "I do business with ———— without money [bil-gada'ana].[5] Me and him, it's neighbors, not *biznis*. That's a colonel and an engineer. We give and take, there's general goodwill. But I feel the social difference between us. We send back and forth customers without money. He's sent me five cars to work on, cars of his brothers, his sister, relatives, and people he knows and sends to me to take care of."

Neighborliness was an important modality through which masters related to families outside the workshop system. Some residents of el-Hirafiyeen had bought apartments intended for the workshop owners and their families because the location was close to their jobs, or because they appreciated the clean air (see chapter 2). Even though these residents were completely outside the workshop world, often masters still developed "neighborly relations" with them. This meant not looking at them in a potentially harmful way, especially the women, and watching out for each other's feelings and interests. "There are something like twenty families of craftsmen in our square. Then there are families, people who have no relation to workshops in the city. We help each other out. If one of the wives is sick, even a wife of a clerk [i.e. someone with a lower level salaried job], we take her to the hospital. In my building, there's a couple, two teachers, who bought an apartment. They teach Arabic and mathematics in elementary school. We take care to respect the other's feelings and privacy."[6]

Samir was gada' in relation not only to his fellow masters but to women. Women who lived in his square told me that they could count on him to offer help whenever they were in need. A man like him would take a woman or child to the hospital in a time of sickness, or give a ride to a woman who had to rely on inconvenient and expensive public transport to get to work. He would not try to elicit sexual favors in return or treat a woman from the community with disrespect, even though he was known as a womanizer (*bita' sitat*). Sometimes women would call on him to help with small repairs in their homes that their husbands hadn't gotten around to.[7] He might reconnect electric lines that had been cut by the company when bills had gone unpaid, fix the plumbing, or repair broken cabinets.

How should we think about the actions and character of a man like Samir? We could start with the anthropological theory of "the gift," in which the concept of barter and the value of individuals replaces the focus in analyses of "the market" on the value of the items exchanged (Strathern 1992, 143–67). But workshops are businesses, and therefore belong to that very market that forms the classic antithesis to "the gift." Workshops produce things for sale on the market. Sometimes they produce commodities that are inputs in the production of large factories. Workshop masters are unabashed about their pursuit of economic interest. Unlike in the Kabyle society of Algeria, where Bourdieu developed his concept of cultural capital, workshops are not characterized by the unending production of cultural capital through the denial of economic interest (Bourdieu 1965).[8] Masters pursue their economic interests openly and with full social legitimacy. But goods and products and profits are not all that the master produces. Clearly, neither "the gift" nor "the market" is an adequate concept with which to think about what is at stake. So let us return to Samir himself.

When Samir spoke about sending people he knew to a colleague's workshop to have their cars worked on for a good price, his action was expressed, verbally, in the simple phrase *illi asharrafhum*. That could literally be translated as "those whom I treat hospitably." But in the context of the workshop, such a phrase means "people I'll do top work for at less than the market price for market quality work." Like the "favor" (*khidma*) or the service performed "for free" (bilgada'ana), a hospitable act toward your relations in one sphere of life, an act made possible by mobilizing your relations in another, is a central part of workshop life. When a master sends a customer to a colleague with instructions to treat him well, networks of relations in the master's "personal life" are meshed with his networks of relations in his "professional life." (The word "meshed" is a misnomer, since that word assumes a prior separation that comes from our conceptual categories and theoretical assumptions.) Similarly, sometimes interactions with a customer inside the workshop are meshed with the master's interactions with what here we can call "the state."

State officials are a common sight in the workshops of el-Hirafiyeen. Masters are happy to enter into exchange relations with state functionaries. They have much to gain from such relations. A general principle prevails in workshops that gaining a customer is more important than short-term economic profit. This principle takes on additional importance when the customer is connected to the state. There are many benefits in apparently unprofitable business relations with low-level functionaries who assess taxes and fines, and who work in the offices of local government where many decisions affecting masters' lives are taken. The master is happy to do a favor for such a customer. The master never knows when he will need to call on an official for a favor in return—perhaps to reduce a tax bill, or to settle a fine incurred for employing child labor or using dangerous chemicals in the workshop. Many workshop practices are socially legitimate but illegal. A master's investment in favors with state officials allows him to move more easily across that fluid boundary of legality without disruption to his production schedules.

It is easy to talk of all this as corruption, and to see el-Hirafiyeen as another example of corrupt Egyptians. From another perspective, we might view such behavior as an example of rent seeking. Egypt is often characterized as a "rent-seeking society."[9] Low-level officials too can be rent seeking, and look to make money not for their labor but because of their position in the state. The current development fashion that attempts to instill the rule of law as a strategy for economic development (Kennedy 2004, 149–68), in fact, treats corruption as a code word for rent seeking (165). Like corruption, rent seeking is a residual category in the moral schema undergirding neoclassical economics. Corruption and rent seeking indicate the pursuit of material interest in areas that lie outside the bounds of where the market is supposed to lie. They are both negative concepts that describe residuals of behavior falling outside these social science assumptions. Informality is another concept that we could invoke to describe the kinds of interactions I describe between workshop masters and tax officials. But that too is a negative category, although one that interests me most in this book as an object of ethnographic inquiry (see chapter 3). I find a different approach more useful. I suggest that by looking at an apparently exceptional case of "corrupt exchanges," we can learn something important about markets in general, and about interventions to impose a particular vision of the market. For every accusation of "corruption" reveals a particular normativity that the observer would like to impose. This commonplace provides powerful tools for anyone trying to understand the constraints and problematics that market economies ruled by the invisible hand tend to produce.[10]

The idea of the "favor" or *mugamala* is essential to understanding this dynamic of workshop life and the multiple registers of value production that it entails. As in all sectors of Egyptian popular culture, performing a mugamla for people is common and important. The importance of favors is expressed in the existence of a verb (*itgammil hadd*) to refer to the action of performing a favor for someone with the knowledge that the favor will be returned in different form at a later time.[11] Performing favors is not the only way the importance of long-term relationships in workshops is expressed. A master might take time off from workshop production to help resolve a conflict between two other masters, or between two of his neighbors. None of my informants thought it strange or a threat to the economic well-being of the workshop to take time off from production for such social obligations. None saw social relations as the inverse of the market. This reality underlines the importance of sociality in life in Cairo, and the importance of the concrete actions that produce that sociality. Sociality shapes the formation of individual subjectivities, the movement of bodies through space, and sensory perception of fullness and emptiness (see chapter 2). People spend a great deal of time intensifying this social fabric.

Exchanges between workshop masters and state employees can be one site where this general rule prevails. But such exchanges are usually looked at in isolation. As a dyadic set, they appear as discrete exchanges of money for services between two individuals. But matters change when three are involved, the minimal number for the existence of a network, and the resulting sociological transformations are not significantly altered if the number is higher (Simmel 1950, 145–69). It is wrongheaded to look at such exchanges in isolation for a number of reasons. First, as I showed in chapter 4, there is no such thing as a purely individual master, or a purely individual workshop. (This is in contrast to the ideal type of the microentrepreneur of the Social Fund project, who works, produces, and sells as an individual.) Each master stands at the apex of a web of relationships. Each master is a node in other masters' networks. Mastery implies the ability to stabilize, reproduce, and extend those networks over time. Workshop networks are the means through which the master produces substances valued within his community as well as economic goods. When masters' networks extend into state institutions, logics of value generation inherent to workshop life are not suspended just because a node of the network is located in the state.

Value, Workshops, and Neoliberalism

What do I mean by value? As noted in chapter 1, there are a number of ways to pursue a notion of value. We might employ Marx's theory of value to see whether workshops are productive of surplus value. We could ask whether unpaid labor in the workshop and home depresses the value of labor power and thus increases the surplus value of capitalist firms. It might also be interesting to ask which workshops produce surplus value and which do not. We could also look at how workshop products fit into the input-output schema of large Egyptian enterprises. Such questions, important as they might be, are not my concern.[12] True enough, workshops produce commodities that have economic value. Some are sold directly to consumers, and others become inputs in the production of capitalist firms. But workshops also produce value that is not inherently economic and which in itself has nothing to do with the production of surplus value or other definitions of economic value. From an anthropological perspective, exchanges among workshop masters "have to be intentional, purposive; without such personal action there would be no relationships. And without knowing how such acts are imaginatively appropriated, economic analysis cannot begin. For all kinds of values can become present" (Strathern 1998, 219).

To pursue this level of analysis, I draw on the work of Nancy Munn to discuss how the popular classes of Egypt in general, and workshop masters in particular, seek "to create the value [they] regard as essential to [their] community viability" (Munn 1986, 3). I look at that value creation in tandem with other, antithetical transformations that undermine this value in the community's perception and block it from being realized (3). I call this value produced in workshop exchanges "relational value," since it expresses the positive value attached to the creation, reproduction, and extension of relationships in workshop life. I have already indicated, through life histories and the ethnography of workshop practice, how masters seek to intensify the production of this value through ongoing exchanges in a spatio-temporal template of their neighborhood, of Cairo, and of Egypt and the region. I have argued that the production of value in workshops is naturalized in metaphors of kinship and a cosmology of the workshop order with deep historical roots. I have also said that the production of value must be analyzed in tandem with negative value as embodied in the notion of the evil eye. In what follows I will substantiate all these claims based on my ethnographic research into workshop life in el-Hirafiyeen and other neighborhoods of Cairo.

The relational value produced in the workshops is based in the cultural logics of Egyptian *baladi*, or popular urban culture. As has been noted by many scholars, relationships make possible the negotiation of daily life in Cairo. A great deal of time and effort is expended in the creation, reproduction, and extension of relationships. The mobilizing of relationships from what social theory has tended to identify as one sphere of life (kinship relationships, for example) into another sphere of life (work relations, for example) is a mode of survival among the popular classes of Cairo in particular.[13] Movement is fluid and constant among nodes of three-dimensional relationships; it does not merely shuttle between dyadic pairs. This characteristic of life in Cairo baladi culture takes on particular dynamics inside the workshop. In their workshop production, masters constantly shift among modalities of value production and transfer the forms of wealth and power that they produce in one domain to another.[14] As I indicated in chapter 4, an indispensable component of mastery is the capacity to modulate from one mode of value production to another.

These other modalities of value produced in workshop networks are central to the workshop master's market success. But that is not all. This capacity to transmute value from one sphere to another, and to transfer the forms of wealth and power that masters produced in one domain to another, is a model for the new wave of market expansion. The master is the beneficiary of his ability to modulate from one mode of value production to another. But in the new context of market expansion based on the incorporation of cultural practices of the poor, this ability provides a model for how the value produced in workshop networks can be transformed into a source of economic value for capital.

Here I must note that this entire field of ethnographic reality is awash with anthropological stereotypes and other pitfalls. The very word "relationships" brings to mind a range of tropes in social theory that are easily mobilized in such an analytic context. For example, whenever we note the importance of relationships in the workshop communities of Cairo, it is easy to fall into a romantic view inherited from Polanyi (and before him Mauss and Durkheim) that while "we" have lost the importance of relationships implied in the concept of an "embedded" economy, "they" whom we study in anthropology do have relationships, economies embedded in society, and thus happiness. It is also easy to start looking for the "real relationships" that lie beneath the surface of things visible in workshop production, as some might use Marx to do. Finally, one could start looking for relationships among individuals in "meaningful" as opposed to accidental relations, as some might draw on Weber to do.[15]

I can also easily fall into some traps particular to Middle Eastern studies. When talking about relationships, I may sound as if I am simply reproducing the work of scholars who have previously pointed out the centrality of relationships in social life in Egypt (such as Early 1993; Singerman 1995; Wikan 1996).[16] Relationships are such a central part of social life in Egypt that I might just seem, on the other hand, to be stating the obvious. For example, Egyptians talk about the need for *wasta*, or connections, to people in positions of power to get anything done. In discussing relational value I could thus seem to be according to a colloquial term of Egyptian Arabic the status of a theoretical concept (which would fall into another trap, the subject of old debates in anthropology about the relationship between emic and etic terms, and between native and theoretical concepts). I think I am doing something different, and would like to clarify for a moment why that is so.

In this book, I place the well-known importance of relationships in Egypt within a broader theoretical framework. I draw on the notion that "entities take their form and acquire their attributes as a result of their relations with other entities" (Law 1999, 3). My approach is one of "relational materiality" (4). Workshop relationships, like workshop markets, are not fixed in abstract space and time. Rather they are situationally produced and performed. Likewise, relationships cannot be analyzed on a one-to-one level, as they randomly occur between two individuals. Workshop masters (and others in Egyptian popular culture) need to be viewed as the nodes of complex networks that are produced over time. Relationships are not a store of value, let alone a store of capital, that masters can cash in. Masters constantly shift their attention among nodes in networks of customers, colleagues, and families in an ongoing and fluid process.

My approach thus moves away from a functionalist approach to relationships as a resource "used" by an individual. Relationships are not a thing that exists outside a previously existing individual and subjectivity.[17] Rather, the centrality of relationships—or relationality—is a habitus shared by the popular Egyptian classes in general, and workshop masters in particular. Relationality is a critical dynamic within a generalized system of value production in Egyptian popular culture that needs to be analyzed simultaneously on material and symbolic planes. An anthropological approach to value makes that dual emphasis possible.

This standpoint of the anthropology of value also allows me to ask the important question about the amazing resources and resourcefulness of the Egyptian popular classes, which have been well noted by scholars of Egypt. What happens to those resources? Who benefits from them? My approach opens up the possibility that the resources produced through relationality can be captured by others. In the era of neoliberalism, when the individual and community are increasingly urged to rely on themselves rather than the state, there is a curious convergence between this capacity of the Egyptian popular classes and the aims of neoliberal rule. I am not the first to notice that convergence. It has been cultivated in many policies and programs to actively incorporate the social networks and cultural practices of the poor into the market. The question of who captures the positive relational value produced among workshop masters in particular, and Egyptian popular classes in general, is a political issue with broad implications.

The anthropology of value has seemed to many to be an obscure field based on fieldwork in areas of little strategic importance. Some of the most important theorizing about value has been carried out in ethnographic settings that seem quite remote from dominant global power relations. Cairo, on the other hand, is anything but marginal. Whatever goes on in Cairo is of global strategic importance. Egypt is the second-largest recipient of foreign aid from the United States, after Israel. It is at the center of the Arab world. What happens in Egypt has reverberations throughout the region, and thus throughout the world. Moreover, Egypt has been repeatedly cited by the World Bank and the IMF as a hallmark of economic reform. Even the "local" setting where I carried out most of my research, el-Hirafiyeen, was deeply enmeshed in global power relations in the most direct sense. Key players in the global and national politics of Egypt were actors in my field site. Microenterprises like those established in el-Hirafiyeen (understood as any place where fewer than ten are employed) have been hailed by the World Bank and writers such as Hernando de Soto (1989, 2000) as the most important component of the private economy. Workshops are subsumed in this definition of microenterprise as small places of employment. As such, they are implicated in the global mobilizations of power under way in the region, which the United States has gone to war to reshape in the name of the free market.

In this context, it is imperative to link any discussion of value production in workshops in Cairo to a broader analysis of changing forms of power on a global scale. The value produced in workshop networks exists in a broader field of power of which the state, IOs, and NGOs are a part, and has been implicated in global regimes of power ever since the "informal economy" began to assume such importance in the thinking and planning of IOs. I see a key transformative moment in the development and spread of the concept of "social capital" in economic theory and development studies.[18] Following the insights of science studies and Michel Callon's work on markets, I suggest that this concept needs to be analyzed in tandem with the social technologies and practices to which it is linked. Within the framework of "social capital," the cultural practices of people once condemned as backwards and in need of development became an important terrain for the accumulation of capital and a strategic resource through which new forms of governance could be reproduced at little cost to the downsized, neoliberal state. When the exchange practices of the poor and disenfranchised of Egypt and elsewhere became the focus of immense attention on the part of IOs around the globe that are entrusted with maintaining necessary conditions of global stability for the functioning of politico-economic order, those practices became implicated in much larger processes. If I am right, then the issues that I am discussing here should be of concern to scholars other than those few who work on under-researched topics like the evil eye or the economic anthropology of the Middle East.

Spheres of Interest

Masters in el-Hirafiyeen did not talk directly about value. But they did talk about interest. Interest, to them, was something negative. By interest I do not mean *ribh*, or interest earned on money without the expenditure of labor, which is forbidden in Islam.[19] Rather, I am referring to *maslaha*, or interest as in "vested interest." I heard this term most often when masters were complaining that other masters were pursuing their personal interests by means of the NGO. Members of the steering committee of the NGO, these masters said, were taking part in politics only because they had an interest to pursue ('*andu maslaha*). Here maslaha meant the pursuit of short-term individual interests in the name of the public good. The board members took part in NGO life, their neighbors complained, only to pursue their own individual interests. Those interests, moreover, and their ambitions, lay beyond the scale of what could be pursued within the schema of ongoing life in el-Hirafiyeen (I pursue this further in chapter 6).

The word *maslaha* can be translated in many ways. The first sense in

Badawi and Hinds is "the common good" (Badawi and Hinds 1986, 508). Another translation is "welfare," as in welfare economics. The premise that individual interests and the common good can be in harmony, and that the balance between the two must be mediated, is important in the region, and was historically codified in law. For example, in Ottoman Egypt, the historian Nelly Hanna writes, one of the bases on which a judge could rule on a case was maslaha, which she defines as either private or public welfare. In one example that she cites, inhabitants of a residential quarter were allowed by a judge to build a gate to protect their quarter, although the street was public, because doing so was a question of maslaha. Likewise, pious foundations (*waqf—awqaf*), which by definition held property that could not be privatized or alienated, were sometimes allowed to sell properties on the ground that a sale could be in the interests of the foundation as a whole, such as for the repair of a building (Hanna 1995, 52).

The idea that the long-term common good can, and must, be reconciled with individual interests is not unique to the Middle East. According to Parry and Bloch, many societies are characterized by concern about maintaining the balance between a sphere of short-term exchanges, in which the pursuit of individual gain is legitimate, and "a cycle of long-term exchanges concerned with the reproduction of the social and cosmic order" (Parry and Bloch 1989, 2). The pursuit of individual interest must be in equilibrium with other kinds of needs. Such a notion is part of the history of political thought and moral philosophy in the West as well. Even in the history of western thought, the maximizing agent of neoclassical economics does not always reign supreme and run free. The individual agent pursuing his interests is neither as universal nor as timeless a concept as folk notions of "the market" would imply. In the tradition of welfare economics, for example, the common good is reconciled with individual interest.[20]

Pursuing one's interest in the economic sphere is legitimate and assumed to be the prime interest of any craftsman. Workshop life is not a context where the economic is persistently denied. But to be legitimate, the pursuit of economic interests must lie within certain bounds. A master has to make his workshop go, since that is the source of his and his family's survival and well-being. This is a legitimate form of interest. But such a legitimate pursuit of interests is quite different from the competition pursued by the agent of neoclassical economics. The word commonly used in Egyptian Arabic for such competition (*munafsa*) is linked to the negative values of envy and the evil eye. According to *A Dictionary of Egyptian Arabic*, the verb meaning to compete with someone (*naafis*) has the same root as the verb "to be struck by the evil eye" (*itnafas*) (Badawi and Hinds 1986).[21] If the maximization of individual utility without regard for others or long-term relationships marks the agent of neoclassical economics, then that agent is at one with the evil eye.

But the agent of neoclassical economics is not the only actor in workshop markets. Not all action is guided by the agent of the evil eye. In general, the master's market life is guided by the presence of a different kind of eye, that which Adam Smith called the "invisible spectator." In Smith's moral philosophy, the invisible spectator insures that the individual agent in commercial society acts with an eye to what others might think. The individual internalizes the multiple eyes of others and their moral judgments on his behavior in market and non-market spheres. Workshop masters spoke often about the existence of such an invisible spectator guiding their ethnical conduct in the market. This invisible spectator was the conscience (*dameer*), the internalized knowledge of what is right. This notion is expressed in the phrase commonly heard in Cairo to discuss issues of ethical conduct when there is no one standing over to watch: "it's between you and your conscience" (*da beinak wa bein damirak*).[22] This conscience is not an externalized notion of God who watches and judges from on high. Nor is it an externalization of internal psychological processes. Rather, this conscience embodies the eyes of one's neighbors and community and is part of the formation of the self. He who ignores the internalized eye of the conscience, and pursues short-term individual interest without constraint, invites the attack of another eye, the evil eye. An attack of the evil eye can wipe out all the gains made by a master over a lifetime of work. The confluence of the evil eye and interest makes sense only when we better understand the nature of workshop production.

Networks and Names

The workshop, as I have shown, does not exist in isolation. The very phrase "individual workshop" is an anomaly. While they appear to be individual and separate, in fact workshops are not. Each apparently individual workshop is but one node of a complex system of social relationships. That web of workshops can be usefully discussed as a network.[23] Networks are not static things fixed in space or time. They exist only in practice and, as such, are culturally distinct. This does not mean, however, that workshop networks have no physical aspect. All the networks that I am discussing here, for example, could be traced out in el-Hirafiyeen by following the physical movement of certain key media: the movement in space of boy "apprentices" among workshops, homes, and service shops; the exchange of small items that although worthless to one had value as an input of production to another; the movement of customers and workers between workshops, with the body carrying and conveying the substance of exchange; and patterns of movement of money among workshops.

Along with the movement of people, money, and things, furthermore, goes the movement of information, the exchange of sociability, and the creation of place infused with meaning for those living in it. These exchanges among the workshops, which are the "stuff" of workshop networks, are not only material in their nature. They are simultaneously a symbolic, conceptual world, the articulation of which can be heard and seen in the course of daily life through the mobilization of symbols and phrases of popular and official Islam, and in language spoken and understood within the bounds of a social world defined by the range of those who understand.

Workshop masters carry out regular exchanges with a network of customers. This network is "the market" of a workshop master. It is neither a group of random individual relations nor a formal institution. The master speaks of this market in terms that make it seem as if the market is semi-attached to his person. This sense of the market is captured in a phrase used by some of my informants to describe a successful newcomer: "he brought his market with him." My informants in this case went on to describe what made up the market that the newcomer had brought with him. They spoke about his kin. By kin, they did not mean that the newcomer's relatives bought each good that he produced, but rather that they provided channels for him to sell to others. This market in turn was a form of kinship; a sense of physical relation, of shared physical substance between the newcomer and his market, was implied. I suggest that this sense of a shared substance, of a physical continuity, between the master and his market is more general than this one example

cited by my informants. The market of the master is always, in one sense
or another, semi-attached to his person, and thus is a form of kin.

If you don't have kin, you have to then have a name. Like kin, the
name is attached to one's person. "To make it in the city, especially with a
big ambitious project, you have to have a name and a customer base,"
explained one young man. Name is also a synonym for reputation.[24] The
name or reputation of a workshop, or the renown that the craftsman has
built up over the years, is a condensation of his relations and networks.
In el-Hirafiyeen, I suggest, positive and negative value production are
systematically expressed in terms of a craftsman's social standing, personal qualities, and name. The master's name is an abstraction of the
history of his interactions with his neighbors, customers, and colleagues.
The name reveals in the present a history of the craftsman in his workshop lineage. It is historically constructed over a series of lifetimes.

The name was central to masters' recounting of their work history.
Acquiring a "name" was the decisive marker of their ability to open a
workshop. Craftsmen waited to open a workshop until they had a large
enough network of customers, among whom their name circulated out
to even a wider network. Craftsmen would describe as critical the moment when customers were "asking for them by name" within the workshop of the master they worked for. The journeyman would then attempt to open a workshop within the same geographic vicinity as his
former master's workshop. Telling of his experience in the last workshop
he had worked for as a waged worker before opening a shop "on the
street," one mechanic said: "I made a big name for myself in that garage.
Customers would come and ask for me."

A master will go to great lengths to preserve his name. When work
goes wrong, "it's the usta who pays the price," losing the customer and
hurting his reputation. And likewise, until the journeyman begins to
establish his own independent reputation, good work done by anyone in
the workshop accrues to the master, to his name, as the reputation of the
workshop is identified with him personally. Even if a workshop has
become successful, and its master relatively rich, preserving the name
remains paramount, and the need to do so can shape decisions about
how to handle money.[25] This overriding consideration can lead to seemingly irrational investment decisions if we view them in terms of short-
term gain alone and do not understand the value represented in the
name. For example, when excess cash accrues, the master may put a

certain amount in reserve, not necessarily to invest it in expansion or to accumulate interest on the money as capital, but as a reserve fund to protect his name if the market turns against him. "I manage my accounts to keep things going O.K., so I can cover eight months of expenses, since here in the city things go well for three months and then are hit bad for another month. I have some obligations where the payments are postponed, where I don't have to pay right away. I have to be able to cover them. My name is at stake. I don't want there to ever be a moment when I can't pay and ruin my name."

When workshops were moved to el-Hirafiyeen, many of the masters lost their markets. They spoke of this often as a loss of their name. The loss of their market was more than a material loss. It was a loss of self as well. Masters had spent their entire working lives building up their name. With the move, that name was rendered worthless. And as the proverb says, having a name is more important than wealth (*el-seet walla el-ghena*). "Money comes and goes," but building renown is a lifetime task. In this case, as in so many others, the state produced only negative value for the workshop masters. Its exercise of institutional power in the move to el-Hirafiyeen was a direct attack on the masters' markets, on their names, and thus on their selves. But not all losses are negative for a workshop master.

The Value of Loss in Workshop Interactions

Loss is a constant part of workshop life.[26] Masters constantly lose customers, work, and workers. They often lose business on purpose. In other words, the modeling of workshop markets must account for loss as a positive outcome. How can a master create a market by sending away business? To answer that question one needs to shift the market model away from short-term transactions of profit and loss to longer-term logics of value creation particular to workshop life.

Masters' actions are certainly oriented toward the production and sale of goods and services to individuals and firms. Their actions are also oriented toward intensifying the depth of the social world in which they live. Masters modulate these two logics of production quite instinctually: that modulation constitutes part of their mastery. What might be a "loss" from one point of view (of work, of money, or of a worker) is sometimes a "gain" for the master from another. Sending away financial gain and directing workers and customers out to other workshops can be productive of relational value.

Masters talk about this modulation of different value systems in their daily life. A master might send out work *bil-'umula*, by taking money payment or commission; as a good neighbor (*'ilaqat gira*), without money (*bil-gad'ana*); or with a keen eye on short-term gain (*bil-biznis*). These categories of exchange are productive of different degrees and kinds of value. They also exist in different time scales. Sending out work bil-'umula elicits a money payment but produces little relational value. Like relations bil-biznis, it is short term and not oriented toward the reproduction of relationships into the future. Sending out work bil-gad'ana elicits no immediate gain but is highly productive of relational value. Such forms of exchange are oriented toward the future.

Let me explain.

Workshop markets are not stable. Good periods can be followed by bad in rapid succession. In good periods the market appears, as I have said, as an extension of the self. It is a network that is semi-attached to the actor. But masters also spoke of the market as a distant, unknowable, and hostile force. It could have supernatural powers. When the market turned against them, it was a hostile force outside their control, like the weather.[27] The market could turn from good to bad quite rapidly. "Here in el-Hirafiyeen, you can be so busy for four months that you don't have the time to say good morning to your neighbor, and then sit right after that for thirteen months with no work at all."[28]

In an unstable market situation, masters were reluctant to take on new workers when they were busy. Nor could they hire a worker away from another workshop without the master's permission.[29] One option was to temporarily hire an outsider, but that arrangement took time and energy. Workshop labor relations rely on patriarchal relations of power as much as direct labor exploitation: when a worker is from "outside" the workshop (*min barra*), it is difficult for the master to exercise his power over the worker. Another and better option is thus to take "on loan" a worker from another workshop, but still inside the workshop system. Finally, if such an option is not available and the master has no other way to increase his work capacity temporarily, he will send work (or a customer, to say the same thing) to another workshop of the same type with which he has ongoing exchange relations, in the knowledge that this "favor" will be returned in the future, perhaps when work is slow and he is really in need.

When a master sends a customer to another workshop, the customer should say who sent him so that each side can keep track of the balance of exchanges. If the customer doesn't offer the information, the master might ask. One blacksmith used those words to explain how things work in relations between workshops: "If I send a customer to someone else, he has to tell the other workshop owner who sent him, that —— sent me to you, so we can all keep track, and the master remember the favor [*mugamla*]."[30] The master gains, in other words, when he sends work away from his workshop.

Sending work away from the workshop can also produce immediate financial gain. "There's a system of commissions ['umula]. No one gets angry about it," explained one master. If a master receiving this work has to pay a commission, he then tries to get this money back from the customer: "If someone who is not a blacksmith brings me work for a few hundred LE and asked for 40 LE commission, I'll take the 40 LE out of the customer [*min el-zubun*]."[31] Exchanges with commissions imply the highest degree of social distance in the workshop world. They are the closest to a classic market exchange devoid of social ties or obligations. However, exchanges based on commissions, or the payment of money to get access to a customer, are clear and clean and indicate no bad relation between two masters.

In contrast, an exchange bil-biznis does imply an attempt to get whatever you can from an exchange partner. Biznis involves the extraction of a bit more money from a customer or competitor with a sort of clever trickery (*hiyla*) that has a hallowed place in Egyptian and Arab popular culture as a whole.[32] After Sadat the use of such trickery and clever moves entered the sphere of economy and exchange relations with a vengeance. And the qualities that the popular classes and workshop masters saw as characterizing the new world of "business" after Sadat—that is, cheating and a fast deal on the basis of no substance—led the speakers of this language to turn the table on those who benefited from the new system, in both action and language: business became biznis, and the cheater, where possible at least, was himself cheated.

None of my informants reported having biznis relations with anyone in their own trade. Nor would they even take commissions ('umula) from masters in the same trade. This practice of not taking commissions from a master in the same craft harkens back to practices referred to in the literature about the "craft guilds" in the Ottoman era.[33] Traces of the historical roots of the workshop system remain in these practices, which enact the substance of what made "sons of the craft" (*abna el-hirfa*) like kin. The impossibility of taking a commission from a master practicing the same craft is a clear example of this. In the words of one blacksmith: "If I have extra work, I might send something to another blacksmith, and likewise he might send work to me. If another blacksmith sends me work he won't ask for money [*'umula*] in return, but we'll both know and keep track. It's impossible that he would ask money in return for sending me work—because he's a blacksmith [*hadad*], because these are ongoing back and forth exchanges [*di khadamat mutabadla*]."

But not paying money in the present does not imply that there is no calculation. Masters "keep track" of these exchanges. "If another blacksmith sends me work . . . then I have to return the favor [*mugamla*]. He remembers that he sent me something and I remember. I might then give him a very low price [*akrimu*] the next time I do some work for him, or send him some work in return."

The only time we saw masters taking commissions from other masters in the same craft was when wealthy masters' automatic paint ovens (*furn—afraan*) were used by those who did not have such high technology to finish off a job for a demanding customer paying a higher price for an expensive, factory-like effect. In these cases, of which there were a few in el-Hirafiyeen (which had the highest concentration of these machines in Egypt, according to my informants), a paint job man would prep a customer's car himself, and then rent the high-tech paint "oven" to finish off the job.[34] But apart from this exceptional case, craftsmen within the same craft shared the use of each other's machines.

Lathe or machinist shops in el-Hirafiyeen were characterized by a particularly high level of cooperation and interdependence. The expensive machinery of one shop was regularly used by the workers of another. Likewise, machinists often used the machines of another workshop to carry out specific aspects of their work. One master was known for having one of the most advanced milling machines (*faraza*) in Egypt; another, for having an especially large lathe that held large pieces of metal. These specialized pieces of equipment attracted customers from both inside and outside el-Hirafiyeen. Machinists relied on their reputation with each other as much as they relied on their reputation with customers. Each machinist had a reputation, and mobilized his particular form of cultural capital to construct his market. The colonel-engineer was like "a computer" because of his ability to diagnose problems and fix them with exactitude. He attracted a customer base in large firms, since the engineers in those companies felt more comfortable dealing with someone educated like them, with an engineering degree, rather than with illiterate masters of a different social class. Another lathe operator was known for being a little expensive, but reliable and consistent.

Machinists were very knowledgeable about the services offered by fellow machinists, not only in el-Hirafiyeen but throughout Cairo. They never purchased a lathe that could be found somewhere else. Rather, masters sent work back and forth. From a purely technical perspective, the workshops collectively could be viewed as one large, integrated workshop, or as a factory.[35] Communication among these workshops was high, with information passed along quickly about who was charging what, and who needed what kind of workers—both inside and outside of town.[36] These masters sent customers back and forth to each other. And prices remained within an accepted band, since the masters had learned, a few of them explained, that competition in the market over the price of their services was bad for all.

The Agency of Workshop Life

Market logic explains many of the exchanges with commissions, and the integration of complementary workshops to form a de facto "center" or integrated, one-stop car repair shop. But this is not the logic of an individual market agent, the maximizing agent of neoclassical economics. The master is not engaged in a monolithic quest to allocate scarce resources so as to optimize his monetary returns. As masters often said, they would often close down the workshop to perform a social obligation in the community, although that might lead to financial loss. They would also deliberately court economic loss to extend relationships, for example. Nor can the master be characterized as a strategizing agent of game theory who takes into account the anticipated actions of others (Breslau 2003).

Anthropological theory of the gift at first seems more useful here than economic theory to describe the agency of craftsmen in el-Hirafiyeen. Their exchange relations were deeply shaped by complex dynamics of giving. Anthropology no longer assumes that gift exchange is a terrain where reciprocity and human kindness reign, in contrast to the cruel individualism of the market. But theory of the gift is also inadequate for understanding workshop agency. After all, we are talking about men whose lives were organized around profit-making economic enterprises. It is important to realize that those profit-making enterprises were also the locus of gift exchange. Gift exchange did not exist in a boxed-off terrain outside the market; it was right inside. (Here I could point out that the very search for the boundary where the market ends and the gift begins is a misplaced exercise.) Rather than search for either the atomized individual market agent, typical of neoclassical economics, or an agent submerged in society, as is typical of classical theory of the gift, we would do better to take seriously the ease with which masters modulated among different registers of agency. A more useful way to think about agency in the workshop, I suggest, is in terms of actor-network theory.

Both in relation to his market and in relation to his colleagues, the master can be seen as an actor-network (Law and Hassard 1999), since the master and the market designate "two faces of the same phenomenon, like waves and particles" (Latour 1999, 19). The notion of the actor-network emphasizes the erasure of traditional social science divisions between the individual on the one hand and the group on the other. With this erasure of the duality between individual and social, master and market, it is easier to see how the workshop habitus of sociality allows masters to negotiate the movement between self and market in a range of modalities. Within this range, loss is not always what it appears. Masters draw on loss as much as gain when they create markets. Loss, as in the sending of work away from the workshop, can be highly productive. When a master loses profit from a job, he may produce financial gain in the 'umula and improved business relations with his neighbors. He may also produce relational value in an exchange bil-gad'ana. Thus we can see why it is such a serious assault on a master's authority if a journeyman sends away a customer. (One such incident during my fieldwork led to the firing of a journeyman.) Such an act not only denies the master a chance to make money and gain a customer. It also denies him the value of loss and the benefits of generosity.

The Evil Eye and Neoclassical Economics

Evil eye beliefs abound among craftsmen in Cairo. Accusations of the evil eye are not made directly, but complaints about it are common.[37] In el-Hirafiyeen unpopular craftsmen were the most likely to complain of the evil eye. Those whose actions were oriented toward producing relational value, and whose personalities were shaped through the act of accumulating this positive value creation with the markers of being "popular" (mahboub) and generous (gada'), were less likely to be hit by the evil eye or to accuse others of the evil eye. Masters who were less well liked, and who lived their lives in el-Hirafiyeen as isolated individuals, more along the lines of the microentrepreneurs, were more concerned about attacks of the evil eye from their neighbors.

The evil eye has received much less attention in anthropological theory than witchcraft has (Ghosh 1983; Herzfeld 1981; Maloney 1976; Siebers 1983). Studies on Egypt are rarer still. Ghosh's article (1983) and his novel *In an Antique Land* (1992) remain the best examples in English.[38] Dundes (1981) notes an abundance of research on the topic of the evil eye, but rarely by anthropologists. This curious neglect may be attributable to the limited range of interests that has characterized anthropological research and theorizing on the Middle East (Abu-Lughod 1989), where evil eye beliefs are common, and to the sharp division of labor between those who study Europe and those who study the Arab world. Evil eye beliefs unite those two regions in the geocultural world that once stretched across the Mediterranean. Religion and economy, moreover, have tended to be strictly separated in studies of the Middle East (Elyachar 2005). But study of the evil eye demands attention to both. In this book I bring together those two spheres by looking at the evil eye in terms of negative and positive value production.

Positive value production among workshop masters appears as the intensification of personality attributes such as generosity and popularity.[39] The masters known as gada' kept their distance from activities marked by the pursuit of individual interest in illegitimate spheres, activities that were therefore imbued with negative value.[40]All the masters pursued their economic interests, as I have said: one could be gada' and do well on the market as well. It was the unrestrained pursuit of economic gain, or the pursuit of individual interest in the name of the community, that was most productive of negative value. In the terms of

Parry and Bloch (1989), transgression of the fluid bounds between short-term and long-term cycles of interest, and between individual and community needs, was marked by the presence of the evil eye. When there was an overproduction of individual interest at the expense of relational value, a crisis could appear as an attack of the evil eye.

Here it is useful to remember that in the cosmology of workshop life, income from the workshop comes ultimately from God. It is the master's responsibility to run his workshop well and to provide for the well-being of his family and dependents. But it is not for man to strive, at least openly, to endlessly increase his income and wealth. Income flowing from the workshop is a blessing from God that moves to people *through* other people and things, but not because of their individual actions. A good man strives not for endless riches but to have the needs of himself and his family "covered" (*mastour*), or taken care of. To be mastour is to be protected from evil by God, and to be covered so that one cannot be seen by the evil eye. It also means to have one's human needs taken care of. Need here is relatively stable. Needs are not endlessly elastic, as is typical of consumer society. Needs can be satisfied, as in the classic response (even in the most dire of circumstances) to an inquiry into well-being: "Thank God, we are covered, our needs are satisfied" (*ilham-dulilah, ihna mastoureen*). The evil eye, however, cannot be satisfied. It is endlessly desirous, and knows no bounds. It does not represent a form of desire in which distance can be overcome to produce value (Simmel 1990, 69). He whose needs cannot be satisfied, and who pursues individual gain at the expense of relations and sociality, is more vulnerable to attacks of the evil eye.

The move into el-Hirafiyeen intensified problems with the evil eye. Masters felt exposed in their new location. Others in the same craft could peer into their workshops and see how they were doing. In the old neighborhoods workshops were situated on busy streets, next to complementary rather than competing workshops. In el-Hirafiyeen, however, with open squares devoid of the constant activity that marks popular neighborhoods, empty space abounded. Such empty spaces lacking in sociality are not a positive value in Cairene life (recall the discussion of empty and full space in chapter 2). Masters stood exposed to the eyes of envious neighbors in el-Hirafiyeen, particularly in the early days of the neighborhood. An envious neighbor, either next door or across the shared public square, could cast an envious glance whenever a customer appeared.

Problems with the evil eye also intensified because competition in the sense of *munafasa*—the pursuit of individual interest without regard for neighbor or colleague—was liberated from its bounds. The link between competition and the evil eye became apparent. With the master's name rendered worthless, each master had to scramble to find new customers in competition with his neighbors and colleagues. Some masters attempted to move toward a shorter-term schema of value by means of investment schemes in land or politics (which meant here pursuing individual interest through the NGO). Those who managed that move badly became vulnerable to attacks of the evil eye.

Likewise, when an individual master made rapid economic gains while the community did not, his overinvestment in short-term gain could become a bubble phenomenon. Then an attack of the evil eye would rectify the overproduction of individual short-term gain and restore the homeostasis between cycles of short- and long-term exchange. When transitions from one schema of value to another were badly managed, a complete collapse of the bubble could ensue. This could happen if a scandal (*fadiha*) erupted that rendered one's name worthless on the market and in the community. Such an erasure of positive relational value could also affect an individual master's "market." That is what happened, for example, when one workshop master who joined the governing board of an NGO began assiduously using his new position to attempt an expansion of his workshop. He became arrogant and disdainful of his neighbors, and harassed a woman from the neighborhood who declined his advances. Another master on the governing board was similarly attempting to use the NGO to expand his workshop production, but he was careful to retain his reputation as a man who respected "the craftsman's way." The first became the victim of a scandal and had to leave his position on the NGO, while the second did not.

Masters also blamed the influx of new money and buyers-in for problems with the evil eye in el-Hirafiyeen. One master put it like this: "In Heliopolis I was well known. All the workshops, each had its own customers. If someone walked down the street, you'd know whose customer he was. Not like in Hirafiyeen where everyone is watching you and trying to catch a customer. There, everyone had his own customer. Here, it's complete chaos [*moulid*].[41] In the old place, only those who learned the craft from the bottom up became a master. Here in Hirafiyeen, any old guy with money has opened up a workshop. Everybody's a master [*usta*]."

Everyone agreed that a neighbor should not "bear a grudge" or have malice (*hiqd*) toward another neighbor. But, some of the masters said, bad will and fear take over when the master's market takes a hit and loses its character as a set of long-standing relationships. In Heliopolis, everyone "had enough," was "satisfied" (*shab'an*); they didn't need to seek their survival on the backs of their neighbors. But when things got tough, and without strong social links and a solid community to sustain them, people became nasty, it was said, trying to steal customers, and looking enviously at those who were doing well. Neighborliness receded; envy and bad will expressed through the evil eye became prominent: "60 percent of the craftsmen sold their apartments, 20 percent made them warehouses, and 20 percent live here. But [even if you don't live here] you need to feel that this is your place, the place you work in, the place you spend a lot of time. You should be gallant, one of the people [*shahm, gada', ibn balad*] with your neighbor. Things should be like that, but unfortunately they're not. Here, if I have work and my neighbor doesn't, he'll hold a grudge against me." When each has enough, then people do not look at one another, do not envy and resent what the other has. "Hunger teaches you real life"; it brings out bad behavior you won't see when everyone has enough. "I only started learning about the realities of life and seeing the world straight after getting here. Here, hunger started teaching people about real life. I've been in war, but there people stuck together. And in the days of Heliopolis, things were easy. People only start looking at you with envy and bad will when they're in need. People started going bad with hard times."[42]

Protection from the Evil Eye

Ibrahim had been hit by the evil eye soon after the move to el-Hirafiyeen. In a situation where others were suffering, his work had taken off. He enjoyed his success and did not try to hide it. "At first [after the move], there wasn't much work in the city. I was hit with the evil eye, because I was still a young guy [and doing so well]. I got into an accident with the car of a customer while he was with me in the car. A millionaire in a '91 Mercedes. . . . He fixed the car and it cost 40,000 LE. I wanted to pay for the repairs but he said never mind, the insurance will pay for it. I repaired the other car, and that cost 6,000 LE. People began to say, 'Look at how Ibrahim is doing, he does better than anyone else in the city.' Anybody who didn't have work, he came to look at me to see how many cars I had to work on. But then, I made good relations with people. Now, anyone who comes by and needs something, I give it to him." In Ibrahim's telling of this story, the attack of the evil eye is a moral lesson. The attack teaches Ibrahim that he must change. He realizes that he cannot simply work on increasing his number of customers or his income. Ibrahim worked hard to rid himself of his previous bad reputation. He became publicly religious. He was soon asked to manage the finances of the main mosque, the one built by the state. Another workshop owner in charge of finances before him had been stealing money from the mosque contributions box, and someone new was needed to take over. Soon after, Ibrahim was approached by the head of the craftsmen's NGO and asked to join their organization. His reputation changed. As his actions became oriented toward the production of positive value, he became known as a good man. He was no longer seen as young and overly greedy, but rather as shab'an, and thus trustworthy. His involvement with the mosque gave him cover from the evil eye, despite his rapid economic success. Leaders of the NGO then tried to mobilize the cover he had gained from the sanctity of Islam and his good works to provide cover for themselves. (In this they were only partially successful.) For Ibrahim as an individual, giving provided protection from another attack of the evil eye: "I was in charge of the finances of the main mosque . . . I made a room in which to keep things of the mosque, and a special room for the women to pray in. I painted the mosque and made the garden. I did all this in honor of the memory of my father. Money came from contributions that people leave in the mosque. From there, people started telling me to take over responsibility for the finances of the NGO and to do like what I did for the mosque. So I took over the treasury and started getting the NGO back into shape."

At the time of our fieldwork Ibrahim was the only master in the steering committee of the NGO who was called a good man by others. Joining the NGO did not cost him the goodwill he had gained through his sustained acts of giving to those in need, both through the mosque and outside it. Masters also appreciated that he had stood by the man accused of stealing money from the mosque and arranged to have him repay the missing funds in installments, rather than report the theft to the police. (The state, in baladi culture in general and in the workshops in particular, is a strong site of negative value, as I will discuss in chapter 6.) All his actions after being hit with the evil eye successfully protected Ibrahim from future attacks.

Such positively valued behavior in the social world is not the only means of protection against the evil eye. Other forms of protection move through the medium of the sacred. The most common of these is writing on workshop walls of words, phrases, and sentences from the Quran and sayings, or *hadith*, of the Prophet. Likewise, material symbols without language are rendered on the wall as displays of the goodwill and pious actions of the master. The walls of workshops in el-Hirafiyeen, as elsewhere in Cairo, are often inscribed inside and out with writing and symbols that communicate with neighbors, other workshops, and possible customers.[43] Through sacred words and symbols, the workshop master communicates with the world of believers in God, and with God himself. Of the symbols that can be found displayed on the internal walls of the workshop, three are most common. First is the imprint of a palm dipped in the blood of the sacrificed lamb (*kaf mitghatas bidam el-debiha*). The master sacrifices the lamb on the occasion of 'Eid al-Adha, with the meat distributed to the poor of the community in fulfillment of his religious obligations. This iconic mark of the master's action of giving to his community and to God protects him from the evil that can befall man from the bad will of another through the evil eye. Two other symbols for protection against the evil eye are commonly found in the homes and workshops of both Muslims and Christians: a palm frond (*za'af*) and a ceramic hand with an eye in the center (*el-'ain el-zar'a fi el-kaf*), a symbol whose roots go to Pharaonic times. Any customer or potential competitor who enters the workshop and sees these symbols, common as they are, is communicated the unconscious message, through the same eye from which envy might flow and render its evil effects, that evil thoughts will be, and are, blocked.[44]

Language can also block the evil eye. But only a particular form of language: the words of the Prophet as written in the sacred books of Islam. Inscribed in formal script, the words and phrases of the Quran and the hadith render sacred the space in which work is carried out and protect it from the evil eye. Different forms of sayings are commonly found in el-Hirafiyeen (and are typical around Cairo). On the inside of the workshop might be verses of the Quran specifically warning the community of Islam against the evil eye, others calling for God to enable those working to earn a living, and still others more general in nature, invoking the name of God in ways clearly designating the master as part of the community of believers.[45] Also commonly written on the walls of workshops in el-Hirafiyeen are sayings calling for blessings from God upon the place of work (or living) and stating that a living comes from God, is God's will, and is not for another to envy.[46] Names of workshops also make reference to God and bring upon the workplace the blessings of his name. The meaning of the workshop's name may be placed in the context of other writings on the walls of the workshop. In one case, the workshop was called "servant of the noble craftsmen" (*khadim el-hirafiyeen al-shurafa'*). Written on the walls inside and outside the workshop were phrases from the Quran and hadith that reinforced the image invoked by the name.[47]

This visual presentation of sacred language can pose a moral challenge to any neighbor who might engage in unfair competitive practices. At the same time, the master marks out his place in a moral community in the eyes of potential customers, and engages in a form of advance defense in the event of a conflict with a neighbor and competitor. When linked to good works that truly serve the community, the religious man inside formal institutions of Islam and the state can protect himself from the dangers of rapid financial success. Combined with the name of God, community giving can give a man a "good name," to offset a name for gain in the marketplace. The imprint of a palm dipped in the blood of a sacrificed animal whose meat is distributed to the community on 'Eid al-Adha, the inscription of words from the Quran on the walls of the workshop, the symbol of the blue eye—all these do more than ward off the evil eye. They are symbols of the workshop master's production of positive value in his community. From the point of view of the anthropology of value, such symbols can be analyzed as qualisigns of positive value production in el-Hirafiyeen, following Munn's use of Peirce's concept, in that they "exhibit something other than themselves *in* themselves" (Munn 1986, 74).[48] The "name" also has attributes of a qualisign, in that it exhibits the master's value production as embodied in his physical person, forms of speech, and ways of moving in space. Negative value production also takes on physical dimensions in attacks of the evil eye that can result in fires, scandals, and accidents.

When masters were transported into el-Hirafiyeen from other neighborhoods of Cairo, they brought with them more than their instruments of production to reconstitute their market life. An entire *dispositif* of market production was transported with the craftsmen from their previous neighborhoods, one that included Quranic inscriptions, writings on the walls, ceramic palms with an eye in the center, and more. These protected the master as qualisigns that exhibited his positive value production. They can also be seen as material devices that help constitute a dispositif of the market.[49] When transported to a new setting, that dispositif helps produce the same practices that were found in the previous setting. Market practices of the craftsmen, in other words, do not just arise from the mind, or the "culture" of the craftsmen. They are materialities. Their market habitus is a habitat as well. The evil eye is a central part not only of that habitus but also of that material habitat of market life.[50]

From Negative Value to Normal Biznis

He who looks only for gain in the marketplace is a practitioner of biznis. The agent of biznis, like the agent of the evil eye, pursues individual gain at the expense of others. But masters of el-Hirafiyeen pursued biznis with strangers alone. They did not explicitly seek illicit gain from members of their community. Biznis marked the point where community ended, and positive value production ended as well.

From the days of the Infitah and Sadat, however, biznis came to pervade huge segments of Egyptian society. The pursuit of biznis was no longer an isolated trick. Rather, in a context where the pursuit of individual gain at the expense of others pervaded the political climate and the ideology of economic life, biznis became a rightful and righteous pursuit of the popular classes. Here it is important to keep in mind that the Egyptian craftsman has a distinct history. In the words of one master, he has nothing to do with microenterprise and microentrepreneurs: "that's something that came in from outside, like a parachute." The poor craftsmen of Cairo, as portrayed by Naguib Mahfouz in his brilliant novel *al-Harafish*, for example, are more than an occupational category or social stratum. They are also a key site of legitimate opposition to the state. The *harafish* of Cairo consolidated their power, and their "alternative economic identities" (Community Economies Collective 2001), in opposition to the ever-present power of the Egyptian state.

Like those harafish of Naguib Mahfouz, the workshop masters or hirafiyeen of Cairo produced more than just goods in their workshops. They produced the value that they regarded as essential to their viability (Munn 1986, 3). They produced subjectivities rooted in their economic practices. How resilient those economic identities can be is an open question. What will be the outcome of an interaction in laboratories like el-Hirafiyeen between the social practices of workshop masters and the entire spectrum of quite different social technologies associated with neoliberal policies enacted in Egypt, from structural adjustment policies to empowerment debt? Will the incorporation of the social networks and cultural practices of the poor into the market proper regenerate the free market? Or will it cause that market to implode?

Will the alternative subjectivities and positive value production of workshops in Cairo provide a barrier to emergent forms of power? Or will the practices analyzed in this chapter become another terrain for "accumulation by dispossession" (Harvey 2003)? Will the inculcation of social technologies that mirror, in inverted form, the practices of workshops in places like el-Hirafiyeen help to regenerate the market, or will it help to unleash the power of the evil eye? I have suggested in this chapter that the agent of economics in its neoliberal version, as an isolated individual who seeks short-term gain in an abstract market, has strong echoes with the agent of the evil eye in the workshops of Cairo. The inculcation of that agent, through social technologies taught in laboratories such as el-Hirafiyeen around the world, could have unexpected results. The irony is that the individualistic agency of neoliberalism was being produced in the name of social networks, through the concept of social capital. I will explore the meaning of that irony in chapter 6.

6. NGOs, Business, and Social Capital

Becoming a Capitalist through the NGO

Fou'ad was a member of the governing board of the NGO. He was also a wealthy man. He owned seven workshops outside of el-Hirafiyeen (not currently in production), and four inside. One workshop he had received from the state in compensation for his workshop closed down in Heliopolis. In that one he had installed a *kabina*, or automatic paint-spraying chamber, that had been made in France. He had bought that kabina in the late 1980s in Italy, where he had it made up and installed to his own specifications, for about 100,000 LE (about $30,000). In contrast to the regular duko job of spray-painting cars out in the open air, the kabina needed special synthetic paints that had to be used at high temperatures to dry correctly. The result looked identical to a factory finish. Fou'ad also owned a machine for mixing paints, with over five hundred colors. This machine had cost 30,000 LE (about $9,000). There were twenty of the kabinas in el-Hirafiyeen, according to Fou'ad, the largest number in Egypt.

Fou'ad had started his working life as a sabi in a workshop in Heliopolis in the 1950s. The master he had worked for was a khawaga—a man of European origin whose family had been resident in Egypt for a few generations. While workshops were not affected by the nationalization of economic enterprises under Abdel-Nasser, most of these khawaga masters left Egypt over the course of the 1950s and 1960s. As with many of the other craftsmen from Heliopolis in el-Hirafiyeen, the exit of this social group gave Fou'ad a crucial chance to get himself established in the business. When his master left, Fou'ad was able to make himself a master by taking over some of the customer base. Since he was still young, and didn't yet have a workshop of his own, Fou'ad worked informally— before the term existed—on the cars of his former master's customers at home in 'Abdeen. Soon he got his own workshop in Roxy, Heliopolis, that he rented for 2–3 LE a month. (After the workshop was closed down by the state, he converted it into an office and shop for ready-made car upholstery, and for accessories.)

He expanded his business further when he took over a workshop for metal and paint work on cars in the informal part of Masr el-Gedida, on Geser el-Sawais Street, in the 1960s. He then joined forces with another workshop master in Roxy, who made spare parts for cars. By the time the workshops in Heliopolis were closed down in the 1980s, he had control of seven workshops outside el-Hirafiyeen. By the mid-1990s, in addition to the workshop and apartment that he had been given at subsidized rates by the state in el-Hirafiyeen, he had acquired two apartments and a number of workshops (he wouldn't say how many) bought out from craftsmen whose businesses had failed after the move. (Fou'ad never bought out workshops from "youth microentrepreneurs," because they had too many debts on their heads for his tastes.) He had already constructed a building for a full car service center, but the land was not yet zoned for industrial use. Through all the changes, he had kept his old customer base. Customers called Fou'ad on the telephone when they needed some work on their cars. Three of his six boys worked together with their father; he would send one of them to pick up and return the customers' cars.

Even though Fou'ad's property holdings were extensive, and the technology that he used in his workshop was advanced, the way he had learned, come up in the business, and run his workshops made him a workshop master. Like other masters, in his economic practices he moved fluidly across the boundaries of legality. As his business got larger, he complied with more regulations than before. More important to him than legality or illegality at this point was gaining access to the means to change the rules. As such, the NGO was critical to his business plan. While the land he had bought for the full car service center was legally his, he needed a change in zoning to be able to use it as he wished. For an illiterate if wealthy man, the NGO provided an invaluable means for contacts with local officials.

The time he spent on NGO activities was a counterpart to other strategies that he used for economic accumulation. The labor that he could mobilize through his sons, and the connections he had established with former apprentices in his workshops who were now masters in their own right, had proved important to his ability to survive the move to el-Hirafiyeen and to benefit from the crisis that the move created for his poorer colleagues, who had to sell out. Fou'ad was adamant in his talk about the need to "obey the law." He had passed the stage when he needed to work on the street to survive. At this point he needed to get the state to work for him. Large as his business was, located as he now was in a place where the eyes of the state were wide open, he needed official approval to violate the law. Work in the NGO was the best way for him to arrange the "exceptions" to the law that could make his business expand into a proper full-service center, one that could compete with the centers carrying the names of Mercedes and BMW. To become a real capitalist, he had to become part of the NGO.

NGOS and Grassroots Globalization

In an article published in the journal *Public Culture* in 2000, Arjun Appadurai called for a "serious commitment to the study of globalization from below, its institutions, its horizons, and its vocabularies" (Appadurai 2000, 17). NGOS, he wrote, were the most visible and obvious of those institutions of grassroots globalization and a potential site for the generation of alternative forms of knowledge and power that could counter the weight of "the state-capital nexus" (17). In this chapter I will show how NGOS are often an important part of the very state-capital nexus that Appadurai identifies with globalization from above. NGOS need to be analyzed as part of—rather than as something lying outside— the dominant mode of political economy in the world today. If, as Eric Wolf has argued, we want to look at the "instrumentalities through which individuals or groups direct or circumscribe the actions of others within determinate settings," then those relations that Wolf calls structural power are located in NGOS and IOs as well as in the state. Even more, the modality of power identified by Wolf as "structural power," which organizes and orchestrates those determinate settings and specifies "the direction and distribution of energy flows," cannot be understood without taking into account this broader frame that includes NGOS (Wolf 1999, 5).

NGOs are central to global political economy. According to the World Bank, an estimated $10 billion in aid was channeled through NGOs to developing countries in 1998 alone.[1] By the early 1990s NGOs collectively channeled more development aid to the South than the World Bank and the IMF put together (Agrawal 1995, 416). In important and ever increasing parts of the world, NGOs are the main provider of services that in theory should be provided by the state. All this is an important transformation in the nature and direction of development aid. It may be useful to remember how different things used to be. Before the Latin American debt crisis of 1982, loans and grants to the third world went largely to states that were themselves to generate economic projects employing their citizens.[2] The unemployed were mobilized in nation-building projects, or in public works programs of the state. But state spending as a vehicle for growth, and the Keynesian economics that provided the theoretical justification for it, have both been long discredited. Neoliberal attacks on the state, together with criticisms launched by critics of development and the World Bank, helped create a new mode of development lending and foreign investment. By 1998 another variation of international debt relations was firmly in place: from IOs and bilateral development agencies to individuals via the intermediation of NGOs.

To analyze these relations of power ethnographically, states, IOs, and NGOs must be approached as part of the same analytical unit of analysis (Elyachar 1996; Elyachar 2002; Elyachar 2003). We need to understand better how those organizations work as part of an evolving political economy, and system of governance, that includes the state, NGOs, and IOs. In this emergent field of power, the sharp divisions that we often assume among these three institutional forms of power are obsolete. In the approach I have suggested, NGOs cannot be assumed to be the inverse of the state. As pointed out by Ferguson and Gupta, this approach entails overcoming the assumptions of a spatial hierarchy in which the NGO represents the local, encompassed at a higher level by the state, with the local and the state together encompassed in something called the international order (Ferguson and Gupta 2002). As they and others have indicated, the global and the local can rather be mutually constructed categories (Agrawal 1995; Ferguson and Gupta 1997; Mato 1997; Rofel 1999). Once we drop the assumption that NGOs exist in a different political and analytical sphere from the state or the IO, new research questions can emerge. For example, the idea contained in the notion of "grassroots globalization"—that NGOs should be the representative of the poor and disenfranchised in opposition to a globalization that aids the rich and powerful—cannot be taken for granted.

NGOs are of many forms and shapes.[3] In Egypt they are highly regulated. During the fieldwork on which this book is based, Egypt's "Law 32," a legacy of the Nasser regime, regulated all NGO activity. (Since that time, the regulations concerning NGOs have only tightened.) Through the Ministry of Social Affairs, the regime had the right to decide if an NGO was legal, non-superfluous, constituted in a permissible fashion, and managing its finances correctly.[4] The NGOs that I talk about in this book mediated the distribution of "microloans" funded by IOs and bilateral development funders. Such NGOs became prominent in Egypt, as elsewhere in the world during the 1980s, in spheres of life usually seen as part of economy—laboring and earning a living, for example. The profusion of NGOs related to economic activity in Egypt is in part due to the common assumption that "economy" is not political. (Political organizations that are not explicitly sanctioned by the state in Egypt are illegal.) Together with the international NGOs and IOs that provided much of their funding, these NGOs became important players in the political economy of Egypt. In that political economy, locating new sources of rents has long been crucial (Vitalis 1995; Sadowski 1991). NGOs and the informal economy became an important source of those funds. Although most of the finance that came into Egypt to support "micro-enterprise" or the "informal economy" moved through institutions of, or partially integrated into, the state, the NGO microlending programs were organized around the slogan of strengthening "civil society," which is supposed to lie outside the boundaries of the state.

The People, NGOs, and Civil Society

A few things have impeded the kind of agenda that I argue for here, over and above the lack of ethnographic research on NGOs. One is a lingering assumption that NGOs represent "the people" and are the opposite of the state. Such assumptions are clearly not true of NGOs organized in the name of economy in Egypt. It is not only that these NGOs explicitly serve the market—most blatantly in the case of BONGOS (business-oriented NGOs). In many places other than Egypt, the World Bank organizes NGOs like those of the youth microentrepreneurs in el-Hirafiyeen.

GONGOS (government-organized NGOS) are also a common phenomenon in many parts of the world as a way to obtain rents accessible only to
NGOS. Rather than view such hybrids as aberrations, as violations of the
natural order of things—with the state in one place, NGOS in another,
and IOs like the World Bank in a third—we need to look at how such hybrid structures actually function. Growing ethnographic evidence about
NGOS still needs to be matched on the analytical plane. That demands an
ethnographic approach in which concepts are included in the field of
analysis. One of the concepts that is often taken for granted in discussions of NGOS is the notion of "the people."

Conventionally, the people were linked to the state or nation. In programs to empower the poor by incorporating them into the market, the
concept of the people was associated no longer with the state but with the
economy. This new association was characteristic of an era in which the
rhetoric of economy had come to prevail. Translated into the language of
economy, the people became the informal economy—those who, without any help from the state, made their own way, depending on themselves or their communities to survive. The people were not attached to
nation-state or even nation.[5] Rather, the people had become a localized
term indicating those who lived together in a particular community.[6]
The market under which they lived, however, was assumed to express
their interests, through NGOS established to serve the "informal economy" or "microentrepreneurs." Where the state had been the site of top-
down development (as portrayed in Scott 1998, for example), the NGO
was here accepted as the legitimate representative of communities of the
people. Sometimes NGOS were taken to be the organizational representation of civil society. Given the link that I have already demonstrated
between the people and NGOS, the conceptual chain of false equivalents
becomes: informal economy = the people = NGOS = civil society.

In neighborhoods of Cairo where workshops were prominent, NGOS
became the vehicle of choice in the 1980s and 1990s for distributing funds
circulating from the coffers of the World Bank and other funders. Unlike
the banks, NGOS as the representative of civil society functioned efficiently as the markers under which large sums of money and instruments of social engineering could circulate in Egypt. Civil society, the
people, and NGOS become semi-concepts, in a terrain of what could be
called, with apologies to Rabinow, middling post-modernity (Rabinow
1989, 13). These terms, together with the money and social technologies

that circulated with them, provided structuring coordinates for actually existing NGOS in el-Hirafiyeen. NGOS in the sphere of "the economy" were a site for maneuvers to accumulate power and wealth in Egypt during the 1990s. They were not a mode of anti-power in the non-state sphere of "civil society." Nor did they represent "the people." Rather, they provided a context—together with the finance and debt that they farmed out to individual borrowers—for new ways to gain and generate power. While all this went on in the name of civil society, in a sphere that was supposedly state free, individuals and groups identified with "the state" were intimately involved.

Stating that NGOS are the bastion of civil society, some might argue, is sloganeering, unserious and thus unimportant (cf. Seligman 1992, cited in Hann 1996, 2). Others might doubt whether anyone still believes that NGOS stand in opposition to the state. But even in academic circles, outdated assumptions about NGOS are still quite common, apart from a few specialists. Appadurai is only the most famous of the scholars who publish such arguments. Outside the academy, in policy circles, such views about NGOS are even more common, and more influential. "Civil society" and "NGOS" were the coordinates for massive programs of intervention and the infusion of billions of dollars around the world in the 1980s and 1990s. One example from Egypt provides a useful illustration. In the mid-1990s the World Bank organized a series of conferences to promote "ownership" of development programs. Meetings were set up between government officials and "civil society" to ensure that civil society and the people, like the state, "owned" and felt attached to development programs funded by the bank. In the words of a bank report: "How strongly a country believes that a program or reform will bring benefits affects the effort put into the activity, the domestic resources contributed, and the commitment to the activity after the donor has left—all substantial determinants of success. To succeed, reforms and projects must foster ownership by the people for whom the policy or project is ostensibly being implemented" (World Bank 2001, 193). Together with this notion of ownership came that of "partnership," which can take shape through a "consultation process involving government, civil society, and the private sector" (194). The bank therefore sponsored "consultations between governments and civil society and between governments and donors" (194). Those accorded recognition as legitimate members of "civil society" gained the right to "partnership" as well, and to consultation with the government.[7] Many of those "NGOs" accorded this status in Egypt were businessmen's associations, such as the Egyptian Businessmen's Association, established with the support of AID after the Camp David accords and based in Alexandria, and the Association of Investors in 10th of Ramadan City.

NGOS like these and others promoting microenterprise became an important conduit for diffusing new social technology and money in Egypt. Despite the disadvantages of NGOS as a financial intermediary, which made some donors prefer to deal with financial professionals in banks, NGOS offered many advantages to those trying to promote civil society. The very existence of these NGOS was taken by many as a sign that microenterprise lending was already strengthening civil society and would thus advance democracy as well. Microenterprise NGOS were to be a market-based way forward to democratic change that would enhance the stability of a regime central to maintaining American strategic interests in the region. How was this supposed to take place? Among development practitioners charged with instilling new social technologies in borrowers from the informal economy, money was a form of empowerment, credit was a human right, and entrepreneurs with money in their pockets and debts to repay were the agents of democracy. They would develop, and express, interests—in the economic and thus in the political sphere. In the words of one of my informants, the pursuit of individual interest in the economic sphere would lead to the democratization of Egypt. Development experts who worked on the microenterprise lending programs in Egypt worked with the concept of "economic interests" promoted by Milton Friedman from the 1960s (Friedman 1962). The spread of the free market would lead to the proliferation of individual interests. Those economic interests would translate into democracy when expressed in the political sphere. Debt, in short, would lead to democracy.

From an Association of Craftsmen to a Development NGO

Workshops were subsumed into this definition of microenterprise, since they were small places of employment. But there was a huge gap between how the development community approached the concept of "interests" and how the masters used a similar concept. As shown in chapter 4, the masters' concept of interests (*maslaha*) was far more complex and diverse than that of Friedman. Only if we interrogate the two concepts side by side—the concept from the West that informs the analytic frame within which we carry out fieldwork, and the concept gleaned from our study of indigenous practices—can this point become clear.[8] The kinds of economic interests that were to be propagated by the microenterprise lending programs and NGOs were in fact associated in workshop culture with the evil eye and the pursuit of biznis. The form of "interest" that the NGO was supposed to propagate was, for the masters, a negative value.

Members of the governing board were often men who had quietly acquired more wealth than their neighbors. Because of concerns with the evil eye, they were reluctant to show their relative wealth. For them to be able to consolidate that wealth, turn it to productive use, and thus let it come to the public eye, they needed to expand their production outside the bounds of el-Hirafiyeen. That need was not merely a technical one that pertained to restrictions on space or zoning regulations in el-Hirafiyeen. Rather, an expansion would allow them to transcend the gaze of the impartial spectator that regulated market life among the community of masters. Membership on the steering committee of the NGO, and the access to favors from state officials that it provided, gave masters better chances to make that jump. On the steering committee they used the sphere of "the public interest" (*el-maslaha el-'ama*) to advance their individual personal interests. But such a conversion was negatively valued among the broader community of masters.[9]

Two kinds of NGOs existed in el-Hirafiyeen. One was the NGO of the youth microentrepreneurs (see chapter 7). That NGO was established as a result of categories, funding, and social technologies implanted around the globe by IOs such as the World Bank. The second was of a different nature. It was formed by workshop masters after they had been moved into el-Hirafiyeen. When the masters found themselves extremely dissatisfied with the conditions there, they held meetings and organized an association, or *rabta*, to facilitate their negotiations with the governorate of Cairo, which is a state ministry. The name that they chose for their association had no relation to the global discourse of NGOs and civil society with which we are all now so familiar. Instead it drew on an indigenous tradition of craftsmen's associations and organizations for self-help among recent migrants to Cairo from the countryside, a tradition that draws on historically diverse forms of interaction and regulation by the Egyptian state.[10] As a civic association, the rabta was regulated by the state through the Ministry of Social Affairs.

The name of the association, and the symbolic frame of reference for interactions with representatives of power that it invoked, were effective in the first years of the association's existence. But when the neighborhood became home as well to microenterprises funded by the Social Fund, the craftsmen had to operate in a new configuration of power. Reference to a long tradition of craftsmen's associations for interactions with the state as the hegemonic form of power no longer made sense. The dominant mode of discourse to refer to civic associations had changed to one in which notions of development organized around NGOs were paramount. Not that either the craftsmen's rabta, or the forms of associational life to which it was linked, were devoid of power. But the rabta and the NGO were each associated with distinct trajectories and configurations of power.

To simplify, the rabta is an indigenous cultural organization that has historically had links to the Egyptian state. The NGO, on the other hand, has its origins on the international stage. NGOs in Egypt are no less "Egyptian" than the craftsmen's rabta, but that obvious point makes it no less useful to delineate the divergent genealogies of power to which different associational forms are connected. NGOs grow out of an international context and development agenda in which funding has flowed through programs to "develop civil society," since the 1980s in particular.[11] The craftsmen's association, and the neighborhood where it had operated, had developed in a dual relation with the state that had forced them to move to this new location.[12] After the graduate microentrepreneurs had become co-residents of the craftsmen's neighborhood, global configurations of power in which the international organizations and NGOs were prominent had become localized as well. Leaders of the craftsmen's association thus changed their name in 1993 to emphasize "development" (*tanmiyya*) as their aim, and began to use the word "NGO" to refer to their organization.[13] This apparently simple name change was effected in recognition of the changing global and national environment in which the neighborhood was located. A simple name change, in other words, reflected crucial shifts in national and global configurations of power. It also indicated the craftsmen's ability to maneuver and exercise power in the locality where they lived and worked.[14] With this transformation, the NGO became a site where negative value associated with the evil eye could be sanctified and rendered licit. The NGO helped to install a set of social technologies and moral schemata alternative to those of workshop culture. Even if it did not have legitimacy among the craftsmen, it implanted in the community an alternative set of practices that had legitimacy outside the community, if not inside.

From Businessman to Microentrepreneur

NGOS were a conduit for many transformations of value and identity in el-Hirafiyeen. Wealthy businessmen attempted to gain tax advantages afforded by the new categories implanted by the state and IOs. They joined NGOS, applied for funding from the Social Fund, and became silent partners behind Youth Graduate microenterprises. When a well-connected businessman appeared in el-Hirafiyeen in the mid-1990s, some of the masters explained that he was hanging out in the neighborhood to gain access, through the local NGO, to funds sent by IOs and bilateral funders to support microenterprise and informal economy. Although he constituted part of the "formal capitalist economy," this businessman decided to reconstitute his identity. To succeed in business ventures, he wanted to gain the identity of a microentrepreneur. That way, he could gain access to IO and NGO funding. But to attach himself to that constructed category, he needed to find a concrete place that symbolized the informal economy to IOs and NGOS. El-Hirafiyeen was such a place. Becoming part of el-Hirafiyeen was an element of his economic investment strategy.

To quickly attach oneself to a physical space, it is useful to enter social networks. But since most of the microenterprises in el-Hirafiyeen had shut down because of unpaid bank debt and unsold commodities, they did not provide the businessman with a social network to enter. Their social reality was, in the main, absence. It was the masters of successful workshops who afforded the businessman the chance to change his identity to that of a microentrepreneur. He entered into generous and high-speed rhythms of gift exchange with local workshop owners to establish his grounding in el-Hirafiyeen. Since the place had become a signifier for microenterprise, on the other hand, locating himself there helped him to gain access to IO and NGO funds. The stated objectives of microenterprise lending—to plant the seeds for future, growing, economic enterprises—were inverted. A successful businessman reconstituted himself as a microentrepreneur to gain access to funds for the "informal economy."[15]

Other entrepreneurial businessmen entered into partnerships with failing "youth microentrepreneurs" to take advantage of the tax exemptions that their social status, as created by IOs, afforded. Two successful youth microenterprises in el-Hirafiyeen were rumored to be fronts for established businessmen. A debate about such businesses raged between two factions of the youth NGOs in town: one side defended the rights of the youth against potential competition from outside businessmen; the other defended the success of businesses, and said it didn't matter how the youth succeeded as long as they did succeed. While the concern of the first group was defending "the youth" as a new social category, the second saw making money as a value in itself that did not have to be attached to ideologies of informal economy, empowerment, or youth microenterprise.

A New Development Model

Many officials spoke to Essam Fawzi and me about the importance of el-Hirafiyeen and NGOs as a new development model. The neighborhood's workshops and microenterprises reduced unemployment and drew noisy workshops away from the center of the urban fabric, and its NGOs were the ideal model for addressing and solving people's needs.[16] State security officers also spoke to me of the importance of this new development model when I was called in for an inquiry into what I was doing in el-Hirafiyeen. There is nothing unusual about a foreign researcher being called in for an interview with state security in Egypt. Research is regulated: one needs a permit to carry out research and the security apparatuses often keep track of what foreign researchers are doing. What intrigued me, though, was that the bulk of the interview involved a long discussion of the importance of NGOs, microenterprise, and the Social Fund. Rather than security of the state, it seemed, the officers were most concerned with the security of the Social Fund and its associated NGOs.

Masters who joined the craftsmen's NGOs also recognized a new development model, but saw that model from a different perspective. The president of the craftsmen's NGO in el-Hirafiyeen put matters like this:

the key role of the NGO was to be the intermediary in distributing money. This gave people in many institutional locations access to what political scientists call "rents" and many call corruption. The hand that can take and distribute the money also gets some money for itself. That was the implication of one local definition of the NGO. "There's money out there now. There's all those banks giving out loans. There's one group alone [an NGO] that got millions for the improvement of the environment. We need to work on that, to make this a beautiful place. My task as head of the NGO is to organize and develop the people who will be the hand that can take and distribute that money."

This environment created a powerful motivation to create the image that funders were eager to see. With microenterprise NGOs, the appearance was one of labor and community. But the performance of labor sometimes became more profitable than labor itself. In el-Hirafiyeen, Callon's notion of the "performance of the economy" (Callon 1998) was often far from abstract. The president of the craftsmen's NGO was well aware of the new value of el-Hirafiyeen and its name in the funding market. He understood that he and his colleagues could more profitably work as native informants,[17] putting themselves on display as bearers of authenticity to foreign donors, than they could as the producers of commodities. This sort of work was the epitome of biznis, of exchanges with outsiders in which one gains by exercising the art of trickery from a positive moral stance. The NGO president spoke of his dreams to showcase el-Hirafiyeen as a "development model" for admiring foreign visitors. He wanted to design distinctive uniforms for all levels of the workshop hierarchy, set up regular reception committees for the new "development tourism," and build a small railroad around the town's periphery from which the workshops could comfortably be viewed. The millions of dollars at stake, and the great interest of the foreign donors in el-Hirafiyeen, gave a logic to his rather surreal visions of a model town.

These were fantastic dreams. The doors of most of the places dubbed microenterprises (as opposed to workshops) in el-Hirafiyeen were padlocked shut. Many of the microentrepreneurs were desperate. They were in debt over their heads, with banks refusing to release further installments of their loans before receiving interest payments. The busy scenes that met the eyes of visitors were peopled by boys and young men of the workshops who knew little about the phenomenon they were supposed to represent. The idea that all this should be made into a Disney World display (or that development tourism was something around which to plan a community) is perverse. And yet the president of the NGO articulated just what his audience wanted to see: a neat and bounded performance of labor with roles easily identified and the smell of sweat kept at bay.

NGOs in the Information Age

Huda was a friend of mine who had got her apartment in el-Hirafiyeen through her brother. He had been offered a workshop and apartment in el-Hirafiyeen in compensation for having his workshop closed down in el-Zeitoun. He didn't want to move to el-Hirafiyeen and offered the apartment to his sister, who was newly married. Huda's boss was a consultant who did research for IOs and development agencies. The Canadians, for whom her boss regularly worked, were a big funder of microenterprise and of projects for women in Egypt. They had long funded a project in Upper Egypt to "empower women through microenterprise." Now they sought to extend that program to Greater Cairo. To help inaugurate the new program, the Canadians wanted to conduct "training sessions" at which the entrepreneurs of Upper Egypt would come to Cairo for training and help with establishing their microenterprises. This was to be kicked off, in the presence of the Canadians, with a series of "Women Microentrepreneur Meetings."

Huda's boss was a higher-level native informant for a large-scale bilateral development program in Egypt. He spoke English, was highly educated, and could produce the kind of low-level research needed by development agencies, IOs, and NGOs to show that their development programs worked. Like other such consultants, he knew that reports were far more convincing when they showed pictures and stories of authentic women from the informal economy. He himself needed cultural brokers to produce appropriate samples of "women" and "the informal economy." Huda was a suitable native informant to him, since she could supply access to the kind of people his funders wanted to hear about. Supplying materials for such research projects was an important part of Huda's job. Here the research task was to come up with a list of women in el-Hirafiyeen who could, on paper at least, train and be counterparts to women from upper Egypt who had been selected as prospective microentrepreneurs. Huda didn't know any such women microentrepreneurs in el-Hirafiyeen, since there were none among the craftsmen. Nor did she know the women who were partners on paper of the male microenterprise owners in town. They had no social interaction with women like Huda who were part of the workshop world.

Huda turned to the researchers in her midst to gather the information she needed to provide her livelihood. As researchers, we began the kind of collaboration through NGOs that Appadurai called for in his essay on grassroots globalization. We pondered who among the workshop masters and microentrepreneurs might be able to produce some women candidates for the meeting. Those whom we approached were eager to send their sisters or wives; they knew that a fee for the "training" conducted would be paid. Meanwhile, we spoke to the president of the craftsmen's NGO about providing the space for the meeting, under the banner of the NGO. He was enthusiastic about the idea; a fee would be paid for the hall, and contacts would be made with potential funders who usually ignored the craftsmen and their workshops.

Meanwhile Huda pursued other tacks of research, using local methods of communication. She called on the child worker of a neighboring workshop to run with messages to workshops that might have women on hand. For his function as a transmitter of information between workshop, IO, NGO, and the state, the boy received a paltry sum. This kind of communications technology might not be recognized as part of the information age,[18] but it is surely a more common form of mediating globalization than many would suspect. Child workers are one of the most exploited categories of workers in Egypt. And yet this form of research, bringing together an NGO, local women, and children with researchers funded by élite western institutions, did not provide alternative forms of knowledge to foster grassroots globalization. Rather, it turned the indigenous forms of value produced in the social networks of Cairo into a resource for the reproduction of dominant social orders. Networks can endlessly absorb new partners in ongoing patterns of exchange. It is a simple matter for the ethnographer or for the local representatives of banks and development agencies to become another node in local social networks. But with the integration of these new elements, the nature of the networks themselves is transformed. The networks became a vein through which the resources of indigenous peoples can be mined in a form of accumulation through dispossession.

Conflict Resolution and Blocking Negative Value

Intervening to solve problems among friends, family members, and neighbors is highly valued in popular culture in Egypt. It is an activity undertaken throughout daily life by anyone who identifies with *sha'bi* culture. Workshop life, again, is an integral part of that sha'bi culture. And thus conflict mediation was an integral part of masters' lives. Masters who were known to be generous and giving (*gada*) were repeatedly called on to help resolve problems among other masters or among their neighbors. The acts that they undertook to help their neighbors and colleagues reinforced their character as gada. If someone was late with a payment to a savings circle, or had had an argument with her husband, or if a problem emerged between two masters, things were resolved whenever possible before crisis fully erupted. Sometimes conflicts among workshop owners erupted into outright fights—over contested rights to a skilled worker, the use of open space in front of the workshops, or explicit public shaming by another master. (Those were the kinds of conflicts that emerged over the course of my fieldwork.) In such cases of overt conflict, masters who had a name and reputation (*siit*) among their peers, as well as the wealth to back up their decisions, were asked to resolve problems. The craftsmen called the meetings a'adat el-'arab, invoking a metaphor of the Bedouin ('Arab), a community that figured prominently in craftsmen's discourse as a model of independent people who lived their lives and solved their own problems without interference from the state. Essam and I were peripherally involved in one of these meetings, and discussed the meetings extensively with a number of the masters.

In these conflict resolution sessions, a few of the masters would sit together with the parties to the conflict, hear both sides of the story, and decide on a fair solution.[19] In moments of crisis, men who combined material wealth with prestige had the power and legitimacy to decide what should be done. The two masters who were parties to the conflict would put a sum of money (the amount depending on their wealth) in a compensation fund to be awarded to the wronged party. The masters in the conflict resolution session would decide who was right and who was wrong, and would decide on the appropriate way to resolve the conflict. Whether the remedy was monetary compensation, an apology, or a worker sent back to his original master, this form of conflict resolution was legitimate. According to our informants, decisions taken in these meetings had never been disputed before an incident that emerged over the course of my fieldwork.

This conflict involved Ahmed Sa'id, who sat on the NGO board. The meeting to settle the conflict marked the first time anyone could remember that mediation had collapsed. It collapsed because Sa'id attempted to affect the outcome of the mediation through the power of the NGO and the state. He had met an official through his work as the secretary to the NGO. The NGO had been a conduit through which Sa'id had attempted to advance his interests and increase his power. He did not comprehend that the power of the state and its associated IO and NGO formations had no currency in this setting. Masters who attended the meeting were furious that Sa'id had attempted to bring in the state. They expressed their anger in the following terms: "We represent five million LE here. We don't need someone [from the state] to come and tell us what to do." According to another, "We're working, aren't we? Just like they tell us to. We're not stealing and not selling drugs. They should leave us alone." (When masters talked about "the state" in contexts like this, they referred as well to global constellations of power that had taken shape and were omnipresent in el-Hirafiyeen, that connected the Egyptian state to the World Bank, the Social Fund, USAID, and important private and public banks.)

Conflict resolution meetings did more than settle individual problems. They reinforced the positive value generated within the community of el-Hirafiyeen and the forms of power generated within the community. This process occurred in part through the exclusion and blocking of the state and the associated IO and NGO formations. As masters confirmed their ability to solve their own problems independently of the state, they reinforced the negative value connotations of the state as well. At the same time, these conflict resolution meetings blocked transfers of value from the workshop community to the power nexus that had evolved in el-Hirafiyeen. Conflict resolution meetings reinforced the forms of power generated within the workshop, and retained the positive value generated for the benefit of workshop masters as a group.

The contrasts with the craftsmen's NGO in this regard are illuminating. The craftsmen's NGO was associated in el-Hirafiyeen with negative value. Its leading members were concerned with the accumulation of personal wealth. The NGO was a site for transforming the community power accumulated by masters into a personal, individual resource separated from their community. This process entailed making connections with state officials and, indirectly, IOs like the World Bank that had funded the Social Fund project. Those connections were not made as part of the ongoing production of workshop life. Rather, they were sought out through the NGO to bypass local systems of value and power altogether. This stratagem was talked about disparagingly by other masters in the community. The NGO governing board had interests (*masalih*) and were "political" (*siyasi*). They used the political sphere to pursue their personal, short-term economic interests. One master who was known as gada expressed this image of the state and the NGO quite clearly:

> Those people in the NGO, they have interests to pursue. I'm not even registered. Some of them have even been put on trial for stealing money. There's no one to tell you where the money's going. They send around a nice young girl in a veil to collect membership fees. I say thanks very much, and send her on. All of their talk about developing the neighborhood, well in principle it's very nice, but in practice . . . until they have a way to show us where the money's going . . . they don't do anything for anyone. There was one guy on our block who paid his fees to the NGO, every month. When there was an electric fire in his shop, did anyone from the NGO do anything to help? . . . Nothing! And he was the one who had been paying his dues, every month. It was only his neighbors, the guys with workshops around him, who helped out and got him back on his feet.
>
> It's just like when the cleaning company comes around from the local government. They want money from me to come and get the garbage. I don't give them a penny. And I save the garbage for the little girl who comes around to collect it [from a Bedouin family who lived in a shack nearby, after they had been evicted from the land on which el-Hirafiyeen was built]. When the cleaning company threatens me that I have to pay for the garbage, I just swear at them and tell them I'll pay them in court. I keep my money to give the little girl.

From NGOs to Social Capital

To many tourists, Khan el-Khalili is the location of authentic, *baladi* Egypt.[20] For those who have read of Egypt through the translations of the Nobel Prize winner Nagib Mahfouz, this is the place one imagines when one thinks of Egypt. It is also the place that most people think of when they think of crafts and craftsmen in Egypt. But in the era of the NGO, Khan el-Khalili came to stand for something else as well. In the World Bank's edited volume *Social Capital: A Multifaceted Perspective* (2000), Khan el-Khalili stands proud as a storehouse not of history but of social capital. Here I refer to the description of the most famous workshop neighborhood of Cairo in James Coleman's seminal article about "social capital" (1988), originally published in the *American Journal of Sociology* and reprinted in the World Bank volume:

> In the Kahn El Khalili market of Cairo, the boundaries between mer-
> chants are difficult for an outsider to discover. The owner of a shop that
> specializes in leather will, when queried about where one can find a
> certain kind of jewelry, turn out to sell that as well—or, what appears to
> be nearly the same thing, to have a close associate who sells it, to whom he
> will immediately take the customer. Or he will instantly become a money
> changer, although he is not a money changer, merely by turning to his
> colleague a few shops down. For some activities, such as bringing a
> customer to a friend's store, there are commissions; for others, such as
> money changing, merely the creation of obligations. Family relations are
> important in the market, as is the stability of proprietorship. The whole
> market is so infused with relations of the sort I have described that it can
> be seen as an organization, no less so than a department store. Alter-
> natively, one can see the market as consisting of a set of individual mer-
> chants, each having an extensive body of social capital on which to draw,
> through the relationships of the market. (World Bank 2000, 18)

It is interesting that Coleman found his exemplar of social capital in Egypt. As with political economists of the nineteenth century (see chapter 1), journeys to "the East" were formative to the making of important social science concepts of the late twentieth century. Hernando de Soto's travels in Egypt, and the fieldwork he supervised there in tandem with a local private consulting firm, were central for his two influential books (de Soto 1989; de Soto 2000). Coleman's impressions of Khan el-Khalili in Cairo found their way into what became arguably the most influential social science concept of the 1990s.

Social capital has its intellectual roots in the concept of human capital (Becker 1963) on the one hand and Bourdieu's concept of cultural capital (Bourdieu 1984) on the other. It was a foundation stone of the "post-

Washington consensus" that came to prevail in the World Bank and across development studies in the late 1990s, and that supplanted the "Washington consensus" of bad state, good market (Fine 1999; Fine 2001). In the post-Washington consensus, workshops, and the ways they are linked in networks, took a central place in ideas about the economy— and, though less explicitly, in ideas about power as well. Rather than attempt to transform workshops into something else, more "modern" and more strongly oriented toward "development," the bank and other development specialists began to argue that institutions like workshops are an important ingredient of economic development writ large.[21]

The revisionist conceptual consensus about social capital was not formed in isolation from the kind of development initiatives that I ana- lyze in this book. Shifts in the bank's conceptual apparatus are inter- twined with the evolution of its lending tools. "Safety nets" such as the Social Fund were originally instituted to offset temporary market dis- equilibrium after the imposition of SAPs.[22] The phrasing, which con- notes a market pregnant with self-regulating equilibrium, had become rarer by the late 1990s. The notion of social capital helped to effect the movement of programs about the empowerment of marginal indi- viduals in the informal economy to the center of debates about the economy at large. It was discovered that the informal economy, and the important ability of the poor to survive without help from the state, had at their core social networks built around community reservoirs of trust. The social networks that lay behind the entity called "the informal econ- omy," it had been found, were a form of "capital." Giving loans to sup- port this reservoir of social trust thus became a way of investing in the economy.

With this conceptual transformation, social networks of the poor could now be seen as an important ingredient of large-scale economic success. What might earlier have been seen as informal economy—that which is not state, that which is not the real economy—was being ab- sorbed into prevailing notions of *the* economy. The nature of microen- terprise NGOs made this easy. Money is exchanged, interest is collected, enterprises are established, unemployed women become entrepreneurs, at least on paper. At the same time, the concept of social capital rein- forces the idea that this is all about economy, and that social networks are at the core of what makes economy, and society, function. Theorists put all this in different ways. Some have argued that social networks were the essence of social capital (Burt 1993), others that the civic associations now called NGOS were the core of social capital (Putnam 1993; Putnam, Leonardi, and Nanetti 1993). Still others, such as Turner, have defined social capital more broadly, in an effort to better integrate "sociological knowledge into economic thinking." In this view, social capital became "those forces that increase the potential for economic development in a society by creating and sustaining social relations and patterns of social organization" (Turner 2000, 95).[23]

The cross-cutting social relations that characterize social networks had long been an object of study by anthropologists. In an influential analysis, Max Gluckman called them "multiplex relations" (Gluckman 1967). These cross-cutting relationships had long been seen as a characteristic of underdevelopment. In notions of modernity that built on Weber, the economic practices of the "underdeveloped" world had formed a contrast for sociologists and anthropologists alike. Relationships inside a large corporation were, at least theoretically, guided by the norms of the corporation, and cross-cutting relationships of kinship ties or religion or ethnicity were supposed to be irrelevant, and restricted to the private sphere. In contrast, the economic practices of the underdeveloped were seen to be overdetermined by many factors other than the pursuit of economic gain. This theoretical orientation framed the terms for central debates within and around anthropology, about whether the "backwards" had their own rationality for their economic systems, or whether the rationality of western capitalist systems was universal. The debate within anthropology between the "substantivists" and the "formalists," which was central to the discipline in the 1950s and 1960s, was framed by the notion of rationality and whether one particular standard of rationality prevailed in economic activity.[24]

The success of social capital as a concept marks the overthrow of the distinction between the "modern" and the "underdeveloped" in the sphere of economy. That revolution had begun with the earlier respect for "the informal economy" and the cross-cutting social networks of the poor. But it was still assumed that the networks were restricted to a particular sphere of social and economic life—even if they were no longer located in a specific geographic space that could be called "the third world." With the notion of social capital, on the other hand, social networks of "multiplex relations" moved to the center of *the* economy, in the United States as well as in Egypt (Putnam 1993). This shift was indicated in Coleman's citations of the work of the anthropologists Gluckman and Geertz in Africa and Indonesia to provide the basis for his analysis of economy and society in the United States (World Bank 2000).[25] When social networks began to be called a form of "capital," the idea grew that social relationships were an important ingredient in the economy, and that investment in social networks gave a payoff in production over the longer term.

What about the usefulness of the category of social capital for understanding workshop markets? My analysis of relational value in chapter 5, for example, might be seen by some as a more confusing way of talking about social capital. Perhaps Coleman's analysis of Khan el-Khalili in terms of social capital was accurate and sufficient. Since I also locate the master at the center of a set of networks and relationships, would it not be better to see those networks and relations as a wealth of social capital possessed by the master? Such an approach is problematic for a number of reasons. Social capital is a concept that I interrogate in this book as part of my ethnographic field of analysis. I cannot take it for granted as an explanatory category. More important, perhaps, is that the concept of social capital reproduces the assumption of a division between the master and his market, the individual and the social, and the individual and the network.[26] Workshop networks are not "owned" by any individual. They are a community resource. When community resources begin to be viewed as an economic value, other things are implied as well. Conceptual shifts do not happen in a void. Rather, as I have shown throughout, new resources are invested, and social technologies implanted, around new social science concepts. In this case, workshops were no longer viewed as an obstacle to becoming "modern" in Egypt but as a source of strategic resources in the age of neoliberalism. NGOS are an important part of the story of how those resources can be accessed.

With community networks conceptualized as social capital, NGOS became a vantage point from which outsiders could gain access to the value that those social networks produce. NGOS can potentially tap the vaunted trust and mutual respect of social networks for capitalist firms. This potential was most nicely illustrated when the Grameen Bank of Bangladesh, the grandfather of the microlending phenomenon, signed a contract with the multinational agricultural firm Monsanto (which has been at the center of debates about genetically engineered foods). Monsanto wanted to use the microloan credit networks of Grameen Bank to distribute its seeds, collect payments, and discipline those peasants who tried to store their seeds for reproduction rather than buying Monsanto's genetically engineered, self-destructing variety. As this incident made clear, NGOs and their microlending networks based on "community trust" can become "low-cost Pinkertons" enforcing financial discipline, just as much as SAPs have enforced discipline on a macro scale.[27]

The Monsanto case is only the most blatant of what we can see in places like el-Hirafiyeen as well. There NGOs functioned as a site for generating economic activity, if by that we mean exchanges mediated by money. NGOs certainly facilitated the creation of what the World Bank calls "linking social capital," defined as the "vertical ties between poor people and people in positions of influence in formal organizations" (World Bank 2000, 128).[28] But it is unclear that those forms of linking social capital advanced the interests of anyone but the wealthiest of the craftsmen in el-Hirafiyeen, and of state officials who had located a new source of funds flowing from the West to Egypt because of its strategic location in the hegemonic global order. Rather than advance the empowerment of the poor, the NGO increased possibilities for the unvarnished pursuit of individual interests.

NGOs in el-Hirafiyeen, in sum, had a strategic place in emerging global orders of the 1990s. The craftsmen's NGO in el-Hirafiyeen was a crucible of value transformation. It was a strategic node from which the transformation of value generated inside workshop communities into an economic resource that could be appropriated by individuals could take place. The NGO provided a legitimate context for negative value transformation, the transformation from positive to negative relational value. Likewise, it was a site from which the financialization of local indigenous communities proceeded apace. Whether NGOs can regularly transform the positive value produced in workshops into a resource of "social capital" for expanded markets and increased profits is another question. Dominant economic subjectivities of craftsmen in el-Hirafiyeen were often quite strong and resilient, and formed a barrier to this kind of expropriation, as I showed in the story of their conflict resolution sessions.

This terrain of contestation about economic subjectivities, and about whether positive relational value can be mined as a source of economic profit, is an important one in the age of late neoliberalism. The transformation of positive relational value into social capital is a form of accumulation by dispossession. That transformation is not effected through analytical moves alone. It proceeds through a range of social technologies enacted in a broad socioeconomic context of structural adjustment, devaluation, and forced globalization. Whether it will be successful is always contingent and open to question. The new economic subjectivities being imposed by the NGO market model jibe too well with negative value production in el-Hirafiyeen for it to be otherwise.

7. Empowering Debt

The Youth Graduates' NGO

In chapter 6 I argued that NGOs have become an important site for instilling economic subjectivities that legitimate short-term gain over community-based norms of value. Through the craftsmen's NGO, modes of market practices that would otherwise have produced negative value and provoked attacks of the evil eye could be pursued with explicit sanction. In this chapter I continue to explore what happens when cultural practices and social networks of the poor become raw materials for market expansion. What happens when cultural practices of the poor are financialized through debt, and tapped as a source of profits for banks? What is the outcome of efforts to instill new economic subjectivities conducive to neoliberal markets through the establishment of NGOs that teach people to conceptualize their lives in terms of profit and loss? What is the meaning of attempts to empower through debt?

To pursue these questions, I turn to another NGO of el-Hirafiyeen, that of the youth graduates, or youth entrepreneurs (*gamaiyet shabab el-kharigiyeen*). This NGO differed in important ways from the craftsmen's NGO, or rabta, that I discussed in chapter 6. The youth graduates' NGO was not grounded in the historical experience of Egyptian craftsmen. It did not grow out of a centuries-old history of associational forms to mediate with the state, or emerge spontaneously out of a moment of conflict with the state. It was rather one of the NGOs organized by USAID, the Social Fund, and other development agencies as a conduit for distributing loans to establish microenterprises in Egypt. This NGO distributed loans from the Egyptian Social Fund for Development, founded by the World Bank together with the Egyptian government. The NGO brought together a group of discrete individuals who had been lucky enough, through different routes, to get access to microenterprise loans. Many of them were over thirty years old and in effect reincarnated as youth only when they joined the NGO. The NGO was designated for "youth graduates," since this category had been targeted as strategically important under conditions of structural adjustment, when former guarantees of state jobs for graduates were being taken away. In Egypt that general concern about youth under structural adjustment was increased by fears in political circles about the attractions of militant Islamic movements for unemployed youth.

The notion of establishing NGOs to support microenterprises grew out of earlier programs to support the informal economy through microloans (see chapter 3). The idea that the market was empowering, which had evolved in informal economy lending programs, became more prominent in connection with microenterprise NGOs. In informal economy programs, it was unclear just what kind of market was empowering. But with microenterprise NGOs, the market had a clear and singular identity. It was the neoliberal market of the invisible hand. NGOs that advanced microenterprises began to train youth for the realities of life after GATT, in the words of the former mayor of Cairo during the Ramadan celebration of microenterprise that opens this book. NGOs became part of a broader process of financialization of the globe.[1] An important part of financialization, in my view, is what I have called "empowerment debt."

Debt as Empowerment and Debt as Oppression

Empowerment debt is a mode of fiscal relations that links IOs and NGOs with individuals outside their relation to the state as citizens. It helps to implant new subjectivities that are more conducive to neoliberal market rule. It is also an important mode of "accumulation by dispossession," through which indigenous forms of production, markets, and sociability are transformed into resources for capital accumulation. Accumulation by dispossession entails the appropriation and cooptation of existing cultural resources as well as overt forms of suppression and displacement (Harvey 2003, 146). Flows of empowerment debt into Egypt intensify the very aspects of market life that donors and outsider observers then cite as a reason why they must intervene in Egypt to reform the market. In all these ways, empowerment debt strengthens the case for neoliberal rule.

To think about empowerment debt, we need to start with empowerment. The idea of empowerment has its roots in the women's movement of the 1970s and has had appeal across a broad spectrum of political opinion. But despite its origins in the women's movement and associations with progressive politics, the notion of empowerment became an important underpinning to neoliberal programs that "respond to the sufferer as if they were the author of their own misfortune" (Rose 1996, 59). In his analysis of advanced liberal democracies, for example, Nikolas Rose points to "the proliferation of the new psychological techniques and languages of empowerment in relation to those subjects now coded as 'marginalized' or 'excluded'" (59). Neoliberalism is characterized by new forms of power arrangements in which the self is a primary agent of the art of governing: the self is both subject and subjected.[2] Empowerment can be the key to that double move.

The neoliberal era is characterized by a "vast, newly articulated set of techniques and tactics that do this work of government," including "all of those tactics that seek to effect the empowerment, consultation, and participation of individuals and groups from the work of community development to the organization of quasi-autonomous nongovernmental organizations, or QUANGOS" (Dean 1996, 223). The empowerment of communities and individuals is part of a new mode of governance or relations of power, in which the individual polices himself or herself rather than being the object of the direct exercise of power by the state. In an era of downsizing states, the exercise of power does not simply disappear but is rather relocated in new spaces that valorize the individual and the community more than the state. But what does this have to do with debt and finance? How is empowerment married to debt?

Debt was first linked to empowerment among NGOs and "people's banks" in the third world. The most famous example is the Grameen Bank of Bangladesh. In this new model of helping the poor to help themselves, long-standing forms of self-help among the poor, as documented by anthropologists, became a popular new model for development. Under the leadership of James Wolfensohn, the World Bank in the 1990s adopted what came to be called microlending as a central tenet of the bank's development programs. Soon the bank became the most powerful proponent of empowerment through debt. Unlike the debt that was seen as enslaving the poor countries of the world, this new form of debt was not proffered to states but to individuals, and to communities designated as "the poor." Credit was seen as liberating when it bypassed the state (which was seen as a negative force in neoliberal thought from the right and from the left) and went directly from financial institutions to NGOS as the direct representative of "the people." Those NGOS, in turn, could directly link "the people" to the global market and to global civil society. The disenfranchised were thus reincarnated as the agents of their own empowerment. Empowerment would come by incurring relations of debt to large IFOS like the World Bank through the intermediation of NGOS. Those NGOS were organized to promote microenterprise as a solution for the problems of the unemployed and disenfranchised in neoliberalism. The market, and not the state, would solve their problems.

In microenterprise lending programs like those that I studied in Cairo, "clients" were taught to view their life choices as a series of financial decisions, and to use the language of accounting to track their family income. Money and accounting became a language through which families were taught to speak about their lives.[3] In cities around the world where state services were being eliminated because of structural adjustment policies, citizens were taught to accept the replacement of state services with market-mediated services as natural and inevitable. Transforming relationships into a cash nexus establishes new and deeply rooted relations of power. Training sessions of microenterprise NGOS in Cairo as elsewhere taught loan recipients to think of life in terms of accounting and budgets. Such training "transforms the activity of the budget holder, increasing choices at the same time as regulating them and providing new ways of ensuring the responsibility and fidelity of agents who remain formally autonomous. Not merely in the setting of the budget, but in the very 'budgetization' of the activity, the terms of calculation and decision are displaced and new diagrams of force and freedom are assembled" (Rose 1996, 55). Some of the training sessions in which I participated in Cairo were led by trainers from AID who usually worked in the United States and Latin America. In those sessions, we were taught to "see the family as a microenterprise" and to "learn to speak the language of money." In all these different settings, individuals were taught to cope with the dispossession they faced under neoliberalism by rethinking their lives in market terms. For example, one exercise we were given showed how a man who had been laid off from a public sector job could help to advance his wife's liberation and increase his family's income by supporting her informal economy projects.

The idea of debt as empowerment arose as one response to a debt crisis and worries about debt that had been increasing in the United States since the 1970s. The rise of unregulated financial transfers outside the territory of the sovereign state in Euromarkets and offshore financial centers had become a source of concern in policy circles in Washington. Massive flows of bank loans to Latin America undertaken by money center banks based in the United States and flooded with cash from oil rents after 1973 were another source of concern. Sovereign states, it had been thought in models of "risk assessment" at the time, were risk-free borrowers. That belief changed when Mexico threatened to default on its debt in 1982 and most of Latin America followed.[4] Debt became further associated with crisis during the "savings and loan crisis" in the United States soon after. It became clear then that debt crises could originate at "home" as well. This mood of concern about debt further increased when a series of debt crises in Russia and Asia threatened to cause a generalized global crisis in 1989. The response in government circles in Washington and among international financial organizations focused on the implications of sovereign debt crises for bank profits and the stability of the global financial system. The IMF and the World Bank imposed structural adjustment policies on borrower states in attempts to ensure that debtor states would have the resources to repay their loans. Those programs entailed new suffering for the citizens of borrower states as health care, education, and infrastructure expenditures were slashed. A new political movement then arose in protest against the implications of these measures for the inhabitants of debtor nations.

The issue of debt became a galvanizing issue with broad appeal by the end of the century. The Jubilee 2000 Coalition built on previous efforts of NGOs and church groups to cancel the debts of the poorest, most heavily indebted countries. Thanks in part to the work of music superstars who adopted the cause as their own, the issue of crippling debts in poor countries was taken up by broad sectors of the population in Britain, in the United States, and around the world.[5] At the same time, an anti-globalization movement erupted into public view with demonstrations in Seattle and Washington, D.C., in 2000, and in Prague in 2001. That movement focused attention on global financial institutions such as the World Bank, the IMF, and the WTO. The GFIS were targeted for forcing poor countries into debt while devastating their social and economic infrastructures. One organization launched an "IMF and World Bank Wanted for Fraud Campaign." The group condemned the bank and the IMF "for committing genocide and robbery" across Africa.[6] Another organization, Drop the Debt, argued that the GFIS could well afford to cancel the debt of the poorest countries without threatening the financial well-being of their organizations.[7] The internet was integral to this globalized movement against debt. A global portal site on international debt, DebtChannel.org, was launched by OneWorld. Edited from Zambia, the site was a partnership of over seventy aid agencies and human rights groups worldwide. The site aimed to "help bring together global civil society to ensure that debt does not bring more human suffering and poverty," in the words of Joe Chilaizya, the editor of Debt-Channel.org.[8] Meanwhile, the Bretton Woods Project provided regular and sophisticated discussions online about debt and financial issues to a broad range of activists and NGOs all across the anti-globalization movement.[9]

Debt and finance, long considered issues for specialists, had become one of the major organizing issues of a global political movement. But by the end of the decade, specialists in IFOS began to sound very much like spokespeople of the anti-globalization movement. The president of the World Bank argued that the bank was against sovereign lending to third world states that was intended to induce them to carry out top-down development programs. Rather, he said, the bank advocated the provision of microloans to women and impoverished communities so that they could develop themselves. Other development officials, and bankers in the private sector, made similar statements and indicated that empowerment of the poor through microloans was better business than sovereign country debt. A curious conjunction became apparent between the views of anti-globalization protestors, the president of the World Bank, and Wall Street bankers (Elyachar 2002). A paradoxical idea of twinning empowerment with debt evolved into a paradoxical consensus between bankers and protestors.

Banks, Microloans, and NGOs as Collection Agencies

It is relatively easy to study the discourse of empowerment. A harder task is to study how mechanisms of empowerment actually work as a mode of neoliberal rule. Empowerment debt works through quite tangible means that we can study by mapping out paths of finance through institutions and networks of individuals. That entails another kind of mapping that I carried out in chapter 2 and 3 of this book. We need to ask the following, sometimes technical questions. Who gave money for empowerment debt? To whom did they give that money? How was that money transferred, how was it distributed, and how was it used? When we follow the paths of that money, see whose hands it landed in, which institutions they represented, and for what they used it, we can begin to think more seriously about how empowerment as a mechanism of neoliberal rule actually functions.

Let me begin with the providers of empowerment debt. IFOs that had been accused of forcing debt on poor countries joined with their NGO accusers from the North in promoting debt for poor individuals and communities. Together with numerous other agents, they joined in a wave of lending to the poor. Even though they had intended to directly finance the poor who had fallen out of the bounds of the state, they could not in fact circumvent the state. The Egyptian state was able to force these donors to move through state institutions (see chapter 3). Programs that had begun as a way to wean the failed third world state from debt, and to support the informal economy as a counterweight to the state, ended up as another source of rents for the state. Transfers for informal economy and microenterprise programs through economic NGOs became an important part of the country's political economy. Funders of microenterprises in Egypt were diverse. They included the World Bank, the EU, a number of Arab agencies, and USAID most prominently. The Canadian agency CIDA, the Danish agency DANIDA, and the Dutch agency NOVIB were also donors, as were the Friederich Ebert Stiftung and the Ford Foundation. These institutions transferred finance to Egypt through a variety of means. Prevented as they were by Egyptian law from directly funding local NGOs, they usually had to move through state or state-approved organizations. Money went from IOs, bilateral funders, or NGOs to banks (both public sector and private), the semi-independent Social Fund, or state-approved NGOs such as those established by AID.

On its way to the poor, this money entered the Egyptian banking system. Banks in Egypt became the intermediary between donors, NGOs, and aspiring microentrepreneurs. Donors had to ensure that someone would be a responsible fiduciary for their funds in borrowing or recipient countries. They would not trust NGOs to play that role. The Egyptian government, on the other hand, strongly discouraged the direct funding of NGOs. After a big debate among NGO and development representatives in Egypt, it was decided that banks could play the role of intermediary. Playing the role of intermediary between donors and microborrowers was good business for Egyptian banks in both the public and private sectors.[10] Loans in hard currency on soft terms from at least some of the donor agencies became part of "bank capital," greatly improving the bank's capital base and balance sheets. Money was kept in dollar accounts and thus was available for trading on international markets. Meanwhile, internal bank loans made these sums available as well in local currency accounts, from which loans were given out at commercial bank rates or higher. The "spreads," or differences between the cost of funds and the interest they brought in, were excellent. Although these funds were technically loans, bankers whom I interviewed said that no arrangements had been made with the donors for repayment, and the funds were treated by the banks as part of bank capital, to remain in perpetuity. On rare occasions, my informants said, the issue of repayment did come up, and the loans or grants to the banks were to be repaid only if the bank's microenterprise or informal economy lending programs were discontinued.

Microenterprise and informal economy lending, moreover, was a reliable business. "The poor" in Egypt as elsewhere were good borrowers: ample research around the world had gone toward proving this. And since the poor entrepreneurs paid market interest rates, lending to them was profitable as well. Charging high rates was not only good business, it was the right and respectful thing to do as well.[11] One reason why the poor were such good business was that NGOs were such good collection agencies.

NGOs have become an important gateway through which financialization of the poor proceeds, and new cycles of the turnover of finance capital are effected. But this function is not without contradictions. Bankers, NGO officials, consultants, and "youth entrepreneurs" whom I worked with in Cairo had different visions of how NGOs should function as mediators in the turnover of bank capital. Funders of empowerment debt wanted loans to be given out as quickly as possible. One AID consultant put this perspective to me most clearly one day, in the middle of a training session for NGO staff who provided loans to microenterprises: "This is empowerment money. We should be helping people get into debt." Debt, in the NGO micro- and informal economy circles, had become highly fetishized. It had acquired the power to generate self-esteem, self-reliance, and liberation from the state. Development consultants were frustrated with Egyptian bankers who had been educated in traditional notions of bank lending, and approached lending as a purely business proposition. In their view, their public sector bank should not lend money unless it could reasonably expect that the project for which the money was being lent was viable and could generate enough income to repay the loan.[12] Funders who lent through NGOs wanted their money returned no less than public sector bankers did. But they had different aims. They wanted to empower, not to see a specific economic enterprise set into motion. They also had different mechanisms at their disposal to get their loans repaid. Those mechanisms were unavailable to bankers who had to rely on the national banking system and the courts.

NGOs had access to more effective legal measures in Egypt than the banks did. Banks had to rely on civil courts in case of nonpayment. And as one banker put it: "That's an endless road with lots of delays. Judicial procedures in Egypt are futile." Things were easier for the NGOs. The dominant model for microenterprise NGOs in Egypt made nonpayment fall under criminal rather than civil law. Microlending in Egypt was constructed that way on purpose by former Egyptian bankers, become consultants to NGOs and development agencies, who knew all too well about the problems of civil courts in Egypt. Since nonpayment of loans fell under criminal law, NGOs could draw on the state's repressive apparatus when they needed to collect back interest. They held, moreover, a kind of undated personal check from each borrower that could be deposited at any time. If funds were not there to back up the check, criminal legal procedures would be instituted. As one of the former bankers who had designed the system explained: "We put psychological pressure on our clients. We have the power of the police to scare them." The banks had no such mechanisms at their disposal.

AID in Egypt, which established the best-known microenterprise NGOs,[13] had a reputation for being "very formal"—turning to legal procedures right away. In other countries debt collection methods relied on the "informal sector." The vast possibilities for informal methods of debt collection were outlined in a microenterprise lending seminar that I attended in Cairo. "Culture" was the key to getting repaid: "In every culture there is something that works, and the thing is to find out what that is. Is it the headman, the religious leader, community pressure, or the police? Find out what it is, and use it." Culture, like NGOs, had become a mechanism of financialization. Culture was also a cost-saving device in the turnover of finance capital.

Debt, Conflict, and Strikes in Egypt

The lessons taught in training seminars about how to promote empowerment through debt and to ensure repayment were pretty clear. But outside the seminar rooms, the lessons being taught by empowerment debt were less neatly drawn. NGO members learned first of all that debt was something for which they should fight. A major conflict emerged in el-Hirafiyeen, pitting NGO members who believed that the debt coming into Egypt to empower the poor was literally theirs against bankers and state officials who didn't want to let the money out of their hands. Bankers and state officials were themselves at odds. A public sector banker who had been responsible for managing the bank branch opened in el-Hirafiyeen complained that the politicians were responsible for the failures of el-Hirafiyeen. Although it was built for the market, in his view, el-Hirafiyeen was a "political project, 100 percent." Speaking of the former governor of Cairo, who had presided over the building of el-Hirafiyeen and the establishment of the Social Fund, and who had spoken so warmly of microenterprise in the Ramadan celebration with which I opened this book, he had this to say: "I had an argument with him. He said to me: 'You've taken money from the Social Fund for twenty million LE, and you haven't paid out from that more than one million LE.' I told him: 'Where's the demand for loans, all those workshops are locked up! We're a government agency, it's our responsibility to be able to get our money back.' . . . We have a loan from the Social Fund of twenty million. I lent out 970,000 LE from that and I won't loan out any more. We've already covered the real projects. The new ones, they're all locked up and closed down." If the microenterprises did not have a market, let alone if they were shut down and no longer producing, then this banker would not release the rest of the loans. Members of the youth graduates'

NGO were furious about this decision. They did not understand why the bank would not release their loans. Some of the NGO members had taken the microenterprise loans with bad intentions and just wanted access to easy money. But others were highly motivated to become entrepreneurs. These had started up their businesses, only to fall on bad times when they confronted the realities of producing and selling to a market they could not find. They had landed in an impossible situation with a triple blow. Their microenterprises were failing, the bank wouldn't release the second installment of their loans, and they were stuck with paying market-rate interest on the full value of their loans. Some of the NGO members, like its first president, saw in this situation a great political battle. In keeping with the new flavor of politics in the NGO age, former party activists took on the battle to get their money from the bank. They decided to go on strike for debt.

The notion that anyone in Egypt would go on strike, and risk arrest, to go into debt was initially surprising to me. It would be odd anywhere. There are, admittedly, precedents of people demanding to be further indebted and more deeply incorporated into the capitalist market. Those redlined from bank lending or denied credit cards in the United States have demanded access to credit as a political right. The Grameen Bank of Indonesia, founder of informal economy NGOs, has even stated that "credit is a human right." But the phenomenon of striking for debt is anomalous in Egypt, because of Egypt's long, rich history of strikes carried out, often at great risk, to fight for working-class and nationalist demands. Egyptian history is replete with accounts of strikes and sit-ins in support of class issues and political battles against the state.[14] The leader of the NGO of youth entrepreneurs had himself been politically active and been to jail for it. Now he and his peers had abandoned traditional politics and were instead joining NGOs and sitting in at banks. Further, Egypt and the rest of the former Ottoman Empire long experienced debt as a yoke through which foreigners exercised control over their land and its resources. The Administration of the Public Debt was established on behalf of mainly western bondholders in the Ottoman Empire as a kind of state within the state in 1879, and granted full property rights to the revenue from important commodities in the Empire, including the right to seek an increase in revenue flows. Egypt had been forced to accept a similar scheme in 1876. Given this history, debt has been an important political topic in Egypt with negative and painful connotations since the nineteenth century, and a common trope of Egyptian nationalist discourse.[15]

That the idea of striking for debt even occurred to the NGO leaders was highly significant in such a historical context. The creation of new institutional forms such as NGOs, new social technologies such as micro-lending, and new subjectivities that embraced market solutions to personal problems was having an effect. The NGO members accurately realized that the mappings of power with which they had to contend had shifted. Capitalist relations of production were not central to their conundrum. Nor was the Egyptian state the primary mover setting the rules of the game of empowerment debt. The bank was, in fact, a logical symbol of new coordinates of power that brought together the state, the IO, financial institutions, and NGOs.

Striking for Debt

One August day in 1993, members of the youth graduates' NGO of el-Hirafiyeen occupied the offices of the local branch of the Industrial Development Bank.[16] They carried out their strike at "the bank" (as it was locally known) in el-Hirafiyeen. This branch of the Industrial Development Bank was both the headquarters of the local Social Fund branch and the fiduciary responsible for mediating between the youth NGO borrowers and donor agencies. The general in charge of the local Social Fund project had his office in the bank, and from there managed the program of lending to the youth NGO. The bank stood in the main square of the neighborhood, with other buildings that marked the official presence of the state: the official mosque and a telephone central (rarely open). A cloth banner hung next to the bank: "Program for the Development of Medinet el-Hirafiyeen, in Cooperation with the Social Fund and the Industrial Bank for Development."

The youth in the NGO were well aware of the amounts being sent to Egypt to support "youth" and "microenterprise." They took seriously the idea that this was their money. In their view, the money was being sent for "the youth" and for "NGOs"—not for the state that owned the public sector bank. They were the youth, theirs was an NGO. The money should be theirs to control. Any attempt by the state to intervene in the management of that money was, from their point of view, illegitimate. When officials attempted to impose funding criteria of their own, or when bankers said that they couldn't have the money right away, the youth saw a form of stealing. They believed the rhetoric of the microenterprise and NGO movement: from the IO to the NGO to the entrepreneurs. To many bankers and politicians who handed them loans, on the other hand, the youth were a bunch of spoiled kids at best and crooks at worst. In the words of one banker, the kids saw this money as their bequest (*tirka*) from the state. Like greedy children after the death of a parent, they fought to get the share they thought they deserved.

Some of the money that they saw as theirs had apparently been privatized by state officials. The path to such appropriations had been paved, however, by the project's donors. Money had begun to flow into Egypt for the Social Fund projects in el-Hirafiyeen long before there was a clear structure for distributing it. The Social Fund allocated 20 million LE (about $6 million) for projects in el-Hirafiyeen in the early 1990s. This money was in addition to loans in the neighborhood from the other banks and development funders. It was decided that 4 million LE (about $1.2 million) of the 20 million LE would be allocated in the first round. Before a system of loan distribution was set in place, however, a period of flexibility and experimentation prevailed. Practical problems emerged in the process.

What would be done with that large amount of money, and who had the power to decide? It was clear to many that el-Hirafiyeen could not "absorb" (*yistaw'eb*) the huge amounts of money that were being sent there. At the same time, it was not yet clear who would be the intermediary and guarantor of the funds being allocated to the youth NGO from the Social Fund. Since these millions of dollars were allocated, in name at least, to the youth, their NGO became the focal point for high-level maneuvers for power and wealth. Many were eager to help. One of the first proposals to the youth NGO, according to my informants, came from a prominent businessmen's association, which had originally been established with the help of USAID, and which functioned as a "civil society NGO" for the purposes of international donor agendas.

The president of this NGO told the leadership of the youth NGO, they claimed, that of the 20 million LE being given them from the Social Fund (about $6 million U.S. at the time), el-Hirafiyeen couldn't absorb even the 4 million that would be dispersed at the first go. He suggested that they should "take 2–3 million, shut up and disappear." They would have "nothing to say about the rest of the money, and in turn no one would ask them about what they did with the 2 million." The youth began to sense just how powerful their new status was, and became a bit nervous that they would lose access to the money attached to the name of "the youth." They were unhappy with this proposal, they said. Not because of moral outrage about corruption. The idea that they were being offered 3 million LE entranced some of them. They realized that the name of the youth NGO, and their new social and political status, must be worth much more. Perhaps the businessmen were going to make business for themselves, rather than to help the youth. They wanted to keep control of the wealth that could be generated by the name of the youth NGO, but could not. The banks were earning interest on loans given to Egypt for the youth NGO and microenterprise, donated funds were used as bank capital on the books of the national banking system, and some officials to whom they turned for help helped themselves rather than the NGO.

In 1993, for example, the board of the NGO appointed an advisor to their NGO, to help in their dealings with officials.[17] The youth issued a letter stating the advisor's position and responsibilities. The advisor circulated with that letter, and developed relationships with local government and high state officials, in accordance with his status as an advisor to the high priority Social Fund Youth NGO. But the advisor had his own agendas to pursue, and he used the letter from the NGO to pursue his own, personal projects. When the youth decided that the advisor was no longer acting in their interests they sought to end the agreement, but through the name of the youth NGO, they discovered, he had already acquired new relationships that they could not annul. In their name, others were making connections and profits that they could neither control nor cancel.

Meanwhile, contracts were signed at the Social Fund for the allocation of the $20 million for the youth, and the Industrial Bank for Development became the custodian and guarantor of those funds. Its local branch then became the "intermediary" with the youth NGO. "The Bank" became, in addition to its function as a mediator of funds, a locus for overt political conflict that at least on the surface pitted "the state" against "the NGO." Members of the NGO were entranced by the vision of the money that was entering Egypt in their name, and frustrated that they could not get their hands on it. They were angry about other things as well. They also fought with authorities over the control of information and the right to decide on what basis funding decisions would be made. This issue of control, of who in practice would have this decision-making power, had been a concern of the World Bank from the start of the project. In an early review of the Social Fund project for the World Bank, concern is expressed that the Social Fund "may be subjected to political pressures that could force subproject choices inconsistent with agreed selection criteria" (World Bank 1991a, 42). That is, patronage relations might become more important than the objectives that had been defined on paper by the bank. But the forms of contestation over the direction of the funds were far more complex than a dualistic conflict between the on-paper formal objectives of a project and the patronage relations of a branch of government. Rather, there were diverse players who entered the field created by the new Social Fund money.

Some of this disagreement played itself out in a dispute over the "questionnaires" that the Social Fund had distributed to the youth to help the NGO decide which projects to fund. The NGO had promised answers about funding within twenty-eight days, but as doubts arose about the wisdom of letting the youth NGO make funding decisions, local officials of the Social Fund began an indirect process of subverting its leading role. According to members of the NGO at the time, the crisis began when the Social Fund officials printed a new copy of the questionnaire, in which the body of the questionnaire was separated from the NGO's comments and evaluation. In place of that page, a new one was added for technical and specialist evaluations of the project brought in by the Social Fund. As the youth saw it, they were being robbed of their legitimate role. The Social Fund was starting to freeze them out from "their" money and "their" decision making. The youth also raised concerns that their ideas for projects were being appropriated by individuals connected to the Social Fund for their own benefit—a charge that I might have thought absurd if I had not seen ample evidence of such appropriations from a number of quite different informants, including one in a private consulting firm. Furthermore, the youth were then denied access to the questionnaires distributed by the Social Fund. During their sit-in, NGO members demanded to see the questionnaires, along with a copy of the contract between the Social Fund and the bank, and an accounting of how much money they were to have received. During this sit-in, the youth later claimed, they found out that the 4 million LE to have supposedly been allocated to them immediately had, in their words, "disappeared." Here they had landed in the midst of the financial crisis of the Egyptian state and its banking sector.

The bank that had been appointed the fiduciary for their loans was in fact in deep financial trouble. Many of the Egyptian banks were known to be in a deep financial crisis at the time, for reasons that have been well reviewed (Mitchell 2002). In an internal accounting of the sort that goes on between central banks and individual banks in any country, this bank was in debt. So when the 4 million LE were deposited into the bank account, the central bank allocated the money to cover some of the red ink of the bank in question. The central bank, in short, blocked payment. To the youth this meant that their money had been stolen. The NGO members organized a sit-in in the local offices of the Social Fund. Starting as it did with great words of confrontation and calls for justice, the event came to a close without the conflict, and the publicity, that some had hoped for. The event marked the high point, and then the collapse, of the NGO in its first incarnation.

A New NGO for the Generation of Structural Adjustment

After the sit-in, in the words of some of the NGO leadership, the bank managed to "break up" the youth and set them against each other. The officials convinced the youth that the confrontational style of the old leadership had been a mistake: "With your rough style and rudeness, you'll never get a thing." To restore calm, eleven of fifteen members of the executive board of the first NGO resigned in "the public interest." At the same time, the Program Administration Committee of the local Social Fund administration in the bank evicted the two members of the NGO from the committee. Then applications for funding began to be approved. Other technical arrangements were made, such as an installment plan for disbursement of the loans. This again made good administrative sense, according to some of the youth, since there were so many concerns that the youth were simply taking the money and "getting married on the loan." However, the new arrangement also gave the bank and the other public officials more control over the disbursement of funds in ways that made it impossible for the youth, in their view, to run their businesses. There was great anger among many of the youth, including those who had stayed far from the confrontations initiated by the first NGO, that they had had to shut down their businesses because they didn't have their second installment, couldn't purchase materials to continue working, and yet had to pay interest to the bank on the entire value of their loan.

With the appointment of the new NGO board, however, the confrontational tone of the NGO faded away. The new leadership had closer links to the authorities. The new leading figure in the NGO, Ali, was an expert producer of official state discourses regarding youth, NGOs, and microenterprise. Cooperation with the authorities was far more productive of results. Most of the youth became convinced that they had more to gain by cooperating with the authorities. A "struggle" had become a "conflict" in which the system was reproduced, not challenged at a systemic level (Gluckman 1967). This could be seen in the different ways in which participants talked about the strike. In the words of two organizers of the sit-in, this event marked an important phase in the struggle for the rights of youth in Egypt. Moustafa translated all the problems with the banks into an issue of politics, of the social rights of the youth, and a great struggle for justice. Galal, on the other hand, who had little interest in politics, analyzed the issues at hand in purely economic terms. When he spoke about the strike, his discursive referents were rather the Asian Tigers, the economic problems of Egypt, and the problems of small business around the third world in the wake of GATT. From the point of view of the bankers who were in charge of the lending program, these were all spoiled children waiting for their take, as well as a bunch of crooks who had no intention of paying back their money to the state. And to those who took over the NGO after the event, the organizers of the sit-in were of "a bad social class." Mohammed, the new president of the NGO, mobilized a different language of politics—the politics of names and connections, of "who knows whom." His language was dotted with fictive and less fictive accounts of his meetings and contacts with state officials, from local officials to the president of the Republic himself. His discourse was also marked by phrases about microenterprise from the press. To him the leaders of the sit-in were troublemakers, "from the worst social environments." They had a wrong attitude, making trouble with the officials rather than working with them.

The story of the sit-in was recounted only in local lore, among local contenders for power. The new incarnation of the NGO functioned far more efficiently. It was a partner of state officials responsible for overseeing the flow of funds from international agencies for "civil society," it represented a vibrant civil society on the media stage, and it demonstrated the success of microenterprise lending as a strategy for the "generation of structural adjustment," to cite the memorable phrase used by the president of the youth NGO of el-Hirafiyeen during the Ramadan celebration of microenterprise with which I opened this book. When he told us about the sit-in at the bank, the former president of the youth graduates' NGO emphasized that it hadn't been aimed at the state: "This was a strike, [but] it wasn't against state institutions, nor against the president of the Republic." By this he implied that there was nothing illegal in what they were doing, and that the state security police should have let them be. But his statement was more significant. It emphasized that young men who might once have gone on strike for political demands that could have got them into serious trouble were now striking over the right to become indebted to international lending agencies and their local counterparts. The language and rhetorical style of the strike and labor militancy were being mobilized to demand the opportunity to get into debt. The greater object of the strike, if there was one, was not to increase the power of the working class, but rather to become "entrepreneurs" through debt relations. The sit-in at the bank was a strike for incorporation, along with many individuals and groups on the financial feeding chain set into motion by the World Bank and others, into the neoliberal market. How shall we understand the meaning of that strike? What shall we make of the NGO of youth graduates that carried it out? What did the NGO teach its members about the market?

The Success of Failure and the Lessons of Success

There were certainly success stories among the NGO members in el-Hirafiyeen. But those few who were lauded as successes had in fact succeeded through fraud. The microenterprise of the new president of the NGO, for example, was mere showcase. With the help of outside investors who had come to el-Hirafiyeen to benefit from tax breaks and who had formed silent partnerships with youth entrepreneurs, he had bought out a failed neighbor and expanded his weaving enterprise into two rooms. Two giant looms stood in the middle of his expanded microenterprise, but they were completely still every time Essam Fawzi and I visited during the two years that we worked in el-Hirafiyeen. An assistant sat by, waiting for the visitors from foreign delegations or local governments who stopped in from time to time to talk to the NGO president, keeping the place open on museum-like display. When the looms had been busy, my informants said, it had been on contract for the outside investor who had set him up in business. Meanwhile, another NGO member lauded even by that critical banker as one of the rare successes of the microenterprise experiment in el-Hirafiyeen, had in fact succeeded only because of his successful exercise of what the Egyptians call *hiyla*, or trickery. He had allegedly forged an order for suitcases from a public sector company, and used the forged document at a bank to get his loan released. Thus was he able to establish himself in the market, although he was reputed to be a front for outside businessmen. The only other microentrepreneurs who were a success were those who had, in the words of one informant, "brought their markets with them" and could function, and make markets, like craftsmen.

What does it mean that fraud and trickery were the most important paths to market success among the NGO members? Why were the only other successful entrepreneurs those from families of craftsmen who had brought their markets with them? So few succeeded on the market in el-Hirafiyeen, in no small part, because the market to which the NGO members had been told to sell did not in fact exist. There was no "the market" out in abstract space that they could reach through the internet or trade fairs. To actually sell products they had to create markets as craftsmen did. They had to have a practice of market life. This, with rare exceptions, they did not have. Like the youth graduates, the craftsmen had been transplanted to el-Hirafiyeen as the objects of a market experiment carried out on human beings. They had been left to reinvent their rules of the game of market life in an empty desert setting. They had to solve the tricky problem of reconstructing their social life and markets just as outsiders were moving in with a completely different project and program. Those outsiders, meanwhile, were installed in the neighborhood with little capacity for social or market life. Despite all these challenges, the craftsmen managed to create a viable market life while the youth entrepreneurs did not.

When masters were transported into el-Hirafiyeen from other neighborhoods of Cairo, they brought with them more than their instruments of production to reconstitute their market life. They brought with them an entire *dispositif* of market production, which included Quranic inscriptions, writings on the walls, and ceramic palms with an eye in the center (see chapter 4). They had a lifetime of experience in the market inscribed in their bodies. Even when transported to a new setting, that helped them to produce the same types of practices that were found in the previous setting. Market practices of the craftsmen did not just arise from their minds, or from the "culture" of the craftsmen. Their market habitus was a habitat as well. The youth had no habitus of market life on which to rely. They lived outside the habitat of workshop markets, even though they were the neighbors of the craftsmen. They shared the same geographic space, but did not experience it in the same way. The emptiness in which they lived was mirrored by the emptiness of their market life (chapter 2). Only those few youth who had other sources of mastery—through kinship or through trickery—could successfully maneuver in such a situation.

What of the shortcomings of el-Hirafiyeen? Those, for certain, were many. By the end of my fieldwork, all the Egyptians I talked to considered the place a complete failure. Different reasons were given for that failure. Some people, like the new president of the NGO, liked to blame the "social character" of the first NGO leadership. The public sector banker who had provided loans to the neighborhood said it was too politicized. Too many turf battles were being fought among politicians for the place to function as a proper home for the market. Other commentators blamed the youth who had "married on the loans." If those NGO members had not thrown their loans away on the costs of reproduction and instead focused on production, this line of thought went, then el-Hirafiyeen would have been a success.

The failure of el-Hirafiyeen was always attributed to the misdeeds of some individual or group. Maybe the fault lay with the youth who had misused loans to ensure their generational reproduction. Or with the rent-seeking attitude of Egyptian society, or with corrupt officials who had stolen money. The notion that there was something wrong with the concept of the market that was being imposed through empowerment debt never came up. The legitimacy of the neoliberal market idea was reinforced with every failure of the microenterprise project.[18] Every complaint voiced by the youth entrepreneurs, including those who struck for debt, reinforced the legitimacy of the market. Even the most militant of the NGO members, who had organized the strike for debt at the bank, fully embraced the new market subjectivity with which they had been endowed.

Empowerment debt in Egypt did more than earn profits for banks, new rents for the state, and new sources of illicit income for state functionaries. It helped to reshape a field of power in which the poor had to change, even if they remained poor.[19] It helped create new economic agencies predisposed to accept the strictures of debt and to embrace empowerment through the market. Even when enraged at others (or perhaps especially when enraged at others), these subjects recognized that their failures on the market were *their* failures—to be good entrepreneurs, to understand marketing, or to force the bank to release their second installments. If they were failures, then others must be better than they, and more deserving of the privileges they themselves had failed to accrue.

Empowerment debt taught other lessons about the market. The lessons that these NGO members learned best were not those taught in training sessions. For they soon learned that the market did not function as they had been taught. They learned that there was no point in trying to succeed by the rules of that fictive market. Since they were unable to mimic the market practices of their craftsmen neighbors, and since the market as the meeting place of supply and demand was a chimera, they were left with nothing but the daily lessons of empowerment debt on which to model their market life. Those lessons were simple. Market success came through trickery and a clear-eyed focus on short-term gain. They should take for themselves what they could, while they could, for if they did not then someone else would do so instead. Officials took what they could, employees took what they could, and youth took what they could. A generation without the means to reproduce itself did what it could to survive. The youth graduates perceived the ill-wisdom of using microenterprise loans as they were instructed to do, since that would have left them stranded in the outer space of the fictive market. Exercising their survival instincts if not entrepreneurial know-how, many instead used the loans to buy the apartments they needed to get married and start a family, or forged order forms from public sector stores. Established businessmen also learned the lessons of empowerment debt. They migrated to the new forms of market life implanted into Egypt and developed new, hybrid forms of market life. Jobless youth created new careers as spokesmen for the importance of microenterprise to foreign donors. All this too is a form of the market. But it is a particular form of market life that many call corrupt. Empowerment debt thus intensified the very aspects of market life that donors and outside observers cite as a reason why they must intervene in Egypt to reform the market. Empowerment debt began as a way to downsize the corrupt third world state and give freer rein to the invisible hand of the market. By the 1990s this thinking had changed. The state could not be eliminated altogether. Market practice had to change. Corruption in the market was the new bugbear that intervention had to reform.

Mutual charges of stealing and corruption were rife through all levels of the social field created by empowerment debt. Members of the state security forces were nervous that I would hear about those reports, and local informers took care to tell me that anyone who reported theft was himself a thief. They were right to be nervous, and not just because of local scandals about corruption that were rife in the opposition press at the time. Anecdotal reports of corrupt practices, after all, are the data on which the influential transnational NGO Transparency International constructs its Corruption Index. On the basis of information like that index, IFOs like the World Bank make decisions about what degree of market intervention is needed to finally, this time, get the market right. The lessons of failure were endless, the success of the failures apparently endless as well.

Conclusion

The Free Market and the Invisible Spectator

My aim in this book has been to question prevailing ideas of the market. I questioned those ideas by analyzing a particular mode of neoliberal market expansion in the 1980s and 1990s. That expansion involved integrating the poor into the neoliberal global market by taking possession of the social networks and cultural practices that enable the poor to survive. Expansion of the neoliberal market, I showed, is simultaneously a mode of dispossessing the poor. In opposition to the prevailing acceptance of the neoliberal market as "the" market I showed that in the world today (just as in the worlds of yesterday), there exist other markets. One such market is the market of workshops that I studied in detail in Cairo.

On the basis of that research, I argued that expansion of the neoliberal market should not be understood as bringing the market to those who had known it not. To the contrary, those on whose account the neoliberal market is expanding lived their market lives long before the idea of the neoliberal market began to haunt us. I have shown how the neoliberal market expanded in this period by integrating those existing markets into its midst. But the integration of existing markets into the neoliberal market was a complex process. It was predicated on deconstructing existing markets, not through academic exercises but through concrete forms of intervention that undermined the very basis for those forms of market life. Integration of those existing markets into the neoliberal market also required that neoliberalism betray key tenets of the liberal credo from which it stemmed, such as the notion of progress. That notion was thrown away when the cultural practices of people once seen as backward became a key to market success in the guise of social capital. Agents of workshop markets resisted the unmaking that was visited upon

213

them and found ways to recreate, in new conditions, that which was set to be devoured—and yet they themselves were drastically changed in the process. I have shown, in sum, how the neoliberal market embraced as vital for its own survival-through-expansion that which used to be seen as backward and a block to the successful functioning of the market; how it integrated that other-of-itself as a necessary condition for its own functioning; how it failed in realizing its own utopias; and how, through failing, it nevertheless succeeded.

My analysis makes clear that the market is not a technical instrument that can be put to use for the benefit of all. Expansion of the neoliberal market is not the application of an instrument or model that has been scientifically proven to work best. Markets are social and political worlds with their own cosmologies. Each is a cosmos of its own, an intricately functioning field of power. The expansion of the neoliberal market is much more than the selling of an economic device. It is a political project par excellence; it is a massive exercise of power aiming at no less than creating a world—the whole world—in the image of neoliberalism. As such, the expansion of the neoliberal market is bound to be a struggle for power.

Expansion of the neoliberal market rarely involves the overt use of violence, even though military force has become ever more visible as the ultimate free market argument. But even when arms don't speak, policies like forced privatization and structural adjustment are a form of violence perpetrated against those who pay a real price in their health and very lives. Indeed, expansion of the neoliberal market is an experience that changes people, and changes life itself. The expansion of the neoliberal market may be practiced in the name of scientific objectivity— implementing the objectively best model—but it can succeed only if it creates new subjectivities on the ground. Certain mechanisms as well as certain ethical attitudes must take hold for that free market to be es- tablished. In my fieldwork in Cairo I observed how the onslaught of the neoliberal market involved the formalization of titles and property rights. It involved figuring out who was a master and who would go back to being an apprentice. It involved taking on new forms of debt that would, when not repaid, call forth the repressive apparatus of the state or the NGO to close workshop doors, evict current owners, and take over the premises. This process required disentangling the webs of mutual obliga- tions and rights that characterize workshop markets in Cairo, to create individual subjects free to own and to sell. It is a massive undertaking to create microenterprises out of workshops, to expand the market through dispossession.

Agents of neoliberal market expansion did not deny that a reshaping of power structures was at stake. Acknowledgment that a power struggle was taking place could be found in the very notion that the poor were to be empowered. The poor, of course, didn't live in a power vacuum. The idea that they had to be empowered implied that a new form of power was entering their lives and that the power they had was being taken away. The power entering their lives laid claim to the cultural resources of the poor as a source of neoliberal market regeneration. A wide array of programs that purported to empower the poor and accord new value to their cultural resources then helped to undermine the basis for workshop life in Cairo. This process seems quite similar to the way that programs intended to support the family farm during the Great Depression in the United States indirectly aided a broader tendency toward their extinction (Harvey 2003, 156). But while workshops in Cairo, with a proven ability to survive many forms of political rule over many centuries in Egypt, struggled to adapt to new realities, life became more tenuous, more difficult, and yet more challenging for the masses of Egyptians who work in workshops and practice the form of market life analyzed in chapters 4 and 5. In Cairo the influx of empowerment debt to microenterprise took resources and attention away from the craftsmen who had, through their daily practices of market life, created the template on which the social science model of microenterprise had been constructed.

In the era of structural adjustment, when the poor were being encouraged to take care of themselves and to wean themselves from their dependence on the state for basic human services, it might be natural to expect those who were particularly independent to see their situation improve. But they did not. The studied neglect of workshop communities was most simply expressed in the words of the former governor of Cairo who spoke at the Ramadan celebration of microenterprise that I cited in chapter 1. A man who had championed the needs of craftsmen now scoffed at them: they just made a piece of something and that was it. As any reader knows quite well, that statement could not be farther from the truth. It and similar statements caused pain for a few master craftsmen who had found comfort in having such a powerful advocate during the short time when workshops held the attention of policymakers in Egypt. But his statements did more than that. They represented a flow of resources away from workshop communities that went beyond the earlier oversight of small enterprises to the advantage of large industry. This time, craftsmen were passed over for a market mirage.

In that market mirage, the idea came to hold sway that the poor could be empowered by undertaking debts to IFOs, banks, and NGOs. Rather than stand as citizens in a field of power defined by the state, the poor would be empowered by joining NGOs funded by IFOs, and by opening microenterprises. They would exist in a field of power where financialization wove together institutions once seen as discrete: the state, the international organization, and the NGO. Those who were to be empowered by this form of debt did not passively receive the lessons they were taught in training sessions and NGO meetings. They turned the tools of empowerment to their own ends through weapons of the weak: they used loans that would get them into hopeless debt to buy apartments and get married; they forged order forms from public sector stores to get their loans released from the bank; they made their microenterprises into shells for wealthy businessmen seeking new ways to escape government taxes. Since empowerment debt reconfigured relations of power, apparently technical fights over business arrangements and the flow of loans were simultaneously a struggle over power.

Those most powerful in Egypt, who benefited most from the inflow of money and power associated with the Social Fund, did not seem to take too seriously the vision of the market that they were selling. They were not deluded by the mirage. But they did take very seriously the market practices that empowerment debt helped to spread. Those practices made a mockery of the notion that if the individual pursues his self-interest, then everything will fall into place for society through the invisible hand. Empowerment debt did, in a way, "afford means to the multiplication of the species," as Adam Smith said the invisible hand would do (Smith 1976a, 185). But it is unlikely that Smith was thinking of appropriating training grants, marrying on the loans, or pursuing the arts of trickery as an acceptable means of generational reproduction.

Because of this power struggle, the idea of empowerment debt did not materialize as intended. Those who saw their experiment go awry were then quick to apportion blame. My informants were very much concerned to figure out what had gone wrong and try to design solutions.

Each iteration of empowerment debt reinforced its basic underlying logic of dispossession through empowerment. Social scientists in the academy observing all this might easily apportion blame to the rent-seeking capacity of the Egyptians, or celebrate the weapons of the weak used against an attempt to discipline the poor. Both explanations may be true, to a degree. But one should not look for blame at the poor alone, even though empowerment teaches us to blame victims for their problems. Rather, we should think about the problems with the ideas themselves. Why, after all, should the neoliberal market utopia be spared the critique leveled at the other utopias that it seemed to dislodge?

We need to take more seriously the market model set in motion with empowerment debt in Egypt. That market harkens back to the image of commercial society critiqued by Adam Smith in *A Theory of Moral Philosophy*, in which he condemned the tendency of the rich to display a "natural selfishness and rapacity" and to seek only "the gratification of their own vain and insatiable desire" (Smith 1980, 49). But here the poor too were empowered to act like the rich of Adam Smith. They too were taught to display selfishness and rapacity. The market that empowerment debt helped to unleash was like a wild west of private appropriation without productive investment. Much as the details of this story are particular to Egypt, the broad sweep can be found in many places where installing neoliberal markets has led to looting and lawlessness as a dominant form of market life.

On its own, the enshrinement of the cultural practices of the poor as a mode of free market expansion might seem marginal. But we need to remember that it is part of a broader phenomenon of accumulation by dispossession. Empowerment debt evolved in a historical period when neoliberal economic policies demanded forced privatization, structural adjustment, and the elimination of basic institutions of public education, health, and welfare. The periodic devaluations of the Egyptian pound that made food prices skyrocket and the child workers in el-Hirafiyeen go just a little bit hungrier each day; the factory closings that created opportunities for laid-off husbands of entrepreneurial wives to learn lessons of women's liberation through the informal economy; the cutbacks in services that made youth learn they had only themselves to rely on—all this was the broader context in which empowering through debt, and drawing on the resources of the poor for market expansion, took place. The notion that empowerment through the market could substitute for a viable development strategy was a sad joke. It was no easy job to present this vast process of dispossession as a form of empowerment. Nor will it be easy to control the resonance of this form of market life with particular aspects of workshop culture.

The subjectivities instilled through empowerment debt and NGOs in el-Hirafiyeen were not completely foreign to workshop market life. The incessant search for short-term gain was an important modality of market practice. Such a modality of market life produced negative value and could result in attacks of the evil eye. Those who adopted the neoliberal subjectivities of pure self-interest, and the pursuit of short-term gain without attention to the reproduction of longer-term cycles of community life, exposed themselves to dangers. Among these were not only bankruptcy and market failure but also spiritual dangers with real bodily consequences, including accidents, illness, social humiliation, or even death. I have discussed some attacks of the evil eye: the apartment of one master who had got much richer than his neighbors and bragged of his success caught fire; a master whose workshop was a great success when his neighbors were barely getting by got into a car accident with a client's car; and an ambitious master and NGO board member who had alienated his neighbors and flaunted his success was publicly shamed by a woman he was pursuing in a scandal that evicted him from social life.

An invisible presence thus could be said to have guided the market practices of workshop masters. But it would be hard to call that invisible presence a hand. One could think more usefully of what Adam Smith called the "invisible spectator." In Smith's moral philosophy, the invisible spectator ensures that the individual agent in commercial society acts with an eye to what others might think. The individual internalizes the multiple eyes of others and their moral judgments on his behavior in market and nonmarket spheres. Workshop masters spoke often about such an invisible spectator guiding their ethical conduct in the market. This invisible spectator was the conscience (*dameer*), the internalized knowledge of what is right. This notion is deeply rooted in Egyptian popular culture. It is expressed in the commonly heard phrase "It's between you and your conscience" (*da beinak wa bein damirak*). In the context of market life, he who ignores this conscience, and pursues only his short-term individual interests, invites an attack of the evil eye. The evil eye, like other elements of the market dispositif among craftsmen such as the customary assemblies through which they solved their conflicts, formed a barrier to the forward march of the neoliberal market. The irony is that without those barriers, the neoliberal market that absorbs all into itself and transforms positive into negative value might all the sooner implode.

In *The Wealth of Nations*, Adam Smith put forward a solution to a central dilemma of moral philosophy: Could a system of private property rights be reconciled with the moral rights of the poor to survive? Smith was sure that the answer to that question was positive. Thanks to the invisible hand, and increased application of the division of labor, an economy of plenty would overcome the contradiction between property rights and the moral rights of the poor. Extension of the market would solve moral dilemmas. In our own times extending the free market has also been posed as a moral imperative. Attempts to extract new economic value from the cultural resources of the poor have been presented as a moral value. Adapting to the neoliberal market has been presented as an ethical project that empowers those who embrace its grasp. But those who attempt to use the free market as a tool to help the poor cannot resolve the moral dilemma bequeathed to us by Adam Smith. Nor can they honestly claim him as their own.

NOTES

Chapter 1: The Power of Invisible Hands

1. On organizational and other forms of power see Wolf 1999, 4–6.

2. Here the reader might compare my findings with those of Michael Taussig (1980) in a quite different ethnographic setting, in South America.

3. The reader will have noticed here that the debate of this time was about "free trade," not the "free market." The story of the shift from free trade to the free market as the object of political debate is not one that I can pursue here.

4. For some of the most influential accounts of the economic history of Egypt see Owen 1969, Owen 1981, Issawi 1963, Landes 1958, Davis 1983, and from the point of view of labor history, Beinin and Lockman 1987. For an important collection that opened new paths to research on labor history in the Middle East see Lockman ed. 1994.

5. For a critique of this perspective from the labor historian of Egypt whose seminal work on the Egyptian working class helped consolidate images of large industry as the site of the economy, see Lockman ed. 1994.

6. For classic statements of this view see Raymond 1958, Baer 1964, Baer 1969. For a critique of this assumption, and evidence that the assumption of decay and backwardness is wrong, see Chalcraft 2004.

7. But for discussion of the exceptions among writers in the French language, both locals and foreigners, who argued for the need to revive local crafts, see Koptiuch 1994. For an important analysis of the elision of crafts and then their recasting as the informal economy see Koptiuch 1999.

8. Pierre Bourdieu uses the term "field of power" in Bourdieu 1999, 58. For my own use of the term see Elyachar 2003. Ali (2002) reveals the interaction of the state, NGOs, IOs, and local practices in Egypt in the social field of family planning.

9. On the notion of "the field" see Gupta and Ferguson 1997, Koptiuch 1999, 46–48. On the history of anthropology, including the so-called Malinowskian revolution, see Vincent 1990, Gupta and Ferguson 1997.

10. This propensity to truck, barter, and exchange is actually not the only explana-

tion that Smith gives for what motivates human beings in their market behavior. He also points, throughout *The Wealth of Nations* and *The Theory of Moral Sentiments*, to the obsession with imitating the wealthy (in a manner that foreshadows Bourdieu in *Distinction*) and the wish to act in accordance with the "impartial spectator."

11. Arrow and Hahn 1971, 1, Tobin 1992, 117, and Rothschild 2001, 116.

12. This section of the essay is titled "Of the Origin of Philosophy." For more on the origins of the phrase "the invisible hand," see a footnote by the editors of *The Theory of Moral Sentiments* about Smith's first use of the phrase in this context. (Smith 1976a, 184–85 n. 7). See also Macfie 1971 and Rothschild 2001, 116–56.

13. St. Thomas Aquinas, *Summa Theologiae*, vol. 38, ed. M. Lefebure, general ed. T. Gilby (London, 1975), cited in Hont and Ignatieff 1983, 27. It is worth noting that this line of argument was key throughout the debates over the "tragedy of the commons" in the twentieth century. For an excellent review of those debates see Peters 1994, 12.

14. The argument for the importance of reading *The Wealth of Nations* together with *The Theory of Moral Sentiments* is put forward by the editors of *The Theory of Moral Sentiments*, D. D. Raphael and A. L. Macfie, who argue in their introduction that the "so-called 'Adam Smith problem' was a pseudo-problem based on ignorance and misunderstanding" (Smith 1976a, 20–25). On the relation of the two works also see Skinner 1979 and Winch 1983. According to Hont and Ignatieff, *The Wealth of Nations* "was centrally concerned with the issue of justice" (2). Rothschild (2001) makes a similar point about the relation of the two books, as indicated in her title, *Economic Sentiments*.

15. I am indebted to Bill Maurer for this point and for directing me to sources about this intellectual history.

16. Aquinas was the student of Albertus Magnus, who "had taken upon himself the massive task of making the new Aristotelian learning, including in that a good deal of Islamic commentary and of other related material, available, so far as possible, as a whole in Latin commentary and exposition" (MacIntyre 1990, 115). Aquinas, Albertus's most notable pupil, mastered the "two rival, incompatible and apparently incommensurable traditions" of Aristotle and Augustine (115–16).

17. Such a perspective was very influential in the informal economy and micro-enterprise lending project as adopted by Hernando de Soto in his books *The Other Path* and *The Mystery of Capital*, in which the state became the enemy of a robust and overregulated informal sector (de Soto 1989, de Soto 2000).

18. Anthony Giddens wrote in 1985 that certain types of locales form "'power containers'—circumscribed arenas for the generation of administrative power." Rob Walker used that concept of "container of power" to talk about the state in 1993 in a fashion that was drawn on by Akhil Gupta in his article on the state published in *American Ethnologist* in 1995 (Gupta 1995, 337).

19. On the relevance of experiences in the East India Company to the rise of political economy, see Mitchell 2002, 6, 294. Key figures of nineteenth-century politi-

cal economy such as James Mill, Robert Malthus, and John Stuart Mill served in the East India Company (Mitchell 2002, 6). The Levant was equally important to the evolution of political economy. Like his colleagues, Nassau Senior formed his theories of political economy in concert with his involvement in practical matters, like the abolition of the Poor Laws. In his obituary it was stated that he "grew up with a determination to reform the English Poor Law and re-establish English agriculture on a tolerable social basis" (Bowley 1937, 238). In his journals of his travels in Egypt and Ireland, he "collected information, just as if he were organizing one of the many government reports he had prepared" (Perelman 2000, 317). Those experiences helped him crystallize his thinking about why England had to reform the Corn Laws and end the Poor Laws—both of which were central to primitive accumulation in England. Senior traveled and held extensive conversations in Egypt that he wrote of in his journals (Senior 1882). Numerous Englishmen served as officials of the Ottoman Empire, the Ottoman Imperial Bank, and the Ottoman Public Debt Adminstration, and subsequently took part in political debates in England that were decisive in creating the field eventually known as political economy (Elyachar 1991).

20. [Henry Martyn] Considerations upon East India Trade (London, 1701), in *Select Collection of Early English Tracts of Commerce*, ed. J. R. McCulloch (London, 1856), 593–94; cited in Hont and Ignatieff 1983, 42.

21. Mauss's analysis of archaic societies was based in part on the areas now known as the Middle East. His note "on Alms" is particularly interesting in this regard. In it he lays out the "beginnings of a theory of alms," as "the result on the one hand of a moral idea about gifts and wealth and on the other of an idea about sacrifice. . . . Originally the Arabic *sadaka* meant, like the Hebrew *zedaqa*, exclusively justice, and it later came to mean alms" (Mauss 1967, 15–16). My thanks to Bill Maurer for pointing out to me the importance of Mauss's note for my argument.

22. This is actually too simple an account, since, as Bill Maurer pointed out to me, "the commons" is a residual category after the creation of private property.

23. The term "the commons" tends to be used in a simplistic fashion by Roy and others in the broad range of movements called "anti-globalization." What might be lost in academic exactitude is gained in political effect. For a useful discussion of how the notion of "the commons" was used in political science to justify privatization, and in debates about development in Botswana among colonial administrators and postcolonial state officials, see Peters 1994, 1–21.

24. Harvey does note that these processes occur in a complex relationship with international financial organizations and NGOs (Harvey 2003, 167), but this insight does not have analytical status in his argument. Rather, it is an empirical observation.

25. It could be important to explore systematically the relationship between the "third" in the philosophy of Charles Peirce and in the work of Georg Simmel.

26. I am indebted to Ashraf Ghani for suggesting that I pursue this line of thought.

27. Those called "research assistant" in the production of ethnographic work run

the gamut from illiterate peasants, to professional translators, to young students with little experience in research, to professional academics rendered jobless by structural adjustment policies. Throughout the third world, local intellectuals provide knowledge for sale to young academics who are moving through the American academy and have resources to distribute. NGOS, as I will discuss in this book, are an important institutional framework in which there are unequal relations of exchange between the educated classes of countries like Egypt and aspiring academics of the United States

28. The relevance here of Crapanzano's use of Simmel was suggested to me by Ashraf Ghani.

29. On the production of ethnographic knowledge as opposed to writing ethnography, see Fabian 2001. The issue of "the field" is analyzed in Ferguson and Gupta 1997. James Ferguson (1999) incorporates the observations and comments of his research assistant into the text, which raises the issue of the production of ethnographic knowledge in his mode of presentation. In first projects of anthropologists privileged enough to come from institutions that provide the financial resources for fieldwork (and knowledge about how to get them), there is a strong pressure to render hidden this assistant, since academic advancement is premised on individual production.

30. I am indebted to Ashraf Ghani for this point.

31. I also drew on initial research that I had carried out during a previous year's stay in Cairo for language study at the American University in Cairo.

32. While Essam did not have an MA or PhD, he did have a great deal of experience in fieldwork and was a published writer in Arabic when we worked together. Therefore the materials that we were producing were of value to him just as they were to me. Our decision was that the outcome of the research belonged to each of us. This included all written materials that we produced over the course of our partnership, as well as the knowledge that we gained from working together.

33. This formulation is Michel Callon's. I take the term "economic subjectivities" from J. K. Gibson-Graham (forthcoming 2006).

34. When we worked together, Essam and I approached informants with certain questions in mind that shaped the course of interviews. Those interviews were more structured than the participant-observation part of my fieldwork, which I conducted alone. We never recorded informants as they talked. We would talk about the interview immediately afterward and make extensive and intensive notes, recording the exact speech of informants wherever possible. That evening, or the next day, I would translate the notes into English, and write my own ongoing fieldnotes about the visit from my own perspective. I would then give to Essam my English translation of the interviews, and my own fieldnotes, and we would renew our conversation about the materials, including words or phrases that I did not adequately understand, and some of the implications for the further conduct of the fieldwork.

35. The debates about ethics in anthropology are complex. For an important discussion see Pels 1999 and comments.

Chapter 2: A Home for Markets

1. On the "New Settlements" see Jossifort 1991, Jossifort 1993.

2. Interview with Yehiya Sa'id, undersecretary for housing, Governorate of Cairo, June 1995.

3. He says "teamwork" in English: *el-masryeen ma beyeshtaghalush tiym werk kwayyes.*

4. Details on the building of Heliopolis can be found in Ilbert 1981. For an analysis of colonial building projects and the garden city movement, see Buckingham 1849 and Tafuri and Dal Co 1986. My thanks to Daniel Monk for those references. On colonial building projects in Morocco see Rabinow 1989.

5. Of the workshop owners in el-Hirafiyeen from whom we took in-depth life histories, thirteen were moved from Heliopolis. Of those families, we took eight family histories back to the grandfather's generation. The case histories were taken in colloquial Egyptian Arabic.

6. On the Empain group in the context of the relations between local and foreign investors in Egypt see Vitalis 1995.

7. On the effect of the financial crash of 1907 on real estate markets see Owen 1972.

8. Ilbert calls Marcel and Jaspar the urban planners of the project. Habib Ayrout was in charge of executing much of the plans and conceded that Empain himself was not much of a technician, let alone a planner (Ilbert 1981, 76).

9. On the very different kinds of problems that arise from lumping all kinds of workers together in an assumed "working class," see Lockman ed. 1994.

10. According to company correspondence for the years 1915–25, the company most commonly resorted to the local engineer H. Ayrout to give an authentic and yet sound critique of their plans. For example, he was the expert consulted on appropriate furniture for "the muslims":

> The technique was quite simple: plan-types were conceived that were transformed according to the population that was going to live in it. Egyptian entrepreneurs were used to go to the sites, assess a list of needs, and propose appropriate transformations. It is thanks to them that the long blocks of building were abandoned. It was judged that other housing types were more appropriate. On site visits to the early inhabited building sites established that the "muslims" living in small houses designed as an alternative lived outdoors as much as possible, and barely used their balcony, terrace, or courtyard. Such needs studies also suggested the installation of *mashrabiyyas* or *salamliks* over the balconies of the garden-city type buildings, since the muslims were particularly sensitive to their neighbors looking into their homes. (Ilbert 1981, 110–11)

11. For an analysis of what is "local" and what "foreign" in the Egyptian context of the beginning of the twentieth century see Vitalis 1995, 13–15. Vitalis argues that those often called "foreigners" on ethnic or religious grounds in the historiography of

Egypt are better understood as locals, or "foreignized" (217) locals, who benefited from possibilities of access to multiple passports. "As in Argentina and Brazil among other countries, local capitalists in Egypt carried many different kinds of passports (or equivalents) and, as individuals, claimed a variety of national identities" (13). For an anthropological audience, it is instructive to keep in mind the parallels with "cultural logics of transnationality" analyzed by Ong in Asia at the end of the twentieth century (Ong 1999). The present era of "globalization" is not the first time that citizens with options have acquired multiple passports and identities to advance their business interests.

12. Ilbert's statement about Alexandria is also apt for the project of Heliopolis outside Cairo: "for each group corresponded a type of habitat and a type of neighborhood . . . In the name of . . . hygiene, there remained a strong taste of exclusion and ethnic segregation" (Ilbert 1989, 278).

13. When Heliopolis was incorporated into the city of Cairo in 1909, against the will of its owners, the municipality assessed fees on the company for the provision of "services" to its inhabitants. The company protested that in fact it provided its own services, and that the charges should thus be dropped (Ilbert 1981, 57). The resonance of this for current debates about neoliberal privatization schemes, and who is responsible for providing services, will not be lost on most readers.

14. Note that the phrase is "begin to learn," rather than "begin to work." This is the language typically used to describe the child's apprenticeship in the workshop, in line with the notion that "the workshop is a school."

15. Marriage of an apprentice to the master's daughter was a common practice in the craft guilds of Egypt ('Abd al-Halim 'Amr 1993, 37).

16. Here I echo Paul Stoller's call for the need to "incorporate into ethnographic works the sensuous body—its smells, tastes, textures, and sensations" (Stoller 1997, xv). His analysis of the apprenticeship of sorcery, and the way in which the apprentice's body "is the locus of learning" (13), is highly relevant to an analysis of workshop markets, in particular to why workshop apprentices and masters experience labor and the market as embodied, while the microentrepreneur experiences space and the market as empty and abstract. Also see Lave and Wenger 1991.

Chapter 3: Mappings of Power

1. On the military as an important owner of land and businesses in Egypt, see Henry and Springborg 2001, 150–52, and Bianchi 1989, 5. According to Henry and Springborg, "the military controls vast tracts of valuable land, much of it along Egypt's coastline or the Suez Canal, in prime tourist development sites. The conversion of such land . . . into other uses provides a major source of revenue directly to the military. It also enables it to enter into joint ventures with public sector and private developers, thereby forging linkages with strategic elites" (150–51). They add that a significant part of military manpower is absorbed in productive activities such

as "the raising of crops and livestock" (151). The case that I discuss here of the poultry farm is not an anomaly.

2. During the 1990s in Egypt, for example, some divergences between the use of property and official accounts provoked a strong response from the security apparatus of the state, and others were systematically overlooked.

3. For some discussions of the link between informal housing and migration, and the relation to other factors, see for example Hoodfar 1997, Nada 1991, Oldham, El Hadidi, and Tamaa 1988, Tekçe, Oldham, and Shorter 1994, and Rageh 1985. For some good summaries of the literature on Egyptian migration to the Gulf see Amin and 'Awny 1985 and Choucri 1983.

4. For a good overview of Islamic Investment Companies see Roussillon 1988, Rycx 1987, and Sadowski 1991, 219–53.

5. For an anthropologist who analyzes both offshore banking in the Caribbean and Islamic banking, see Maurer 2000, Maurer 2001. On the implications of unregulated banking and the new computer technology, with good references on the relationship to the Latin American debt crisis of 1982, see Castells 1996, 119–25. After September 11 the U.S. government targeted such informal banking networks as "financiers of terror." The links between offshore banking and informal migrant financial networks became front-page news in November 2001, when the government shut down financial organizations accused of funding the al-Qaeda network. See the *Financial Times, Wall Street Journal,* and *New York Times* of 8 November 2001 for reporting about informal financial networks, or *hawala* funds, and the article "Quartermasters of Terror" by Patrick Radden Keefe in the *New York Review of Books,* 10 February 2005.

6. In the late 1990s, on the other hand, in a different period of globalization and triumphant financial deregulation, similar practices, called arbitrage, were made famous by the financier and civil society advocate George Soros.

7. Mitchell 2002, 275, citing *Economist Intelligence Unit (EIU), Country Report: Egypt, Third Quarter 1998,* 10. Furthermore, as Mitchell goes on to say, "Indeed it may have become the largest non-oil sector, since most tourism investment went into building hotels and vacation homes, another form of real estate."

8. For study of the historical precedents in another period of "globalization," see Owen 1969 on the real estate boom in Cairo at the beginning of the twentieth century.

9. The desert surrounding Cairo is historically state-owned.

10. See Denis 1994, Ghannam 1998, and Ghannam 2002, 41, for useful discussions of the security concerns of the state about informal neighborhoods. Denis provides an excellent survey of the press debates of the time. See Denis 1995 for a more complex typology of the sociology of housing in Cairo than that provided by the duality of "informal" and "formal" housing. That duality is also critiqued by Tekçe, Oldham, and Shorter (1994, 10).

11. In fact by 1992 the originator of the term, the anthropologist Keith Hart, was

writing that the dualism of "state" versus "informal economy" was dubious at best (Hart 1992, 225).

12. Asef Bayat (2002, 3) makes a similar point. For examples of the notion that informality refers specifically to "the poor" and "survival strategies," see Wikan 1996, Singerman 1995, and Hoodfar 1997.

13. A statement like "informality had become part of the state" can be read as a rhetorical device to illustrate the problems of the duality of "state" and "informal." But for the historical processes that are captured by such a statement, see Castells 1998 on the informalization of the state, Bayart, Ellis, and Hibou eds. 1997 on the criminalization of the state, and Hibou 1999 on the privatization of the state.

14. On this issue see Fine 1999, Callon 1998, Elyachar 2002, and Mitchell 2002.

15. On categories and counting in the colonial context see Cohn 1986, Cohn 1996. The studies inspired by Foucault on such issues are numerous, but Cohn's analysis of state building as a cultural project actually precedes Foucault (Dirks 1996), as pointed out by Stoler and Cooper (1997, 11).

16. For anthropological contributions to a rethinking of property see Verdery 1998, Verdery 1997, Hann ed. 1998, Ghani 1996, and Strathern 1998.

17. My point is not that the Egyptian government draws no maps. Official maps of the area did eventually come to include el-Hirafiyeen. My point is rather that there are ample forces, even within the state itself, that impede mapping, contra Scott (1998).

18. On the change in the World Bank to alleviating poverty see Finnemore 1997 and Escobar 1995.

19. Research on the informal economy is voluminous and sometimes contentious. For a sample of different perspectives on informality that also include good summaries of the debate, see Assaad, Zhou, and Razzaz 1997, Peattie 1987, Tripp 1997, Meagher 1995, and Lubell 1991. I do not include here some of the more commonly cited works, since they are well summarized in these.

20. As Meagher points out, the analysis of informality and flexible accumulation was developed in regard to Latin America, Asia, Europe, and the United States (Meagher 1995, 265). Meagher also points out that structural adjustment reforms "now enforce a process of systematic deconcentration of capital in the public sector, thereby creating conditions more favorable to informalization" (264).

21. For example, the growing sections on small business in large bookstores like Barnes and Noble during the 1990s, or special issues of Business Week on small and microenterprises. For discussion of the informal sector as a potential "engine of growth," see Handoussa and Potter eds. 1991 and Handoussa 1992. For a critique of the idea that the large corporation is outdated in the global age, see Harrison 1994. A good summary of the debates about the importance of small business in the "information age" can be found in Castells 1996, 155–56.

22. Those numbers were commonly used in the development literature for Egypt in this period.

23. The Egyptian Businessmen's Association, for example, was set up to lobby for the peace treaty with Israel, sponsored by the United States but the subject of much criticism among all sectors of Egyptian society.

24. It might be more accurate to write, "to invent as a problem of development intervention based on the production of knowledge about legitimate practices on the ground that did not proceed according to the rule of law." But considering the central role of the ILO in the history of the concept, my statement is not really a glib exaggeration, as one reader suggested. According to Keith Hart, the inventor of the term, the ILO applied the concept to a report on Kenya in 1972 even before his original paper coining the term had been published (Hart 2001, 150). See Hart 1992 and Hart 2001, 148–51, for his own reassessment of the debate about the informal economy and his role in that debate. As I hope is clear from the thrust of my argument, I do not deny the existence of the processes captured by the analytical concept "the informal economy." Rather, I am interested in an interactive process whereby social realities are studied by anthropologists such as Keith Hart, under the auspices of specific forms of institutional power such as IOs, and those concepts then play a crucial role in mobilizing organizational and tactical power, in the sense defined by Eric Wolf (1999), in specific ethnographic settings. My thanks to Bill Maurer for alerting me to the publication of Hart's 2001 book.

25. For a critique of the impact of fundamentalist neoliberal theorists in the International Monetary Fund on third world countries, and a representative sample of one of the main views inside the World Bank, see Stiglitz 2000.

26. "Continuation of Administrative and Legal Reform," *el-Ahram*, 17 May 1995, 1 (in Arabic).

27. I was not able to ascertain final figures on the size of these loans and grants coming into Egypt in the name of informal economy and microenterprise in the 1990s. A paper written by a senior economist of the World Bank who headed up the resident mission in Egypt, and a consultant who did regular work for the bank, cited (in a report whose statements were not attributed to the World Bank) "millions of dollars annually" (Giugale and El-Diwany 1995).

28. The name of the agency reflects its origins in the period of Abdel-Nasser, when gathering statistics was seen as part of a nation- and state-building project. As an anonymous reviewer pointed out, statistics have long been seen as a security issue in Egypt.

29. Such conferences are advocated by the World Bank to solve the dilemma of "ownership": the problems that occur when developing nations forced by conditionality agreements to sign on to development programs do not feel that those programs are really "theirs." The conferences are seen as a way of mobilizing "civil society" in a dialogue with the state and the IOs over development policies. Theoretically, such conferences should help lead to a consensus among "civil society," the state, and IOs about development policies, and increase the possibility that development policies will actually be carried out. At the conference in Egypt for which my

informants were preparing, the representatives of "civil society" were, in the main, businessmen's associations. For a discussion of the concept of "ownership" see World Bank 2001, 191–94.

30. One of the main authors of the 1994 report was in fact a development consultant who is cited by de Soto as an important resource for his research in Egypt (de Soto 2000). I mention this not to point to any "conspiracy," as one reader implied, but because informal networks of knowledge creation about the informal economy, and their place in broader fields of power, are a central topic of mine. At the same time, it is important to realize that views on these and many other matters are the subject of debate within the bank itself. For example, the World Bank Development Report for 2000–2001, written under the leadership of Ravi Kanbur, clearly states that "microfinance"—loans to support the establishment of microenterprises—is "no panacea for poverty" (World Bank 2001, 75), and repeats throughout that the state has an important role to play in development. In turn, it is important to realize that Kanbur resigned from the bank because of controversies inside the organization about the views that he advanced. This debate can be characterized (if simplified) as one between the "Washington consensus" and the "post-Washington consensus." On that debate see Fine 1999, Fine 2001, and Elyachar 2002.

31. See Ghannam 1998 and Ghannam 2002 for a parallel discussion of how the users of government-constructed housing who were moved from central Cairo to Zawiya el-Hamra reordered their built environment.

32. Maps of the region began to include el-Hirafiyeen some years later.

33. I emphasize my foreignness in this context because of its centrality in Sa'id's decision to bring me to the meeting. At first he thought it a bad idea, and only wanted Essam to attend, posing as a craftsman. But then he decided that more pressure would be exerted by the presence of a foreign researcher with a local assistant.

34. For important examples of this approach by scholars who combine fieldwork with theoretical inquiry, see Herzfeld 1992, Gupta 1995, and Mitchell 1991, and the ensuing debate about Mitchell's article in the *American Political Science Review*. Gibson-Graham's identification of the strengths and limits of deconstructive and other approaches to the question of "global versus local" was helpful to me in this formulation (Gibson-Graham, forthcoming).

35. On the changing nature of state sovereignty see for example Hibou 1999 and Smith, Solinger, and Topik 1999.

36. Reginald Dale, "A New Debate on 'Global Governance,'" *International Herald Tribune*, 25 July 2000.

37. That comment is made in the context of the debate surrounding Mbembe 1992, in which Coronil took part. The citation here is from Coronil 1997, 73 n. 8.

38. On the notion of economic citizenry see Sassen 1996. For a critique see Spivak 1999, 400 n. 116.

39. Bianchi (1989) argued in the 1980s for the importance of understanding "hybrid forms" and the uselessness of the usual binary oppositions for understand-

ing the Egyptian state and its relations to civil society. Stark's use of hybridity to analyze what he calls "recombinant property" in Eastern Europe is also relevant here, particularly in the context of his argument about the uselessness of the search for divisions between "private" and "public" sectors in post-socialism (1998). See also Callon's discussion of hybrid forms (1998).

40. I am grateful to Sally Moore for challenging me to think about these issues in a panel she organized at the annual meeting of the American Anthropological Association in 2000. She develops her argument about institutional attempts to plan the future (Moore 2005).

Chapter 4: Mastery, Power, and Model Workshop Markets

1. *Afrangi* means foreigner or Westerner. The word comes from "the Franks," used to refer to the crusaders as well as Europeans in the Ottoman Empire. An afrangi Egyptian is one whose cultural practice is identified as more "European" than indigenous. In general, Egyptians with higher levels of education tend to be afrangi. *Sha'bi* Egyptians, on the other hand, have a lifestyle indigenous to the popular quarters of Cairo. Workshops and workshop masters are very much rooted in sha'bi culture. Sha'bi is usually translated as "popular." On afrangi versus sha'bi culture see el-Mesiri 1978, Early 1993, and Booth 1990.

2. Note that this is related to, but different from, the traditional Cairene practice of having complementary workshops next to each other on a street.

3. Words like "apprentice" and "master" can be misleading English translations. Imported from the European context to make sense of the economic practices of the Middle Eastern workshop, they carry strong connotations of the European craft guilds and distort as much as they illuminate. For an important critique of the debate about the craft guilds see Chalcraft 2004. For a critique of the use of terms of "apprenticeship" and reference to the terminology of craft guilds to discuss the conditions of workers in workshops of Cairo in the 1990s see Elyachar 1997.

4. Egyptian-born Jews were often called *khawaga*, as were children of Italians and other communities who were born in the country. Foreigners were also *khawagat*. Small businesses like workshops were never the target of efforts to nationalize foreign-owned businesses, but many khawagat emigrated from Egypt in the wake of nationalizations.

5. Many workers whom we interviewed in the workshop spoke of having dropped out of school partly because they had been hit by teachers. They also spoke of the workshop as a school, one where corporal punishment was also necessary for learning. Masters often spoke of the workshop as a school, and of the need to hit apprentices so that they would learn. Children and adolescents spoke of the importance of this form of learning as well.

6. My analysis in what follows is based largely on my fieldwork in el-Hirafiyeen, among the workshops of carpenters, blacksmiths, machinists, mechanics, painters, and others in various trades linked to remaking cars. Many of these activities are far

from what some readers might associate with "crafts" (if not readers familiar with Cairo or other megacities where workshops produce all that millions of residents might need). All the workshops had access to electricity and telephones and some used highly sophisticated equipment. But they are all definitely "workshops" as opposed to "microenterprises." The neighborhood was without doubt "formal," since it was established by the state. But by the definition that equates small size with informality, the workshops would be considered informal. Without a doubt, all the workshops engaged in technically illegal but common practices, which is another definition of informality (see chapter 3). Such practices included employing children, not paying taxes, and using toxic chemicals that were officially illegal.

7. Exceptions to this rule in el-Hirafiyeen seemed to be in the fields with the highest potential profits: machine and paint shops.

8. The need for anthropologists to "incorporate into ethnographic works the sensuous body—its smells, tastes, textures, and sensations" (Stoller 1997, xv) has been noted most powerfully by Stoller. For analysis of direct relevance to my own work, see his chapter "Spaces, Places, and Fields: The Politics of West African Trading in New York City's Informal Economy." In the context of apprenticeship and learning see also Lave and Wenger 1991.

9. Essam Fawzi opened this line of inquiry. He first thought of asking the craftsmen about how they knew whether the work was going well when they were not in the room, and predicted they would talk about the sound or another sensory experience.

10. For connections between the performing arts and anthropology see Denby 1965 and Kondo 1997.

11. The debate about craft guilds in Egypt is complex and must be bracketed here. But for a sampling of perspectives among historians see Baer 1964; Raymond 1973–1974; Massignon 1987; Gerber 1976; Toledano 1990; Ghazaleh 1995; 'al-Halim 'Amr 1993. For a reassessment of the debate, Chalcraft 2004.

12. But not always. One workshop that was moved out of Heliopolis had depended for most of its work, making spare parts on a lathe, on one German company for which a steady supply of work and spare parts was crucial. But the move to el-Hirafiyeen seems to have added too much expense in time and transport for the German firm. After the workshop moved to el-Hirafiyeen, the German managers decided that it would be cheaper and more reliable to hire their own machinist and an assistant—and the machinist had been an apprentice in the very workshop to which they had subcontracted the same work.

13. Since soldiers are paid only a pittance in Egypt, survival is quite precarious for young men without money who cannot arrange their service to be near their families or workplaces. All the craftsmen from Heliopolis, and many of the others, mentioned that they had worked in the workshop during their army service, except for those who were in wars.

14. I do not mean to imply that influence peddling was not common in "modern"

states like the United States in the 1990s. That would be hard to argue. The point is rather that exchange networks with officers in Egypt provide more democratic access to institutions. I have never heard of working-class kids in the United States being able to buy their way out of the army, for example. Furthermore, discussions with Americans high in the embassy made clear to me that at least as far as they would reveal to me, they had little idea of how things operated inside the bureaucracy, while it was common knowledge to the craftsmen how the dreamed-of visa to America could be obtained.

15. On the importance of patriarchy for understanding the workshop and informal economy, and why it is that these workshops can remain "hidden" from the eye of the state, see Wilson 1993.

16. I witnessed one notable exception during a visit to Egypt in 1995 from a representative of the ILO, who was interested in developing a program for the support of children working in the informal economy, based on the successes of similar programs in Istanbul. Essam and I took this official on a tour of el-Hirafiyeen and introduced him to some of the people who appear in this ethnography.

17. More than one husband interviewed, who didn't like the idea that his wife was working, used a clever strategy to persuade his wife to do as he wished. When the new home that they "married in" was farther from her work than her family home, taking over two hours each way in commuting time, he just let her come to the decision herself that the commute wasn't worth what the job brought in. Confrontation was in this way avoided.

18. On the centrality of the value of the family in Egypt see Wikan 1995 and Wikan 1996. Singerman (1995), a political scientist, also points to the "familial ethos" as central in the structuring of Egypt's social and political order.

Chapter 5: Value, Evil Eye, Economic Subjectivities

1. The notion of *gada'* is also related to the position of the *futuwa*, who was more formally responsible for insuring the well-being of his community. For a beautiful fictional treatment of the futuwa within the world of poor craftsmen, see the novel by Naguib Mahfouz, al-Harafish, and the English translation (Mahfouz 1997).

2. The reader should keep in mind that cars considered fit for the junk heap in the United States are usually repaired inside and out in Cairo, with workshops specializing in each particular phase of the restoration.

3. To deal with workshops regularly is, in the original, *benit'amil ma'ahum*. Those workshops that he deals with for a commission are, in the original, *fi bil-'umula*. Those with which he exchanges without money are, in the original, *fi bil-gad 'ana*.

4. Two proverbs about neighbors and neighborly relations express the delicacy of balancing distance and closeness. On the one hand, *el-nabi wasa 'ala sabi' gar*, that is, the Prophet enjoined concern for even the most distant (the seventh) neighbor.

However, according to another proverb, in Egyptian rather than classical Arabic, that concern should be mixed with a degree of distance and respect for privacy: *sabah el-kheer ya gari, enta fi hallak wa ana fi halli.*

5. Note that *it'amil*, which I have translated as "do business," can also be translated, according to *A Dictionary of Egyptian Arabic*, as "manage, conduct oneself in relation to another" or "transact business" (Badawi and Hinds 1986). I would argue that in the workshop, and in popular colloquial Arabic, the two meanings in the dictionary are combined, since one rarely "does business" without face-to-face contact, even, in many cases, within large bureaucracies and corporations. In this context the word could be translated as "do business," but that seems too dry.

6. Taking care to respect each other's feelings and privacy is, in the original, *binra'i shu'ur ba'ad.*

7. Women could not always count on their husbands to take care of such labor. As many masters and their wives said, a master does not want to do physical labor when he gets home. That is the place for rest. One carpenter and his wife laughed as they recounted that the carpenter had finally renovated their kitchen only when the wife had started producing sweets for his coffee shop.

8. "The endless reconversion of economic capital into symbolic capital, at the cost of a wastage of social energy which is the condition for the permanence of domination, cannot succeed without the complicity of the whole group: the work of denial which is the source of social alchemy is, like magic, a collective undertaking. As Mauss puts it, the whole society pays itself in the false coin of its dreams" (Bourdieu 1977, 195).

9. Not all scholars of Egypt resort to this kind of popular description. Diane Singerman, for example, showed the logics that lie behind Egyptian customs that are often called "corrupt" (Singerman 1995, 213–14, also 227–28). Ragui Assaad has analyzed the logics of informal labor markets in a fashion that also touches on the alternative logics of corruption (Assaad 1993).

10. This formulation is Michel Callon's.

11. *A Dictionary of Egyptian Arabic* (Badawi and Hinds 1986) includes in its entry for the verb *itgammil* the expression *ma-yhibbish hadd yitgammil 'alee,* "he doesn't like anyone to do him a favour (thereby making him feel under an obligation)." The part of the definition in parentheses shows what is implicit, and thus understood, to native speakers.

12. I was thinking about such questions when I was carrying out my fieldwork, however. Realizing that those categories were not useful for thinking about workshop production, I attempted to suspend my mobilization of such analytical frameworks while doing my fieldwork, and to develop instead a conceptual framework based on the ethnographic reality that I was studying. Avraham Zloczower and Tomaž Mastnak both encouraged me to do just that. I did not realize with that attempt that I was walking into a crossfire of anthropological theorizing about the relative impact of our concepts on what we see in the field and the impact of the field on our anthropological theory. See the exchange between Carrier and Strathern, for example, in Hann

ed. 1998: Carrier's stance is that an analytic concern does not "emerge spontaneously from . . . naïve contemplation." "Rather, it is motivated by the intellectual assumptions and interests that shape ethnographic perception and production" (Carrier, "Property and Social Relations in Melanesia," Hann ed. 1998, 86). Strathern argues that we can develop concepts from an analysis of ethnographic reality: "My own interest has been in forms of sociality developed without regard to the European/ Enlightenment distinction between individual and society that has driven much anthropological enquiry" (Strathern 1998, 220). She draws attention to the "historical location of analytical constructs" (220). In her view, we should strive to "understand the categories of action people mobilize in pursuing their interests. It is probably redundant to say that anthropologists' own management of knowledge already inheres in the concepts they choose to use" (218).

13. This is related to Gluckman's notion that "multiplex relationships" dominate social and political organization (Gluckman 1967).

14. Here I have benefited from Marilyn Strathern's formulation that the "theoretical problem was to understand a particular conversion process," which in my case occurs in the workshops of Cairo (Strathern 1998, 221). In Strathern's work, women need pigs to produce men—they "need a medium which will make visible their maternal care" (Strathern 1998, 227) in a process of producing persons through the production of things.

15. I am grateful to Bill Maurer for pointing out these possible readings of my work.

16. Singerman, for example, has pointed to the centrality of these informal relationships to political life in Egypt (Singerman 1995).

17. Here the reader might see echoes of the work of Mustafa Emirbayer and relational sociology, which Diane Singerman brought to my attention. His argument that "individual entities and interests are not preconstituted and unproblematic; parties to a transaction do not enter into mutual relations with their attributes already given" (Emirbayer 1997, 296) is clearly also very relevant for my argument about workshop markets.

18. For a critical history of the concept of social capital see Fine 2001.

19. For anthropological explorations of the meaning of interest see Maurer 2003.

20. The idea of "interests" underwent drastic changes in seventeenth- and eighteenth-century thought, as Hirschman (1977) in particular made clear.

21. The usual expression is to be "struck" (*itdarab*) by the evil eye.

22. One master expressed this well when he talked about the economic losses of his workshop while he was ill in the hospital. His journeyman had run the business in his absence, and workshop income had gone down about 50 percent. It was clear to him that the journeyman was stealing some of the workshop's income, but he said nothing. "There's nothing to say," he explained. "It's between him and his conscience." That phrase is heard repeatedly in all walks of life in Egyptian Arabic.

23. Essam Fawzi and I began to talk about workshop interactions in terms of networks (*shabakat*) over the course of our fieldwork. At the time, I knew nothing

about the vast literature in sociology concerning networks, or about actor-network theory, or about more recent critiques of the notion of the network. I still find it a useful term for understanding workshops and the value they produce, and have retained it here. Workshop masters do not talk about their interactions in terms of networks.

24. The word used for the reputation of the craftsman and thus of his workshop, *siit*, is different from the word for reputation more commonly used among educated Egyptians, *sum'a*.

25. Masters with a good name in the community regularly organized "saving circles" to help out families or masters in financial trouble, but these saving circles do not involve protecting the value of a "name." In el-Hirafiyeen, some masters who regularly organized saving circles for colleagues or neighbors in financial trouble did not have a good name in the market in the first place. Moreover, a master concerned with protecting his name would be reluctant to receive help that would mark him as one in need.

26. Material in this chapter is based mainly on fieldwork and in-depth interviews in el-Hirafiyeen, although I also draw on fieldwork from other neighborhoods. My discussion focuses on the rules of the game that govern sending customers back and forth, the use of each other's machinery, and access to another workshop's workers. To account for the possibility that the information given by craftsmen is particular to their craft, I always note which craft is under discussion.

27. Masters sometimes drew on Bedouin sayings about the weather to describe the market. Desert dwellers live at the mercy of the weather in the same way that masters felt they lived at the mercy of the market.

28. In the original: *Heina mumkin tu''ud mashghoul 4 shuhur ma tesabbahshi 'ala garak, we ba'deen mumkin tu''ud ba'adaha 13 shahr ma fish shughl.*

29. Taking another's worker is a challenge to authority that is not tolerated, because it threatens the interests of all the craftsmen. Stealing workers generates conflicts needing mediation to settle, or leads to outright fights. While I did not witness any such fights, they were talked about by craftsmen, skilled workers, and their wives.

30. The language of accounting for these "favors" in the original is as follows. To say whom the customer comes from: *min taraf fullan.* For keeping track of favors: *ni'mel hisabna.* Badawi and Hinds (1986) define this as an "act of courtesy," but in English this implies that there is no keeping of accounts, or expectation of return. I use instead the term "favor," since in English favors generally fall within the scope of what Michel Callon calls "calculability" (Callon 1998).

31. This structure of commissions existed only for work sent back and forth between masters in different trades. Each trade had its own practices regarding commissions. The more intense the ongoing exchanges between two masters, the more their exchanges were productive of relational value, and less of monetary compensation. Buyers-in who did not have the cultural capital of the other masters were apt to rely on money to mediate their interactions rather than the modality of

relational value production. Machinists who used expensive, specialized forms of machinery were more likely to establish ongoing exchange relations without money (bil-gada'ana) than those who used very simple tools.

32. For three brilliant and completely different analyses (one fictional, one centuries old) of achieving one's way while avoiding direct confrontation by cleverly using language and brain as "weapons of the weak" (Scott 1985), or trickery, or ruse (all inadequate translations of the idea of the *hiyla* and the verb *ihtaal*), see Mohamed Rajib al-Najar 1981, Yehiya al-Tahir 'Abd Allah 1994, and Rinih Khawwam 1992.

33. See chapter 4, note 11.

34. The going price for renting a paint "oven" during my fieldwork was 100 LE, or about $30.

35. Stauth 1986 makes note of a similar phenomenon among aluminum workshops in Gamaliyya in the 1970s.

36. The lack of this sort of knowledge of highly segmented markets, and of crosscutting relations with different workshops of the same kind in Cairo, seems to be one reason for the failure of the microenterprises in town and elsewhere in Cairo. Entrepreneurs don't know how to enter the market, which they see as an abstract entity rather than a set of relationships reproduced in space and time through regularized exchanges.

37. This is similar to accusations of witchcraft, which are also rarely made directly.

38. But see also Dundes 1981, 268–69, which bases the statement that "eating in public is thought to be especially dangerous with respect to the evil eye" on materials from Egypt and Morocco.

39. Here one could think about the personality of the master in terms of qualisigns of positive value. Personal characteristics of masters were in fact embodied characteristics. See chapter 5, note 48.

40. They avoided the NGO in particular, which was a site where masters attempted to transform their different forms of wealth into direct monetary gain through the mediation of state officials. See chapter 6 for more on this.

41. The word here used for chaos (*moulid*) literally means a popular religious festival, on the anniversary of the birth of a venerated figure.

42. But the same man said, a minute later, that it is "fast, easy money that ruins people," which happened in Heliopolis when the money started flowing in. While the two statements are contradictory on the surface, they both point to a view that people can be ruined by money—lack of it or its influx—without a grounding in social relations and values. Such statements about "how things were" is also a form of structural nostalgia (Herzfeld 1997), as I argued in chapter 3.

43. Juan Campo offers a related analysis of writings and drawings on the walls of houses in popular neighborhoods among those returning from the hajj to Mecca. He argues that this form of symbolic speech offers to the popular classes a power to restore meaning and harmony to the sacred space of the home, after it was disrupted by incursions of various kinds (Campo 1991). For a critique of his approach to

Islamic space and discourse see Elyachar 1994a. Sayyid 'Uways presented an incisive analysis of the writings of the disempowered on forms of public transport in Cairo that showed the relation between this form of political expression and political religious practices in Egypt ('Uways 1989).

44. This formulation is from Essam Fawzi, who shared with me his extensive knowledge of popular religion in Egypt and first alerted me to its importance in workshop life.

45. Writings on workshop walls included excerpts of verses from the Quran such as al-Talaq, verse 3; al-Naml, verse 40; al-Ma'ida, verse 40; and al-Baqara, verse 212.

46. Examples include:

Ma sha' Allah.
Allahu yarzuq man yasha'
Allahuma barik hadha al-makan. (al-Baqara, verse 212)

47. Elsewhere inside the workshop was written the verse: wa ta'awanu 'ala al-bir wa al-taqwa wala ta'awanu 'ala al-ithm wa al-'uduan. (al-Ma'ida, verse 2)

48. In Munn's analysis, bodily qualities—of heaviness, lightness, slowness, torpor—are qualisigns of positive and negative value production in Gawa. As Webb Keane has reminded us, qualisigns were for Peirce unrealized potential that could be actualized only through a particular embodiment. The determination of "what counts" is "thoroughly enmeshed with the dynamics of social value and authority" (Keane 2003, 415).

49. For an analysis of the global cotton market as a market dispositif see Çaliskan 2003.

50. The formulation is from Michel Callon, who pointed this out to me.

Chapter 6: NGOs, Business, and Social Capital

1. World Bank 2001, 200. This report represents a revision of earlier euphoric support for NGOs among many in the development community as a funding channel alternative to the state. It stresses the importance of the state in general and the rule of law in particular.

2. A good brief review of the issues surrounding the Latin American debt crisis and its aftermath, with many references for interested readers, can be found in Castells 1996, 119–33.

3. On NGOs and the development world see Gardner and Lewis 1996, 107. For the first important statement on NGOs in anthropology see Fisher 1997. Ong 1999 discusses NGOs in the context of the state and transnationality in Asia. For other approaches see Elyachar 2001a and Fisher 2001.

4. For an important analysis of the effect of Law 32 on the workings of NGOs in Egypt see Abdel-Rahman 1993.

5. Theoretical analysis of how "the nation" or "the people" had become unhinged from "the state" was echoed in this development praxis. The work of the political

scientist John Ruggie was the most commonly cited among anthropologists on this issue of the nation-state (Ruggie 1993). For an alternative, historically informed analysis of the crisis of the nation-state see Hont 1995.

6. I am indebted to Mara Thomas for this point. The community is another term that bears deconstruction. For relevant discussions of place, community, and the local see Ferguson and Gupta 1997, Agrawal 1999, Scott 1998, 309–41, and Gupta 1998, 174.

7. For an interesting discussion of how some groups get accorded status as legitimate members of civil society and others do not, see Fisher 2001.

8. I benefit here from Strathern (1998, 8–11).

9. In general, the NGO was a site where inversions occurred and positive value production turned into negative. For example, I have said that mastery entailed the ability to shift with ease from different modalities of value production. I have said that conversion of value from one sphere to another is highly productive in workshop life. But in the NGO, this dynamic became inverted.

10. Civic associations have been under state regulation in Egypt since 1964, when the regime of Abdel-Nasser enacted Law 32. The legacy of self-help associations among internal migrants to Cairo is very much alive. There were 823 such migrant associations in Egypt in 1990, 80 percent of them in Greater Cairo. See Bayat 2002, citing the work of Tanada. Bayat's article provides a good comparative overview of associational life in Egypt. See also the research of Amani Qandil, including Qandil 1998, and Bianchi 1989. The historical legacy of the "craft guilds" in Egypt since at least the Ottoman Empire has been the subject of much debate among historians. For an important recent reassessment of the debate see Chalcraft 2004.

11. I develop this argument further elsewhere (Elyachar 2001a, Elyachar 2001b).

12. See Ghannam 1998 and Ghannam 2002 for analysis of another case where the Egyptian state forced residents of one neighborhood to move to another.

13. The name was changed from Craftsmen's Association (*Rabtet el-hirafiyeen*) to Association for the Development of el-Hirafiyeen City (*Al-gam'iyya li-tanmiyyat madinet el-Hirafiyeen*). In Arabic the word designating the type of association changed from rabta to *gam'iyya*; the latter is ordinarily used in Egypt as the translation of an NGO.

14. In this sentence it would be accurate to speak of "strategic power" in the terms of de Certeau (1988). But the concept of "strategy" has had multiple meanings in anthropology since Bourdieu used "strategy" to develop his theory of practice in opposition to static notions of "the rule" (1977). De Certeau contrasts strategic to tactical power in regard to the individual's or group's relation to external forms of power. A strategy can be a basis for generating relations with an "exteriority composed of targets or threats" (1988, 36), whereas a tactic "cannot count on a 'proper' (spatial or institutional) locus" (xix). See Ghannam 1998 for an excellent mobilization of de Certeau's concepts to analyze a housing project in Cairo. De Certeau's concepts of strategy and strategic power are quite different from those of the anthropologist Eric Wolf (1999; 2001), which I draw upon below.

15. We heard many other such stories from a wide range of informants. In this particular case I knew all the parties involved.

16. Transcript of an interview conducted by Essam Fawzi and me in Cairo, 31 October 1994, with Dr. Hamdi el-Sayyid, local member of Parliament. Dr. el-Sayyid amended his remarks about the importance of microenterprise by saying that of course microenterprise could not solve Egypt's employment problems: "When the Khawaga Clinton wants to solve America's employment problems, he doesn't make microenterprises, he makes large public works projects." That this comment might not have accurately reflected funding policies in the United States in the 1990s is not the point.

17. For a relevant discussion of professional native informants see Spivak 1999. Spivak discussed microloans in the context of what she calls the "financialization of the globe" (418–19).

18. The title of Manuel Castells's three-volume book *The Information Age.*

19. Methods of crisis resolution among the masters were shared by them regardless of their origins in different parts of Cairo. From that we can deduce the relevance of what I am talking about here to a sample far wider than that found in el-Hirafiyeen.

20. On *baladi* culture see for example el-Mesiri 1978. For a critique of viewing such neighborhoods of Cairo as the location of the authentic Egyptian spirit, see Ghannam 2002.

21. On rule of law as a strategy for economic development see Kennedy 2004, chapter 5. On private property as capital and the key for development see de Soto 2000. I discuss informal economy extensively in chapter 3 of this book.

22. On "safety nets" and the establishment of social funds see World Bank 1991b, World Bank 2001, and Graham 1995.

23. For a short summary of different views of social capital, including Arrow's view that social networks cannot be viewed as capital because they "are built for reasons other than their economic value to participants," see World Bank 2001, 129. For an overview of perspectives about social capital, see Dasgupta and Serageldin eds. 2000. Their volume includes the critical remarks of Arrow and others, and recounts some of the different trends of research within the bank, including the resignation of Joseph Stiglitz from the World Bank in a policy conflict in 2000. For a critical review of the concept of "social capital" in the bank's literature in particular, see Fine 1999 and Fine 2001.

24. The leading figure of the substantivists was Karl Polanyi. For classic statements of this position, which argued that the rationality of nonwestern systems was still "embedded" in a broader social and cultural system with its own distinct logics and rationales, see Polanyi 1957a, Polanyi 1957c, Chayanov 1966, Dalton 1971, LeClair and Schneider 1968, and from a different perspective, Godelier 1978. For classic statements of the "formalist" position, which argued that economic logic and rationality were universal, see Bohannan and Dalton eds. 1965, LeClair and Schneider 1968, and Schneider 1974.

25. When Robert Putnam used the concept of social capital to discuss what ailed the United States, the term gained broad mainstream currency (Putnam 1993).

26. Michel Callon makes a similar point about problems with the concept of social capital (Callon 1998, 12–13).

27. "In North America, Monsanto has hired Pinkertons (private police) to enforce farm contracts and technology licencing agreements. The "Monster" [Monsanto] has gone after farmers threatening criminal charges wherever they suspect them of trying to save seed. 'In Bangladesh, the Grameen credit network can do Pinkertons' work for the company at no cost,' Mooney argues." Rural Advancement Foundation International (RAFI), "Grameen Turns Mean? From Poverty-Fighter to the Peasants' Pinkerton: Is Bangladesh's Fabled Grameen Bank Turning Mean with Its Monsanto Deal. . . . or Is the 'Monster' Turning Farmer Philanthropist?" Posted on http://www.rafi.org, 7 July 1998. My thanks to Daniel von Moltke for bringing this article to my attention. The Grameen Bank was founded in 1983 by Muhammad Yunus, who is usually seen as the guiding spirit of the microlending business and had become a virtual superstar, lauded during the 1990s by Hillary Clinton, Ted Turner, and George Soros.

28. The other two types of social capital defined here are "bonding social capital," or "ties that connect people who share similar demographic characteristics," and "bridging social capital," or the "horizontal connections to people with broadly comparable economic status and political power" (World Bank 2001, 128).

Chapter 7: Empowering Debt

1. Spivak calls community-based savings and credit programs that are usually organized through NGOs as a "door through which credit-baiting without infrastructural reform enters under globalization, for the sake of the complete financialization of the globe; or, it provides justification for the opening of the world's poor to the commercial sector" (Spivak 1999, 418). To David Harvey, the wave of financialization that set in after 1973 has been as predatory and speculative as those at the beginning of the twentieth century. "Stock promotions, ponzi schemes, structured asset destruction through inflation, asset-stripping through mergers and acquisitions, and the promotion of levels of debt incumbency that reduce whole populations, even in the advanced capitalist countries, to debt peonage, to say nothing of corporate fraud and dispossession of assets. . . . by credit and stock manipulations—all of these are central features of what contemporary capitalism is all about. . . . the speculative raiding carried out by hedge funds and other major institutions of finance capital [is] the cutting edge of accumulation by dispossession in recent times" (Harvey 2003, 147).

2. See for example Cruikshank's analysis of self-government and self-esteem, and of how "poor single mothers on welfare who are enrolled in self-esteem programmes become subjects even as they are subjected to forms of power and government" (Cruikshank 1996, 249).

3. See for example the introduction to a textbook on accounting for NGOs: "Ac-

counting is basically the 'language of business.' It is the language that businesspeople use to talk about the economic realities of their establishments. Like a language, it has rules and dialects. Also like a language, accounting uses its own vocabulary: money. To interpret its prose, one must understand its rules and the definitions of its major terms" (Bartel, McCord, and Bell 1994, 3).

4. See note 2 to chapter 6. But my statements are largely based on my own experience as a research analyst at the New York Federal Reserve Bank between 1982 and 1984. My responsibilities included analyzing unregulated Euromarkets, the potential impact of the Latin American debt crisis on the American banking system, and the impact on the American banking system of what was then called the "computerization of money." Concern about these issues then was often ad hoc.

5. On the Jubilee Coalition, see www.jubilee2000uk.org. For a discussion of debt relief from the point of view of the World Bank, see World Bank 2001, 200–204.

6. See the report from the Bretton Woods Project on a protest outside the offices of the World Bank in London on 26 May 2001 to mark African Liberation Day, at which protesters carried placards proclaiming, "Africa Needs Liberation Not Charity," "The Debt Is a Fraud," and "IMF and World Bank Wanted for Fraud Campaign." Bretton Woods Update no. 23, part 2, 25 June 2001.

7. See "Reality Check on Debt," Bretton Woods Update no. 23, 25 June 2001: "A new report from Drop the Debt argues that the World Bank and IMF can afford to cancel in full the debts of the poorest countries without putting at risk their finances. A World Bank and IMF report released just prior to the Spring Meetings agrees that debt sustainability is not guaranteed by the HIPC initiative because export and growth projections are likely to be too optimistic and new borrowing, including to fight HIV/AIDS, is likely to push debt burdens up quickly. However, Bank President James Wolfensohn argued that giving more debt relief would take resources away from other equally needy countries." See also http://www.dropthedebt.org.

8. Bretton Woods Update no. 3, part 3, 14 December 2000. See also http://www.DebtChannel.org.

9. On the Bretton Woods Project see the web site www.brettonwoodsproject.org.

10. My account is based on interviews with officials of the Industrial Bank of Egypt, the National Bank of Egypt, USAID, the World Bank, and independent consultants.

11. As argued in one paper that summarizes this kind of research (Christen, Ryne, Vogel, and McKean 1994).

12. Only a few banks in Egypt are Islamic and therefore subject to the Islamic prohibition against paying interest. Nevertheless, the training of informal economy outreach workers did entail finding words other than "interest" to describe what borrowers would pay.

13. NGOs established by USAID for informal economy lending were called "foundations" since, I was told, the usual Arabic word for an NGO had traditional overtones of charity.

14. On this history of the working class in Egypt see Lockman ed. 1994.

15. On the history of indebtedness in Egypt and the Ottoman Empire see, for a start, Blaisdell 1929, Shaw 1976, du Velay 1903, and Landes 1958.

16. This strike took place before I began my fieldwork. I did not witness any of the events myself, but rather heard about them from many different informants and points of view.

17. I do not give a name to this official since my own informants did not want to give me his name.

18. My thanks to Michel Callon for pointing this out to me.

19. For a different analysis of the productivity of debt see Roitman 2003, Roitman 2005.

Bibliography

'Abd al-Halim 'Amr, 'Abd el-Salam. 1993. *Tawa'if al-Hirif fi Masr*. Cairo: Dar al-Mustaqbal al-'Arabi.

'Abd Allah, Yehiya al-Tahir. 1994. *Al-Kitabat at-kamila*. Al-Qahira: Dar al-Mustaqbal al-'Arabi.

Abdel-Latif, Omayma. 1995. "Little Workers." *El-Ahram Weekly*, 12–18 January.

Abdel-Rahman, Maha Mahfouz. 1993. M.A. thesis, American University in Cairo.

Abrams, Philip. 1988. "Notes on the Difficulty of Studying the State." *Journal of Historical Sociology* 1, no. 1:58–89.

Abu-Lughod, Lila. 1989. "Zones of Theory in the Anthropology of the Arab World." *Annual Review of Anthropology* 18:267–306.

——. 2000. "Modern Subjects: Egyptian Melodrama and Postcolonial Difference." *Questions of Modernity*, ed. Timothy Mitchell. Minneapolis: University of Minnesota Press. 87–114.

Adams, Julia. 1993. "Working-Class Politics in Nineteenth-Century Toulouse, France: Paths of Proletarianization Revisited." *Social Science History* 17, no. 2:195–225.

Agrawal, Arun. 1995. "Dismantling the Divide between Indigenous and Scientific Knowledge." *Development and Change* 26:413–30.

——. 1999. *Greener Pastures: Politics, Markets, and Community among a Migrant Pastoral People*. Durham: Duke University Press.

Ahmed, Ali. 1984. *Al-Qur'an. A Contemporary Translation*. Princeton: Princeton University Press.

Ahmed, Jamal Mohammed. 1960. *The Intellectual Origins of Egyptian Nationalism*. London: Oxford University Press.

Ali, Kamran Asdar. 2002. *Planning the Family in Egypt: New Bodies, New Selves*. Austin: University of Texas Press.

al-Nadim, 'Abdallah. 1994. *'Abdallah al-Nadim: al-'Adad al-kamila li majallat al-ustadh*. Cairo: al-Hi'ya al-'amma l-il-kitab.

al-Najar, Mohamed Rajib. 1981. *Al-shuttaar wa al-'ayyarun fi al-turaath al-'arabi*. Al-Kuwait: Al-maglis al-watani lil-thaqafa wa al-fanoun wa al-aadaab.

Amin, Galal, and 'Awny, E. 1985. *International Migration of Egyptian Labour: A Review of the State of the Art: Manuscript Report*. Ottawa: International Development Research Center.

Amin, Samir. 1974. *Modern Migrations in the Middle East*. New York: Oxford University Press.

Anderson, Benedict. 1983. *Imagined Communities: Reflections on the Origin and Spread of Nationalism*. London: Verso.

Appadurai, Arjun, ed. 1986. *The Social Life of Things: Commodities in Cultural Perspective*. Cambridge: Cambridge University Press.

——. 1993. "Patriotism and Its Futures." *Public Culture* 5, no. 3: 411–29.

——. 1995. "The Production of Locality." *Counterworks: Managing the Diversity of Knowledge*, ed. Richard Fardon. New York: Routledge. 204–25.

——. 2000. "Grassroots Globalization and the Research Imagination." *Public Culture* 12, no. 1:1–19.

Arrow, Kenneth J., and F. H. Hahn. 1971. *General Competitive Analysis*. San Francisco: Holden-Day.

Asad, Talal. 1986. "The Idea of an Anthropology of Islam." Occasional Papers Series, Center for Contemporary Arab Studies, Georgetown University.

——, ed. 1988. *Anthropology and the Colonial Encounter*. Atlantic Highlands, N.J.: Humanities Press.

Assaad, Ragui. 1993. "Formal and Informal Institutions in the Labor Market, with Applications to the Construction Sector in Egypt." *World Development* 21, no. 6: 925–39.

——. 1996. "Formalizing the Informal? The Transformation of Cairo's Refuse Collection System." *Journal of Planning Education and Research* 16:115–26.

Assaad, Ragui, Yu Zhou, and Omar Razzaz. 1997. "Why Is Informality a Useful Analytical Category for Understanding Social Networks and Institutions?" MacArthur Consortium Working Paper Series, Institute for International Studies, University of Minnesota.

Badawi, el-Said, and Martin Hinds. 1986. *A Dictionary of Egyptian Arabic*. Beirut: Librairie du Liban.

Baer, Gabriel. 1964. *Egyptian Guilds in Modern Times*. Jerusalem: Israeli Oriental Society.

——. 1969. "Decline and Disappearance of the Guilds." *Studies in the Social History of Modern Egypt*. Chicago: University of Chicago Press.

——. 1982. *Fellah and Townsman in the Middle East*. London: Frank Cass.

Barry, Andrew, Thomas Osborne, and Nikolas Rose, eds. 1996. *Foucault and Political Reason: Liberalism, Neo-liberalism, and Rationalities of Government*. London: UCL Press.

Bartel, Margaret, Michael J. McCord, and Robin R. Bell. 1994. "Fundamentals of Accounting for Microcredit Programs: Tools for Microenterprise Programs: Financial Assistance Section." Gemini Project, U.S. Agency for International Development.

Bayart, J. F., S. Ellis, and B. Hibou, eds. 1997. *La criminalisation de l'état en Afrique.* Brussels: Complexe.

Bayat, Asef. 2002. "Activism and Social Development in the Middle East." *International Journal of Middle East Studies* 34:1–28.

Becker, Gary. 1963. *Human Capital: A Theoretical and Empirical Analysis, with Special Reference to Education.* New York: National Bureau of Economic Research.

Beinin, Joel, and Zachary Lockman. 1987. *Workers on the Nile: Nationalism, Communism, Islam, and the Egyptian Working Class, 1882–1954.* Princeton: Princeton University Press.

Beneria, L. 1989. "Subcontracting and Employment Dynamics in Mexico City." *The Informal Economy,* ed. Alejandro Portes, Manuel Castells, and Lauren Benton. 173–88.

Berry, Sara S. 1995. "Stable Prices, Unstable Values: Some Thoughts on Monetization and the Meaning of Transactions in West African Economies." *Money Matters,* ed. Jane Guyer.

Bertaux, Daniel, ed. 1981. *Biography and Society: The Life History Approach in the Social Sciences.* Beverly Hills: Sage.

Bertaux, Daniel, and Isabelle Bertaux-Wiame. 1981. "Life Stories in the Bakers' Trade." *Biography and Society,* ed. Daniel Bertaux. 169–89.

——. 1997. "Heritage and Its Lineage: A Case History of Transmission and Social Mobility over Five Generations." *Pathways to Social Class: A Qualitative Approach to Social Mobility,* ed. Daniel Bertaux and Paul Thompson. Oxford: Clarendon. 62–98.

Besançon, Jacques. 1958. "Une Banlieue du Caire: Héliopolis." *Revue de Géographie de Lyon* 33, no. 2.

Bianchi, Robert. 1989. *Unruly Corporatism: Associational Life in Twentieth-Century Egypt.* New York: Oxford University Press.

Blaisdell, Donald C. 1929. *European Financial Control in the Ottoman Empire.* New York: Columbia University Press.

Blaug, Mark. 1985. *Economic Theory in Retrospect.* Cambridge: Cambridge University Press.

Boeke, J. H. 1953. *Economics and Economic Policy of Dual Societies as Exemplified by Indonesia.* New York: International Secretariat of Pacific Relations.

Bohannan, Paul, and George Dalton, eds. 1965. *Markets in Africa: Eight Subsistence Economies in Transition.* New York: Doubleday.

Booth, Marilyn. 1990. *Bayram al-Tunisi's Egypt: Social Criticism and Narrative Strategies.* Exeter: Ithaca Press for the Middle East Centre, St. Antony's College, Oxford.

Bourdieu, Pierre. 1965. "The Sentiment of Honour in Kabyle Society." *Honour and Shame: The Values of Mediterranean Society,* ed. J. Péristiany. Chicago: University of Chicago Press. 193–241.

——. 1977. *Outline of a Theory of Practice.* Trans. Richard Nice. Cambridge: Cambridge University Press.

——. 1984. *Distinction: A Social Critique of the Judgement of Taste.* Trans. Richard Nice. Cambridge: Harvard University Press.

——. 1999. "Rethinking the State: Genesis and Structure of the Bureaucratic Field." *State/Culture: State-Formation after the Cultural Turn,* ed. George Steinmetz. Ithaca: Cornell University Press. 53–75.

Bowley, Marian. 1937. *Nassau Senior and Classical Economics.* London: George Allen and Unwin.

Breslau, Daniel. 2003. "Rationalizing Strategy: Game Theory in Management Pedagogy and Practice." *Social Analysis* 47, no. 1:53–64.

Buckingham, James S. 1849. *National Evils and Practical Remedies, with the Plan of a Model Town.* London: Peter Jackson, Late Fisher, Son.

Burawoy, Michael. 2000. "Grounding Globalization." *Global Ethnography,* ed. M. Burawoy, J. Blum, et al. Berkeley: University of California Press. 337–50.

Burawoy, Michael, and Katherine Verdery, eds. 1999. *Uncertain Transition: Ethnographies of Change in the Postsocialist World.* New York: Rowman and Littlefield.

Burchell, Graham. 1996. "Liberal Government and Techniques of the Self." *Foucault and Political Reason,* ed. Andrew Barry, Thomas Osborne, and Nikolas Rose. 19–36.

Burchell, Graham, Colin Gordon, and Peter Miller, eds. 1991. *The Foucault Effect: Studies in Governmentality.* Chicago: University of Chicago Press.

Burgess, John. 2000. "As the World Bank Meets: Serving the Poor, and Serving Time: Staff Asks, 'Why Us?' " *International Herald Tribune,* 14 April, 19.

Burt, Ronald S. 1993. "The Social Structure of Competition." *Explorations in Economic Sociology,* ed. Richard Swedburg. New York: Russell Sage Foundation. 65–103.

Cahen, Claude. 1970. "Y a-t-il des corporations professionnelles dans le monde musulman classique?" *The Islamic City,* ed. Albert Hourani and S. M. Stern. Oxford: Oxford University Press.

Çaliskan, Koray. 2003. "Price Realization in World Markets: The Prosthetic and Actual Worth of a Bale of Cotton." Paper presented at the conference Economics at Large, New York University, 14–15 November.

Callon, Michel. 1998. "The Embeddedness of Economic Markets in Economics." *The Laws of the Markets.* Oxford: Basil Blackwell / Sociological Review. 1–57.

Campbell, Colin. 1987. *The Romantic Ethic and the Spirit of Modern Consumerism.* Cambridge: Cambridge University Press.

Campo, Juan Eduardo. 1991. *The Other Sides of Paradise: Explorations into the Religious Meanings of Domestic Space in Islam.* Columbia: University of South Carolina Press.

Castells, Manuel. 1996. *The Rise of the Network Society.* Vol. 1 of *The Information Age: Economy, Society and Culture.* Malden: Basil Blackwell.

——. 1997. *The Power of Identity.* Vol. 2 of *The Information Age: Economy, Society and Culture.* Malden: Basil Blackwell.

——. 1998. *End of Millennium.* Vol. 3 of *The Information Age: Economy, Society and Culture.* Malden: Basil Blackwell.

Castells, Manuel, and Alejandro Portes. 1989. "World Underneath: The Origins, Dynamics, and Effects of the Informal Economy." *The Informal Economy*, ed. Alejandro Portes, Manuel Castells, and Lauren Benton. 11–37.

Chalcraft, John. 2004. *The Striking Cabbies of Cairo and Other Stories: Crafts and Guilds in Egypt, 1863–1914.* Albany: State University of New York Press.

Charmes, Jacques. 1990. "Une revue critique des concepts, définitions, et recherches sur le secteur informel." *Nouvelles approches du secteur informel.* Paris: Centre de Développement de l'Organisation de Coopération et de Développement Économiques. 11–51.

———. 1992. "Le secteur informel, nouvel enjeu des politiques de développement?" *L'homme et la société* 105–6:63–77.

Chayanov, Aleksandr V. [1925] 1966. *The Theory of Peasant Economy.* Homewood, Ill.: R. D. Irwin for the Economic Association.

Choucri, Nazli, with the collaboration of Peter Brecke. 1983. *Migration in the Middle East: Transformations, Policies, and Processes.* Technology Adaptation Program, Massachusetts Institute of Technology.

Christen, Robert Peck, Elisabeth Ryne, Robert C. Vogel, and Cressida McKean. 1995. "Maximizing the Outreach of Microenterprise Finance: An Analysis of Successful Microfinance Programs." Washington: U.S. Agency for International Development.

Clark, Gracia, ed. 1988. *Traders versus the State.* Boulder: Westview.

Cohen, Jean L. 1985. "Strategy or Identity: New Theoretical Paradigms and Contemporary Social Movements." *Social Research* 52, no. 4: 663–716.

Cohn, Bernard S. 1986. *An Anthropologist among the Historians and Other Essays.* Delhi: Oxford University Press.

———. 1996. *Colonialism and Its Forms of Knowledge: The British in India.* Princeton: Princeton University Press.

Coleman, James. 1988. "Social Capital in the Creation of Human Capital." *American Journal of Sociology* 94:S95–S120 (supplement). Repr. in *Social Capital*, ed. Dasgupta and Serageldin.

Comaroff, Jean, and John L. Comaroff, eds. 1999. *Civil Society and the Political Imagination in Africa: Critical Perspectives.* Chicago: University of Chicago Press.

Community Economics Corporation. 1993. "Lending and Learning: Formal Banks and Microenterprise in Egypt." Prepared for the Ford Foundation, Cairo.

Community Economies Collective. 2001. "Imagining and Enacting Noncapitalist Futures." *Socialist Review* 28, nos. 3–4:93–135.

Cook, M.A. 1970. *Studies in the Economic History of the Middle East: From the Rise of Islam to the Present Day.* London: Oxford University Press.

Cooper, Frederick, and Randall Packard, eds. 1997. *International Development and the Social Sciences: Essays on the History and Politics of Knowledge.* Berkeley: University of California Press.

Cooper, Frederick, and Ann Stoler, eds. 1989. *Tensions of Empire: Colonial Cultures in a Bourgeois World.* Berkeley: University of California Press.

Coronil, Fernando. 1997. *The Magical State: Nature, Money, and Modernity in Venezuela*. Chicago: University of Chicago Press.

Crabbs, Jack A., Jr. 1984. *The Writing of History in Nineteenth-Century Egypt: A Study in National Transformation*. Cairo: American University in Cairo Press.

Crapanzano, Vincent. 1980. *Tuhami: Portrait of a Moroccan*. Chicago: University of Chicago Press.

Cruikshank, Barbara. 1996. "Revolutions Within: Self-Government and Self-Esteem." *Foucault and Political Reason*, ed. Andrew Barry, Thomas Osborne, and Nikolas Rose. 231–52.

Dalton, George. 1971. *Studies in Economic Anthropology*. Washington: American Anthropological Association.

Dasgupta, Partha, and Ismail Serageldin, eds. 2000. *Social Capital: A Multifaceted Perspective*. Washington: World Bank.

Davidson, Sidney, James S. Schindler, and Roman L. Weil. 1974. *Accounting: The Language of Business*. Glen Ridge, N. J.: T. Horton.

Davis, Eric. 1983. *Challenging Colonialism: Bank Misr and Egyptian Industrialization, 1920–1941*. Princeton: Princeton University Press.

Dean, Mitchell. 1996. "Foucault, Government, and the Enfolding of Authority." *Foucault and Political Reason*, ed. Andrew Barry, Thomas Osborne, and Nikolas Rose. 209–30.

de Certeau, Michel. 1988. *The Practice of Everyday Life*. Berkeley: University of California Press.

Delanoue, Gilbert. 1961–62. "'Abd Allah Nadim (1845–1896): Les idées politiques et morales d'un journaliste Égyptien." *Bulletin d'Études Orientales* 17:75–120.

Denby, Edwin. 1965. *Dancers, Buildings and People in the Street*. New York: Horizon.

Denis, Eric. 1994. "La Mise En Scène des 'Ashwaiyyat, Premier acte: Imbâba, Décembre 1992." *Égypte/Monde Arabe* 20.

———. 1995. "Le Caire: Aspects sociaux de l'étalement urbain: Entre spécialisation et mixité." *Égypte / Monde arabe* 23 (3d trimester): 77–130.

de Soto, Hernando. 1989. *The Other Path: The Invisible Revolution in the Third World*. New York: Harper and Row.

———. 2000. *The Mystery of Capital: Why Capitalism Triumphs in the West and Fails Everywhere Else*. New York: Bantam.

Dickson, P. G. M. 1967. *The Financial Revolution in England: A Study in the Development of Public Credit, 1688–1756*. London: Macmillan.

Dilley, Roy, ed. 1992. *Contesting Markets: Analyses of Ideology, Discourse, and Practice*. Edinburgh: Edinburgh University Press.

Dobb, Maurice. 1973. *Theories of Value and Distribution since Adam Smith: Ideology and Economic Theory*. Cambridge: Cambridge University Press.

Douglas, Mary. 1990. "No Free Gifts." Foreword to *The Gift: The Form and Reason for Exchange in Archaic Societies*, by Marcel Mauss. New York: W. W. Norton.

Dube, S. C. 1988. *Modernization and Development: The Search for Alternative Paradigms*. Tokyo: United Nations University.

Dundes, Alan. 1981. *The Evil Eye: A Folklore Casebook*. New York: Garland.

Dunn, John, ed. 1990. *The Economic Limits to Modern Politics*. Cambridge: Cambridge University Press.

du Velay, A. 1903. *Essai sur l'histoire financière de la Turquie depuis le règne du Sultan Mahoud II jusqu'à nos jours*. Paris: Rousseau.

Early, Evelyn. 1993. *Baladi Women of Cairo: Playing with an Egg and a Stone*. Boulder: L. Rienner.

el-Bahr, Sahar. 1996. "The Flash Factor: A Car with a History." *El-Ahram Weekly*, 7–13 March, 13.

el-Kadi, Galila. 1987. *L'urbanisation spontanée au Caire*. Fascicule de Recherches. Tours: URBAMA-ORSTOM.

——. 1989. "Trente ans de planification urbaine au Caire." *Revue Tiers-Monde* 121, January–March. Paris: Presses Universitaires de France. 166–85.

——. 1994. "Le Caire: La ville spontanée sous contrôle." *Monde arabe-Maghreb-Machrek*. Special issue. 1st trimester. 30–41.

El Mahdy, Alia. 1995. "The Informal Sector in Egypt: A Brief Literature Review." Paper presented at the workshop The Dynamics of the Informal and Small-Scale Enterprise Sector, Aswan, Egypt, 1–3 December.

el-Mesiri, Sawsan. 1978. *Ibn al-Balad: A Concept of Egyptian Identity*. Leiden: E. J. Brill.

Elyachar, Julia. 1991. "Talking in Tongues: The Making and Remaking of Knowledge, Finance, and Institutions between the Ottoman and British Empires, 1850–1895." M.A. paper, Department of Anthropology and Center for Middle Eastern Studies, Harvard University.

——. 1993. "The Impact of Gulf Migration on Egyptian Constructions of Identity and Economy as Seen from the Street in Cairo." Paper presented at the Seventh Annual SSRC–MacArthur Foundation Fellows' Conference, May 1993, Istanbul.

——. 1994a. "The Other Sides of Paradise." Review article of Juan Eduardo Campo: *The Other Sides of Paradise: Explorations into the Religious Meanings of Domestic Space in Islam, Harvard Middle Eastern and Islamic Review*.

——. 1994b. "Capturing Informality: The Interaction between the Informal Economy, the State, the Supra-State, and NGOs in Egypt." Research Report, SSRC-MacArthur Foundation, May 1994.

——. 1996. "Developing Informality: The State, International Organizations, and NGOs in a Model Workshop Town of Cairo." Paper presented in the session "Beyond the State: International Organizations, Civil Society, and NGOs in the Global Age" at the 95th annual meeting of the American Anthropological Association, San Francisco, 11 November.

——. 1997. "Masters without Craft, Apprentices without Masters: Properties of Mastery in Three Craft Workshops of Cairo." Paper presented at the panel "Mimetic Practices, Crafted Selves: Labor, Performance, and Formations of Power," 96th annual meeting of the American Anthropological Association, Washington, 19–23 November.

——. 2001a. "NGOs and the Religion of Civil Society in the 'Informal Economy' of Cairo." *Critique Internationale*, October, 139–52.

——. 2001b. "Rural Labor Movements in Egypt and Their Impact on the State, 1961–1992: A Review Article." *American Ethnologist*, autumn.

——. 2001c. "The Illicit Relations of Seattle and Wall Street: Anti-Globalization Movements and Anti-Development in the World Bank." *Časopis za kritiko znanosti*, Ljubljana.

——. 2002. "Empowerment Money: The World Bank, NGOs, and the Value of Culture in Egypt." *Public Culture* 14, no. 3: 493–513.

——. 2003. "Mappings of Power: The State, NGOs, and International Organizations in the Informal Economy of Cairo." *Comparative Studies in Society and History* 45:3.

——. 2005. "Economic Anthropology of the Middle East." *Handbook of Economic Anthropology*, ed. James Carrier. Cheltenham: Edward Elgar.

Emirbayer, Mustafa. 1997. "Manifesto for a Relational Sociology." *American Journal of Sociology* 103:281–317.

Escobar, Arturo. 1995. *Encountering Development: The Making and Unmaking of the Third World*. Princeton: Princeton University Press.

Escobar, Arturo, and Sonia E. Alvarez, eds. 1992. *The Making of Social Movements in Latin America: Identity, Strategy, and Democracy*. Boulder: Westview.

Esteva, Gustavo. 1992. "Development." *The Development Dictionary*, ed. Wolfgang Sachs.

Fabian, Johannes. 1983. *Time and the Other: How Anthropology Makes Its Object*. New York: Columbia University Press.

——. 2001. *Anthropology with an Attitude: Critical Essays*. Stanford: Stanford University Press.

Fergany, Nader. 1991. "A Characterisation of the Employment Problem in Egypt." *Employment and Structural Adjustment*, ed. Heba Handoussa and Gillian Potter.

Ferguson, Adam. [1767] 1966. *An Essay on the History of Civil Society*. Ed. D. Forbes. Edinburgh: Edinburgh University Press.

Ferguson, James. 1990. *The Anti-Politics Machine: "Development," Depoliticization, and Bureaucratic Power in Lesotho*. Cambridge: Cambridge University Press.

——. 1999. *Expectations of Modernity: Myths and Meanings of Urban Life on the Zambian Copperbelt*. Berkeley: University of California Press.

Ferguson, James, and Akhil Gupta. 1997. "Discipline and Practice: 'The Field' as Site, Method, and Location in Anthropology." *Anthropological Locations*, ed. Akhil Gupta and James Ferguson. Berkeley: University of California Press. 1–46.

——. 2002. "Spatializing States: Toward an Ethnography of Neoliberal Governmentality." *American Ethnologist* 24, no. 4:981–1002.

Fine, Ben. 1999. "The Developmental State Is Dead—Long Live Social Capital?" *Development and Change* 30:1–20.

——. 2001. *Social Capital versus Social Theory: Political Economy and Social Science at the Turn of the Millennium*. London: Routledge.

Finnemore, Martha. 1997. "Redefining Development at the World Bank." *International Development and the Social Sciences*, ed. Frederick Cooper and Randall Packard. 203–27.

Fisher, William. 1997. "Doing Good? The Politics and Antipolitics of NGO Practices." *Annual Review of Anthropology* 26:439–64.

———. 2001. "Global Civil Society and Its Fragments." *Critique Internationale*, October.

Foucault, Michel. 1977. *Discipline and Punish: The Birth of the Prison*. Trans. A. Sheridan. New York: Pantheon.

———. 1980. *Power/Knowledge: Selected Interviews and Other Writings, 1972–1977*. Ed. C. Gordon. New York: Pantheon.

———. 1991. "Governmentality." *The Foucault Effect*, ed. Graham Burchell, Colin Gordon, and Peter Miller. 87–104.

Friedman, Milton. 1962. *Capitalism and Freedom*. Chicago: University of Chicago Press.

Frow, John. 1997. *Time and Commodity Culture: Essays in Cultural Theory and Postmodernity*. Oxford: Oxford University Press.

Gardner, Katy, and David Lewis. 1996. *Anthropology, Development, and the Post-Modern Challenge*. London: Pluto.

Geertz, Clifford. 1962. "The Rotating Credit Association: A 'Middle Rung' in Development." *Economic Development and Cultural Change* 10:240–63.

———. 1963a. *Agricultural Involution: The Processes of Change in Indonesia*. Berkeley: University of California Press.

———. 1963b. *Peddlers and Princes: Social Change and Economic Modernization in Two Indonesian Towns*. Chicago: University of Chicago Press.

Gerber, Haim. 1976. "Guilds in Seventeenth Century Anatolian Bursa." *Asian and African Studies* 11:59–86.

Ghani, Ashraf. 1992. "Theory and Mode of Presentation: From Malinowski to Marx." Lecture presented at the Massachusetts Institute of Technology, 18 November.

———. 1996. "Production and Reproduction of Property as a Bundle of Powers: Afghanistan 1774–1901." Paper presented at the Agrarian Studies Program, Yale University.

Ghannam, Farha. 1998. "The Visual Remaking of Urban Space: Relocation and the Use of Public Housing in 'Modern' Cairo." *Visual Anthropology* 10:265–80.

———. 2002. *Remaking the Modern: Space, Relocation, and the Politics of Identity in a Global Cairo*. Berkeley: University of California Press.

Ghazaleh, Pascale. 1995. "The Guilds, Between Tradition and Modernity." *The State and Its Servants*, ed. Nelly Hanna. 60–74.

Ghosh, Amitav. 1983. "The Relations of Envy in an Egyptian Village." *Ethnology* 22, no. 3: 211–23.

———. 1992. *In an Antique Land: History in the Guise of a Traveler's Tale*. New York: Vintage.

Gibb, H. A. R., and Harold Bowen. 1957. *Islamic Society and the West: A Study of the Impact of Western Civilization on Muslem Culture in the Near East.* London: Oxford University Press.

Gibson-Graham, J. K. Forthcoming 2006. *Reluctant Subjects: Ethics and Emotions for a Post-Capitalist Politics.* Minneapolis: University of Minnesota Press.

Giddens, Anthony. 1985. *The Nation-State and Violence.* Cambridge: Polity.

Giugale, Marcelo, and Sherif El-Diwany. 1995. "Informality, Size and Regulation: Theory and an Application to Egypt." Unpublished paper.

Gluckman, Max. 1967. *The Judicial Process among the Barotse of Northern Rhodesia.* 2d ed. Manchester: Manchester University Press.

Godelier, Maurice. 1978. "The Object and Method of Economic Anthropology." *Relations of Production*, ed. David Seddon. 49–126.

Goitein, S. D. 1967–93. *A Mediterranean Society: The Jewish Communities of the Arab World as Portrayed in the Documents of the Cairo Geniza.* Berkeley: University of California Press.

Gordon, Colin. 1991. "Government Rationality: An Introduction." *The Foucault Effect*, ed. Graham Burchell, Colin Gordon, and Peter Miller. 1–52.

——. 1996. "Foucault in Britain." *Foucault and Political Reason*, ed. Andrew Barry, Thomas Osborne, and Nikolas Rose. 253–70.

Government of Egypt, Ministry of Development, New Communities, Housing and Public Utilities. 1991. *Greater Cairo Region Master Scheme: Implementation Assessment Updating Proposals.* Institut d'Aménagement et d'Urbanisme de la Region d'Île de France, General Organization for Physical Planning, Egypt, May.

Government of Egypt, Social Fund for Development. 1995. *Annual Report 1994.*

Graeber, David. 2001. *Toward an Anthropological Theory of Value: The False Coin of Our Own Dreams.* New York: Palgrave.

Graham, Carol. 1994. *Safety Nets, Politics, and the Poor: Transitions to Market Economies.* Washington: Brookings Institution.

Gupta, Akhil. 1995. "Blurred Boundaries: The Discourse of Corruption, the Culture of Politics, and the Imagined State." *American Ethnologist* 22, no. 2:375–402.

——. 1998. *Postcolonial Developments: Agriculture in the Making of Modern India.* Durham: Duke University Press.

Gupta, Akhil, and Ferguson, James, eds. 1997. *Anthropological Locations: Boundaries and Grounds of a Field Science.* Berkeley: University of California Press.

Guyer, Jane. 1994. "The Spatial Dimensions of Civil Society in Africa: An Anthropologist Looks at Nigeria." *Civil Society and the State in Africa*, ed. J. W. Harbeson, D. Rothchild, and N. Chazan. Boulder: L. Rienner. 215–30.

——, ed. 1995. *Money Matters: Instability, Values and Social Payments in the Modern History of West African Communities.* Portsmouth, N.H.: Heinemann.

Haeri, Niloofar. 1997. *The Sociolinguistic Market of Cairo: Gender, Class, and Education.* London: Kegan Paul International.

Handoussa, Heba. 1991. "Crisis and Challenge: Prospects for the 1990s." *Employment and Structural Adjustment*, ed. Heba Handoussa and Gillian Potter.

——. 1992. "Egypt's Informal Sector: Engine of Growth?" Paper presented to the Middle East Studies Association Conference, Portland, Oregon, 28–31 October.

Handoussa, Heba, and Gillian Potter, eds. 1991. *Employment and Structural Adjustment: Egypt in the 1990s*. Cairo: American University in Cairo Press.

Hann, Chris, ed. 1998. *Property Relations: Renewing the Anthropological Tradition*. Cambridge: Cambridge University Press.

Hann, Chris, and Elizabeth Dunn, eds. 1996. *Civil Society: Challenging Western Models*. New York: Routledge.

Hanna, Nelly, ed. 1995. *The State and Its Servants: Administration in Egypt from Ottoman Times to the Present*. Cairo: American University in Cairo Press.

Harper, Malcolm. 1993. "From the Editor." *Small Enterprise Development* 4, no. 4.

Harrison, Bennett. 1994. *Lean and Mean: The Changing Landscape of Corporate Power in the Age of Flexibility*. New York: Basic Books.

Hart, Keith. 1973. "Informal Income Opportunities and Urban Employment in Ghana." *Journal of Modern African Studies* 11:61–89.

——. 1992. "Market and State after the Cold War: The Informal Economy Reconsidered." *Contesting Markets*, ed. Roy Dilley. 214–26.

——. 2001. *Money in an Unequal World: Keith Hart and His Memory Bank*. New York: Texere.

Harvey, David. 2003. *The New Imperialism*. Oxford: Oxford University Press.

Haykal, Muhammad Hasanayn. 1996. "Al-Nar taqtaribmin al-hatab." *al-Sha'ab*, 3 March.

Henry, Clement M., and Robert Springborg. 2001. *Globalization and the Politics of Development in the Middle East*. Cambridge: Cambridge University Press.

Herzfeld, Michael. 1981. "Meaning and Morality: A Semiotic Approach to Evil Eye Accusations in a Greek Village." *American Ethnologist* 8:560–74.

——. 1992. *The Social Production of Indifference: Exploring the Symbolic Roots of Western Bureaucracy*. Chicago: University of Chicago Press.

——. 1997. *Cultural Intimacy: Social Poetics in the Nation-State*. New York: Routledge.

Heyman, Josiah McC., ed. 1999. *States and Illegal Practices*. Oxford: Berg.

Hibou, Béatrice, ed. 1999. *La privatisation des états*. Paris: Karthala.

Hindess, Barry. 1996. *Discourses of Power: From Hobbes to Foucault*. Oxford: Basil Blackwell.

Hinnebusch, Raymond A., Jr. 1985. *Egyptian Politics under Sadat: The Post-Populist Development of an Authoritarian-Modernizing State*. Cambridge: Cambridge University Press.

Hirschman, Albert O. 1977. *The Passions and the Interests: Political Arguments for Capitalism before Its Triumph*. Princeton: Princeton University Press.

Hobbes, Thomas. [1651] 1968. *Leviathan*. Ed. C. B. Macpherson. Baltimore: Pelican Classics.

Hodgson, Marshall G. S. 1974. *The Expansion of Islam in the Middle Periods*. Vol. 2 of

The Venture of Islam: Conscience and History in a World Civilization. Chicago: University of Chicago Press.

Hont, Istvan. 1983. "The 'Rich Country—Poor Country' Debate in Scottish Classical Political Economy." *Wealth and Virtue: The Shaping of Political Economy in the Scottish Enlightenment*, ed. Istvan Hont and Michael Ignatieff. Cambridge: Cambridge University Press.

——. 1990. "Free Trade and the Economic Limits to National Politics: Neo-Machiavellian Political Economy Reconsidered." *The Economic Limits to Modern Politics*, ed. John Dunn.

——. 1993. "The Rhapsody of Public Debt: David Hume and Voluntary State Bankruptcy." *Political Discourse in Early Modern Britain*, ed. Nicholas Phillipson and Quentin Skinner.

——. 1995. "The Permanent Crisis of a Divided Mankind: 'Contemporary Crisis of the Nation State' in Historical Perspective." *Contemporary Crisis of the Nation State*, ed. J. Dunn. Oxford: Oxford University Press.

Hont, Istvan, and Michael Ignatieff. 1983. "Needs and Justice in the Wealth of Nations: An Introductory Essay." *Wealth and Virtue: The Shaping of Political Economy in the Scottish Enlightenment*, ed. Istvan Hont and Michael Ignatieff. Cambridge: Cambridge University Press.

Hoodfar, Homa. 1997. *Between Marriage and the Market: Intimate Politics and Survival in Cairo*. Berkeley: University of California Press.

Hume, David. 1985. "Of Public Credit." *David Hume, Essays Moral, Political and Literary*, ed. E. F. Miller. Indianapolis: Liberty Classics.

Humphrey, Caroline. 1996–97. "Myth Making, Narratives, and the Dispossessed in Russia." *Cambridge Anthropology* 19, no. 2:70–92 (Ernest Gellner Memorial Issue).

Humphrey, Caroline, and Stephen Hugh-Jones, eds. 1992. *Barter, Exchange, and Value: An Anthropological Approach*. Cambridge: Cambridge University Press.

Hussmanns, Ralf. 1996. "ILO's Recommendations on Methodologies Concerning Informal Sector Data Collection." *Unveiling the Informal Sector: More than Counting Heads*, ed. B. Herman and W. Stoffers. Aldershot: Avebury.

Ilbert, Robert. 1981. *Heliopolis: Genèse d'une ville*. Paris: Centre National de la Recherche Scientifique.

——. 1985. "Heliopolis: Colonial Enterprise and Town Planning Success?" *The Expanding Metropolis: Coping with Urban Growth of Cairo*. Proceedings of Seminar Nine in the Series Architectural Transformations in the Islamic World, Held in Cairo, Egypt, November 11–15, 1984. Aga Khan Awards.

——. 1989. "Égypte 1900, Habitat Populaire, Société Coloniale." *État, ville et mouvements sociaux au Maghreb et au Moyen-Orient*, ed. K. Brown et al. Paris: L'Harmattan.

Inalcik, Halil. 1985. *Studies in Ottoman Social and Economic History*. London: Variorum Reprints.

Issawi, Charles. 1963. *Egypt in Revolution: An Economic Analysis*. London: Oxford University Press.

——, ed. 1966. *The Economic History of the Middle East, 1800–1914*. Chicago: University of Chicago Press.

Jones, R.M. 1988. "Small Scale Industry in Egypt: An Examination of Channels Available to Donors for Activities in Small Scale Industry Sector in Egypt." Final Report Prepared for the Development and Co-operation Division of the Netherlands Embassy, Cairo, June 1988.

Jossifort, Sabine. 1991. *Les New-Settlements: Une Tentative Inachevée d'un Habitat Social au Caire*. Paris: Institut d'Urbanisme de Paris.

——. 1993. "Les 'new settlements' du Cairo." Lettre d'information de l'Observatoire urbain du Caire contemporain, Supplément à la Lettre d'information, Numéro 33, July.

Kaji, Gautam S., and Percy S. Mistry. 2000. "Streamline the International Financial System." *International Herald Tribune*, 18 April, 8.

Kapferer, Bruce. 1976. "Conflict and Process in a Zambian Mine Community." *Freedom and Constraint: A Memorial Tribute to Max Gluckman*, ed. M. J. Aronoff. Amsterdam: Van Gorcum.

Keane, John. 1988. *Civil Society and Democracy*. London: Verso.

——, ed. 1988. *Civil Society and the State: New European Perspectives*. London: Verso.

Keane, Webb. 2003. "Semiotics and the Social Analysis of Material Things." *Language and Communication* 23:409–25.

Kelly, Kevin. 1999. *New Rules for the New Economy: Ten Ways the Network Economy Is Changing Everything*. London: Fourth Estate.

Kennedy, David. 2004. *The Dark Sides of Virtue: Reassessing International Humanitarianism*. Princeton: Princeton University Press.

Kharoufi, Mostafa. 1991. "The Informal Dimension of Urban Activity in Egypt: Some Recent Work." *Cairo Papers of Social Science* 14, no. 4.

Khawwam, Rinih. 1992. *Al-Siyasah wa al-hilah 'inda al-'Arab: Raqa'iq al-hilal fi daqa'iq al-hiyal*, al-Tab'ah 2. London: Dar al-Saqi.

Khundker, Nasreen. 1988. "The Fuzziness of the Informal Sector: Can We Afford to Throw Out the Baby with the Bath Water? (A Comment)." *World Development* 16, no. 10:1263–65.

Kondo, Dorinne. 1997. *About Face: Performing Race in Fashion and Theater*. New York: Routledge.

Koptiuch, Kristin. 1994. "Other Workers: A Critical Reading of Representations of Egyptian Petty Commodity Production at the Turn of the Twentieth Century." *Workers and Working Classes in the Middle East*, ed. Zachary Lockman.

——. 1999. *A Poetics of Political Economy in Egypt*. Minneapolis: University of Minnesota Press.

Kumar, Krishan. 1993. "Civil Society: An Inquiry into the Usefulness of an Historical Term." *British Journal of Sociology* 44, no. 3:375–95.

——. 1994. "Civil Society Again: A Reply to Christopher Bryant's 'Social Self-Organization, Civility and Sociology.'" *British Journal of Sociology* 45, no. 1:127.

Landes, David. 1958. *Bankers and Pashas: International Finance and Economic Imperialism in Egypt*. Cambridge: Harvard University Press.

Lapidus, Ira. 1967. *Muslim Cities in the Later Middle Ages*. Cambridge: Harvard University Press.

Latour, Bruno. 1999. "On Recalling ANT." *Actor Network Theory and After*, ed. John Law and John Hassard. 15–25.

Lave, Jean, and Etienne Wenger. 1991. *Situated Learning: Legitimate Peripheral Participation*. Cambridge: Cambridge University Press.

Law, John. 1999. "After ANT: Complexity, Naming and Topology." *Actor Network Theory and After*, ed. John Law and John Hassard. 1–14.

Law, John, and John Hassard, eds. 1999. *Actor Network Theory and After*. Oxford: Basil Blackwell.

LeClair, Edward, and Harold K. Schneider. 1968. *Economic Anthropology: Readings in Theory and Analysis*. New York: Rinehart and Winston.

Levi, Clement, ed. 1952. *The Stock Exchange Year Book of Egypt*. 1950–51 ed. Alexandria: Société des Publications Égyptiennes.

Lévi-Strauss, Claude. 1966. *The Savage Mind*. Chicago: University of Chicago Press.

Lewis, Bernard. 1937. "The Islamic Guilds." *Economic History Review* 8:20–37.

——. 1961. *The Emergence of Modern Turkey*. London: Oxford University Press.

Lewis, Nelson. 1916. *The Planning of the Modern City: A Review of the Principles Governing City Planning*. New York: John Wiley and Sons.

Lockman, Zachary, ed. 1994. *Workers and Working Classes in the Middle East: Struggles, Histories, Historiographies*. Albany: State University of New York Press.

Lubell, Harold. 1991. *The Informal Sector in the 1980s and 1990s*. Paris: Development Centre, Organisation for Economic Co-operation and Development.

Macfie, A. L. 1971. "The Invisible Hand of Jupiter." *Journal of the History of Ideas* 32:595–99.

MacIntyre, Alasdair. 1990. *Three Rival Versions of Moral Enquiry: Encyclopaedia, Genealogy, and Tradition*. Notre Dame: University of Notre Dame Press.

Mahfouz, Naguib. 1997. *The Harafish*. Trans. Catherine Cobham. New York: Random House.

Maier, Charles. 1987. *Changing Boundaries of the Political*. Cambridge: Cambridge University Press.

Malinowski, Bronislaw. 1922. *Argonauts of the Western Pacific*. London: Routledge and Kegan Paul.

Malkki, Liisa. 1994. "Citizens of Humanity: Internationalism and the Imagined Community of Nations." *Diaspora* 3, no.1:41–68.

Maloney, Clarence, ed. 1976. *The Evil Eye*. New York: Columbia University Press.

Mandel, Ruth, and Caroline Humphrey. 2002. "The Market in Everyday Life: Ethnographies of Postsocialism." *Markets and Moralities: Ethnographies of Postsocialism*. Oxford: Berg.

Marcus, George E. 1998. *Ethnography through Thick and Thin*. Princeton: Princeton University Press.

Marsot, Afaf Lutfi al-Sayyid. 1984. *Egypt in the Reign of Muhammad Ali*. Cambridge: Cambridge University Press.

Martin, Germain. 1910. *Les Bazars du Caire et les petits métiers arabes*. Cairo: Université Égyptienne.

Marx, Karl. 1957. *Capital*. New York: Everyman's Library.

Massiah, Joycelin, ed. 1993. *Women in Developing Economies: Making Visible the Invisible*. Providence, R.I.: Berg, in cooperation with UNESCO.

Massignon, Louis. 1987. "Sinf." *E. J. Brill's First Encyclopedia of Islam: 1913–1936*. Leiden: E. J. Brill.

Mastnak, Tomaž. 1996. "Fascists, Liberals, and Anti-Nationalism." *Europe's New Nationalism: States and Minorities in Conflict*, ed. R. Caplan and J. Feffer. New York: Oxford University Press. 59–74.

———. 2002. *Crusading Peace: Christendom, the Muslim World, and Western Political Order*. Berkeley: University of California Press.

Mato, Daniel. 1997. "On Global and Local Agents and the Social Making of Transnational Identities and Related Agendas in 'Latin' America." *Identities* 4, no. 2:167–212.

Maunier, Réné. 1912. "L'Apprentissage dans la petite industrie en Égypte, l'organisation actuelle, les réformes possibles." *Égypte Contemporaine* 3:341–69.

Maurer, Bill. 2000. "A Fish Story: Rethinking Globalization on Virgin Gorda, British Virgin Islands." *American Ethnologist* 27, no. 3:670–701.

———. 2001. "Islands in the Net: Rewiring Technological and Financial Circuits in the 'Offshore' Caribbean." *Comparative Studies in Society and History* 43, no. 3:467–501.

———. 2002. "Anthropological and Accounting Knowledge in Islamic Banking and Finance: Rethinking Critical Accounts." *Journal of the Royal Anthropological Institute*, n.s. 8, no. 4:645–67.

———. 2003. "Uncanny Exchanges: The Possibilities and Failures of 'Making Change' with Alternative Monetary Forms." *Environment and Planning D: Society and Space* 20, no. 3:317–40.

Mauss, Marcel. 1990. *The Gift: The Form and Reason for Exchange in Archaic Societies*. New York: W. W. Norton.

Mbembe, Achille. 1992. "The Banality of Power and the Aesthetics of Vulgarity in the Postcolony." *Public Culture* 4, no. 2:1–30.

Meagher, Kate. 1995. "Crisis, Informalization and the Urban Informal Sector in Sub-Saharan Africa." *Development and Change* 26:259–84.

Melucci, Alberto. 1989. *Nomads of the Present: Social Movements and Individual Needs in Contemporary Society*, ed. J. Keane and P. Mier. London: Hutchinson.

Meyer, Günter. 1988. "Manufacturing in Old Quarters of Central Cairo." *Éléments sur les Centres-Villes dans le Monde Arabe*. Paris: URBAMA.

———. 1990. "Economic and Social Change in the Old City of Cairo." Paper presented at the 24th Annual Meeting of the Middle East Studies Association of North America. San Antonio, Texas, 10–13 November.

Meyer, John W., and Brian Rowan. 1990. "Institutionalized Organizations: Formal Structure as Myth and Ceremony." *The New Institutionalism in Organizational Analysis*, ed. W. W. Powell and P. J. DiMaggio. Chicago: University of Chicago Press. 41–62.

Migdal, Joel S. 1988. *Strong Societies and Weak States: State-Society Relations and State Capabilities in the Third World*. Princeton: Princeton University Press.

Miles, Helen. 1994. "Return of the Entrepreneurs." *El-Ahram Weekly*, 30 June–6 July.

Miller, Daniel. 1987. *Material Culture and Mass Consumption*. New York: Basil Blackwell.

Mitchell, Timothy. 1991. *Colonising Egypt*. Berkeley: University of California Press.

——. 2002. *Rule of Experts: Egypt, Techno-politics, Modernity*. Berkeley: University of California Press.

Mnookin, Robert H., Scott Peppet, and Andrew S. Tulumello. 2000. *Beyond Winning: Negotiating to Create Value in Deals and Disputes*. Cambridge: Harvard University Press.

Moore, Sally Falk. 1987. "Explaining the Present: Theoretical Dilemmas in Processual Ethnography." *American Ethnologist* 14, no. 4:727–36.

——. 2005. "Comparisons, Possible and Impossible." *Annual Review of Anthropology*. Palo Alto: Annual Reviews.

Morsey, Soheir A. 1986. "U.S. Aid to Egypt: An Illustration and Account of U.S. Foreign Assistance Policy." *Arab Studies Quarterly* 8, no. 4:358–89.

Mosley, P. 1987. *Overseas Aid: Its Defence and Reform*. Brighton: Wheatsheaf.

Munn, Nancy D. 1986. *The Fame of Gawa: A Symbolic Study of Value Transformation in a Massim (Papua New Guinea) Society*. Durham: Duke University Press.

Murray, Oswyn. 1993. *Early Greece*. 2d ed. Cambridge: Harvard University Press.

Myers, Fred, and Donald Brenneis. 1991. "Introduction: Language and Politics in the Pacific." *Dangerous Words: Language and Politics in the Pacific*, ed. Donald Brenneis and Fred Myers. Prospect Heights, Ill.: Waveland. 1–29.

Nada, Atef Hanna. 1991. *Impact of Temporary International Migration on Rural Egypt*. Cairo: American University in Cairo Press.

Nader, Laura. 1969. "Up the Anthropologist: Perspectives Gained from Studying Up." *Reinventing Anthropology*, ed. D. Hymes. New York: Pantheon. 284–311.

Nafie, Ibrahim. 1994. "The Pursuit of Wealth: Making Money Is Not Synonymous with Stealing Money." *El-Ahram Weekly*, 3–9 February.

O'Brien, Robert, Anne Marie Goetz, Jan Aart Scholte, and Marc Williams. 2000. *Contesting Global Governance: Multilateral Economic Institutions and Global Social Movements*. Cambridge: Cambridge University Press.

Offe, Claus. 1985. *Disorganized Capitalism*. Cambridge: MIT Press.

Oldham, Linda, Haguer el Hadidi, and Hussein Tamaa. 1988. *Informal Communities in Cairo: The Basis of a Typology*. Cairo: American University in Cairo Press.

Ong, Aihwa. 1999. *Flexible Citizenship: The Cultural Logics of Transnationality*. Durham: Duke University Press.

Owen, Roger. 1969. *Cotton and the Egyptian Economy, 1820–1914: A Study in Trade and Development*. Oxford: Clarendon.

———. 1972. "The Cairo Building Industry and the Building Boom of 1897 to 1907." *Colloque international sur l'histoire du Caire, 27 mars–5 avril 1969*. Cairo: Ministry of Culture of the Arab Republic of Egypt, General Egyptian Book Organization.

———. 1981. *The Middle East in the World Economy, 1800–1914*. London: Methuen.

Parry, J., and M. Bloch. 1989. *Money and the Morality of Exchange*. Cambridge: Cambridge University Press.

Peattie, Lisa. 1987. "An Idea in Good Currency and How It Grew: The Informal Sector." *World Development* 15, no. 7: 851–60.

Pels, Peter. 1999. "Professions of Duplexity: A Prehistory of Ethical Codes in Anthropology." *Current Anthropology* 40, no. 2:101–36.

Perelman, Michael. 2000. *The Invention of Capitalism: Classical Political Economy and the Secret History of Primitive Accumulation*. Durham: Duke University Press.

Peters, Pauline. 1994. *Dividing the Commons: Politics, Policy, and Culture in Botswana*. Charlottesville: University Press of Virginia.

———. 1996. "Anti Anti-Development: A Critical Look at Anthropologists' Engagement with 'Development.'" Paper presented at the 95th annual meeting of the American Anthropological Association, San Francisco, 20–24 November.

Phillipson, Nicholas, and Quentin Skinner, eds. 1993. *Political Discourse in Early Modern Britain*. Cambridge: Cambridge University Press.

Pocock, J. G. A. 1975. *The Machiavellian Moment: Florentine Political Thought and the Atlantic Republican Tradition*. Princeton: Princeton University Press.

———. 1985. *Virtue, Commerce, and History: Essays on Political Thought and History, Chiefly in the Eighteenth Century*. Cambridge: Cambridge University Press.

Polanyi, Karl. 1957a. "The Economy as Instituted Process." *Trade and Markets in the Early Empires*, ed. K. Polanyi, C. M. Arensberg, and H. W. Pearson. New York: Free Press. 250–56.

———. 1957b. *The Great Transformation: The Political and Economic Origins of Our Times*. Boston: Beacon.

———. 1957c. "The Place of Economies in Societies." *Trade and Markets in the Early Empires*, ed. K. Polanyi, C. M. Arensberg, and H. W. Pearson. New York: Free Press.

"Police Arrest 14 Suspected Protestors on Eve of International Economic Summit in Bologna." 2000. *Italy Daily*, 14 June, 1.

Portes, Alejandro, Manuel Castells, and Lauren Benton, eds. 1989. *The Informal Economy: Studies in Advanced and Less Developed Countries*. Baltimore: Johns Hopkins University Press.

Portes, A., and S. Sassen-Koob. 1984. "Making It Underground: Comparative Material on the Urban Informal Sector in Western Market Economies." *American Journal of Sociology* 93:30–61.

Psacharopoulos, George. 1980. *Higher Education in Developing Countries: A Cost-Benefit Analysis*. World Bank Staff Working Paper 440. Washington: World Bank.

Putnam, Robert D. 1993. "The Prosperous Community: Social Capital and Public Life." *American Prospect* 13:35–42.

——. 2000. *Bowling Alone: The Collapse and Revival of American Community*. New York : Simon and Schuster.

Putnam, Robert, R. Leonardi, and R. Nanetti. 1993. *Making Democracy Work: Civic Traditions in Modern Italy*. Princeton: Princeton University Press.

Qandil, Amani. 1998. "The Nonprofit Sector in Egypt." *The Nonprofit Sector in the Developing World*, ed. H. K. Anheier and L. M. Salamon. Manchester: Manchester University Press. 145–46.

Rabinow, Paul. 1989. *French Modern: Norms and Forms of the Social Environment*. Cambridge: MIT Press.

——, ed. 1984. *The Foucault Reader*. New York: Pantheon.

Rageh, Abou-Zeid. 1985. "The Changing Pattern of Housing in Cairo." *The Expanding Metropolis: Coping with Urban Growth of Cairo*. Proceedings of Seminar Nine in the Series Architectural Transformations in the Islamic World, Held in Cairo, Egypt, November 11–15, 1984. Aga Khan Awards.

Raphael, D. D., and A. L. MacFie. 1982. Introduction, *The Theory of Moral Sentiments*, by Adam Smith. 20–25.

Raymond, André. 1958. "Les Porteurs d'Eau du Caire." *Bulletin de l'Institut Français d'Archéologie Orientale* 57:183–203.

——. 1973–74. *Artisans et commerçants au Caire au XVIIIᵉ siècle*. Damascus: Institut Français de Damas.

——. 1993. *Le Caire*. Paris: Fayard.

——. 1995a. "The Role of Communities in the Administration of Cairo." *The State and Its Servants*, ed. Nelly Hanna.

——. 1995b. "Guilds." *The Oxford Encyclopedia of the Modern Islamic World*, ed. John L. Esposito. Oxford: Oxford University Press. 74–77.

Rist, Gilbert. 1997. *The History of Development: From Western Origins to Global Faith*. London: Zed.

Rizq, Su'ad Kamel. 1991. "The Structure and Operation of the Informal Sector in Egypt." *Employment and Structural Adjustment*, ed. Heba Handoussa and Gillian Potter.

Robertson, A. F. 1984. *The People and the State: An Anthropology of Planned Development*. Cambridge: Cambridge University Press.

Rofel, Lisa. 1999. *Other Modernities: Gendered Yearnings in China after Socialism*. Berkeley: University of California Press.

Roitman, Janet. 2003. "Unsanctioned Wealth; or, The Productivity of Debt in Northern Cameroon." *Public Culture* 15, no. 2:211–37.

——. 2005. *Fiscal Disobedience: An Anthropology of Economic Regulation in Central Africa*. Princeton: Princeton University Press.

Rose, Nikolas. 1996. "Governing 'Advanced' Liberal Democracies." *Foucault and Political Reason*, ed. Andrew Barry, Thomas Osborne, and Nikolas Rose. 37–64.

Rothschild, Emma. 2001. *Economic Sentiments: Adam Smith, Condorcet, and the Enlightenment.* Cambridge: Harvard University Press.

Roussillon, Alain. 1987–88. "L'Égypte dans le regard des sciences sociales." *Égypte Recompositions: Peuples Méditerranéens / Mediterranean Peoples* 41–42:87.

———. 1988. "Sociétés islamiques de placement de fonds et l'ouverture économique." Dossier 3. Cairo: CEDEJ.

Roy, Arundhati. 2001. *Power Politics.* Cambridge: South End.

Ruggie, John Gerard. 1993. "Territoriality and Beyond: Problematizing Modernity in International Relations." *International Organization* 47, no. 1:139–74.

Rycx, J. F. 1987. "Islam et dérégulation financière: Banques et sociétés islamiques d'investissement: Le cas égyptien." Dossier 3. Cairo: CEDEJ.

Sachs, Wolfgang, ed. 1992. *The Development Dictionary: A Guide to Knowledge as Power.* London: Zed.

Sadowski, Yahya M. 1991. *Political Vegetables? Businessman and Bureaucrat in the Development of Egyptian Agriculture.* Washington: Brookings Institution.

Sampson, Steven. 1996. "The Social Life of Projects: Importing Civil Society to Albania." *Civil Society*, ed. Chris Hann and Elizabeth Dunn. 121–42.

Sassen, Saskia. 1996. "On Economic Citizenship." *Losing Control? Sovereignty in an Age of Globalization.* New York: Columbia University Press. 33–62.

———. 1999. "Embedding the Global in the National." *States and Sovereignty in the Global Economy*, ed. David Smith, Dorothy J. Solinger, and Steven C. Topik. 158–71.

Schneider, Harold K. 1974. *Economic Man: The Anthropology of Economics.* New York: Free Press.

Schumpeter, Joseph A. 1954. *History of Economic Analysis.* Oxford: Oxford University Press.

Scott, James C. 1985. *Weapons of the Weak: Everyday Forms of Peasant Resistance.* New Haven: Yale University Press.

———. 1998. *Seeing like a State: How Certain Schemes to Improve the Human Condition Have Failed.* New Haven: Yale University Press.

Seddon, David, ed. 1978. *Relations of Production: Marxist Approaches to Economic Anthropology.* Trans. H. Lackner. London: Frank Cass.

Seligman, Adam. 1992. *The Idea of Civil Society.* New York: Free Press.

Sen, Amartya. 1989. *Education and Training in the 1990s: Developing Countries' Needs and Strategies.* New York: UN Development Program.

Senior, Nassau William. 1882. *Conversations and Journals in Egypt and Malta, Edited by His Daughter, M. C. M. Simpson.* London: Sampson Low, Marston, Searles, and Rivington.

Serageldin, Ismail. 1985. "Some Economic and Philosophical Issues." *The Expanding Metropolis: Coping with Urban Growth of Cairo.* Proceedings of Seminar Nine in the Series Architectural Transformations in the Islamic World, Held in Cairo, Egypt, November 11–15, 1984. Aga Khan Awards.

Serageldin, Mona. 1984. "Planning and Institutional Mechanisms." Conference intervention. Aga Khan Award for Architecture, Cairo, 121.

Serageldin, Mona, with William Doebele and Kadri el-Araby. 1979. "Land Tenure Systems and Development Controls in the Arab Countries of the Middle East." *Housing: Process and Physical Form*. Aga Khan Foundation.

Seton-Williams, Veronica, and Peter Stocks. 1993. *Blue Guide: Egypt*. New York: W. W. Norton.

Shanks, Andrew. 1995. *Civil Society, Civil Religion*. Oxford: Basil Blackwell.

Shaw, Stanford J. 1976. *History of the Ottoman Empire and Modern Turkey*. New York: Cambridge University Press.

Siebers, Tobin. 1983. *The Mirror of Medusa*. Berkeley: University of California Press.

Simmel, Georg. 1950. *The Sociology of Georg Simmel*. Ed. and trans. Kurt H. Wolff. New York: Free Press.

———. 1990. *The Philosophy of Money*. Ed. David Frisby, trans. Tom Bottomore and David Frisby. New York: Routledge.

Singer, David. 2000. "World Bank Defends Itself to Critics." *International Herald Tribune*, 17 April, 18.

Singerman, Diane. 1995. *Avenues of Participation: Family, Politics, and Networks in Urban Quarters of Cairo*. Princeton: Princeton University Press.

Skinner A. S. 1979. "Adam Smith, Science and the Role of the Imagination." *A System of Social Science*. Oxford: Oxford University Press.

Smart, Alan. 1999. "Predatory Rule and Illegal Economic Practices." *States and Illegal Practices*, ed. Josiah McC. Heyman. 99–128.

Smith, Adam. [1759] 1976a. *The Theory of Moral Sentiments*. Ed. D. D. Raphael and A. L. Macfie. New York: Oxford University Press.

———. [1796] 1976b. *An Inquiry into the Nature and Causes of the Wealth of Nations*. Ed. R. H. Campbell and A. S. Skinner. Oxford: Clarendon.

———. [1795] 1980. *Essays on Philosophical Subjects*. Ed. W. P. D. Wightman and J. C. Bryce. Oxford: Clarendon.

Smith, David, Dorothy J. Solinger, and Steven C. Topik, eds. 1999. *States and Sovereignty in the Global Economy*. New York: Routledge.

Spivak, Gayatri Chakravorty. 1999. *A Critique of Postcolonial Reason: Toward a History of the Vanishing Present*. Cambridge: Harvard University Press.

Spooner, Brian. 1976. "Concluding Essay 1: Anthropology and the Evil Eye." *The Evil Eye*, ed. Clarence Maloney.

Stallard, Janice K., and Debjani Bagchi with Soha El Agouz. 1995. "Small and Micro Enterprise Development in Egypt: Opportunities for Outreach and Sustainability." Cairo: National Cooperative Business Association/Environmental Quality International.

Stark, David. 1998. "Recombinant Property in East European Capitalism." *The Laws of the Markets*, ed. Michel Callon. 116–46.

Stark, David, and Laszlo Bruszt. 1998. *Postsocialist Pathways: Transforming Politics and Property in East Central Europe*. Cambridge: Cambridge University Press.

Starrett, Gregory. 1998. *Putting Islam to Work: Education, Politics, and Religious Transformation in Egypt*. Berkeley: University of California Press.

Stauth, Georg. 1986. "Gamaliyya: Informal Economy and Social Life in a Popular Quarter of Cairo." Working Paper no. 87. Bielefeld: University of Bielefeld, Faculty of Sociology, Sociology of Development Research Centre.

——. 1991. "Gamaliyya: Informal Economy and Social Life in a Popular Quarter of Cairo." *Cairo Papers in Social Science* 14, no. 4.

——. n. d. "Gamaleyya: What Is It That There Remains: An Essay on 'Popular Habitus' in a Cairean Quarter." Unpublished paper (from CEDEJ).

Stiglitz, Joseph. 2000. "The Insider: What I Learned at the World Economic Crisis." *New Republic*, 17 April, 56.

Stoler, Ann Laura, and Frederick Cooper. 1997. *Tensions of Empire: Colonial Cultures in a Bourgeois World*. Berkeley: University of California Press.

Stoller, Paul. 1997. *Sensuous Scholarship*. Philadelphia: University of Pennsylvania Press.

Strathern, Marilyn. 1988. *The Gender of the Gift*. Berkeley: University of California Press.

——. 1992. "Qualified Value: The Perspective of Gift Exchange." *Barter, Exchange, and Value*, ed. Caroline Humphrey and Stephen Hugh-Jones. 169–91.

——. 1998. "Divisions of Interest and Languages of Ownership." *Property Relations*, ed. Chris Hann. 214–32.

Tafuri, Manfredo, and Francesco Dal Co. 1986. *Modern Architecture*. Trans. Robert Erich Wolf. New York: Electa/Rizzoli.

Tanada, Hirofumi. 1996. "Survey of Migrant Associations in Cairo Metropolitan Society (Egypt), 1955–1990: Quantitative and Qualitative Data." *Social Science Review* 42, no. 1.

Taussig, Michael. 1980. *The Devil and Commodity Fetishism in South America*. Chapel Hill: University of North Carolina Press.

Tekçe, Belgin, Linda Oldham, and Frederic Shorter. 1994. *A Place to Live: Families and Child Health in a Cairo Neighborhood*. Cairo: American University in Cairo Press.

Tignor, Robert T. 1989. *Egyptian Textiles and British Capital, 1930–1956*. Cairo: American University in Cairo Press.

Tinker, Irene. 1993. *Evaluation of the Organization for Development and Support of Street Food Vendors in the City of Minia: Model for Empowering the Working Poor*. Cairo: Social Planning, Analysis, and Administration Consultants.

Tobin, James. 1992. "The Invisible Hand in Modern Macroeconomics." *Adam Smith's Legacy: His Place in the Development of Modern Economics*, ed. Michael Fry. London: Routledge. 117–29.

Toledano, Ehud. 1990. *State and Society in Mid-Nineteenth-Century Egypt*. Cambridge: Cambridge University Press.

Touraine, Alain. 1980. *L'Après socialisme*. Paris: Bernard Grasset.

——. 1985. "An Introduction to the Study of Social Movements." *Social Research* 52, no. 4.

Tripp, Aili Mari. 1997. *Changing the Rules: The Politics of Liberalization and the Urban Informal Economy in Tanzania*. Berkeley: University of California Press.

Turner, Jonathan. 2000. "The Formation of Social Capital." *Social Capital*, ed. Partha Dasgupta and Ismail Serageldin.

Turner, Terence. 1978. "The Kayapo of Central Brazil." *Face Values*, ed. A. Sutherland. London: BBC.

——. 1979. "Anthropology and the Politics of Indigenous Peoples' Struggles." *Cambridge Anthropology* 5:1–43.

United Kingdom, House of Commons. 1906. "Report by H.M. Agent and Consul General on the Finances, Administration, and Condition of Egypt and the Sudan." *House of Commons Sessional Papers* 137:572.

'Uways, Sayyid. 1989. *L'histoire que je porte sur mon dos: mémoires*. Trans. Nashwa al-Azhari, Gilbert Delanoue, and Alain Roussillon. Cairo: CEDEJ.

Vallet, Jean. 1911. *Contribution à l'étude de la condition des ouvriers de la grande industrie au Caire*. Valence: Imprimerie Valentinoise.

Verdery, Katherine. 1997. "Political Identities and Property Restitution in Transylvania, Romania." National Science Foundation grant proposal, published in POLAR: Political and Legal Anthropology Review 2, no. 1:120–41.

——. 1998. "Property and Power in Transylvania's Decollectivization." *Property Relations*, ed. Chris Hann. 160–80.

Vincent, Joan. 1990. *Anthropology and Politics: Visions, Traditions, and Trends*. Tucson: University of Arizona Press.

Vitalis, Robert. 1995. *When Capitalists Collide: Business Conflict and the End of Empire in Egypt*. Berkeley: University of California Press.

Waterbury, John. 1976. *Egypt: Burdens of the Past, Options for the Future*. Bloomington: Indiana University Press.

——. 1983. *The Egypt of Nasser and Sadat: The Political Economy of Two Regimes*. Princeton: Princeton University Press.

Weiner, Annette B. 1992. *Inalienable Possessions: The Paradox of Keeping-While-Giving*. Berkeley: University of California Press.

Westermarck, Edward. 1926. *Ritual and Belief in Morocco*. Vol. 1. London: Macmillan.

Wikan, Unni. 1995. "Sustainable Development in the Mega-City: Can the Concept Be Made Applicable?" *Current Anthropology* 36, no. 4:635–55.

——. 1996. *Tomorrow, God Willing: Self-Made Destinies in Cairo*. Chicago: University of Chicago Press.

Wilson, Fiona. 1993. "Workshops as Domestic Domains: Reflections on Small-Scale Industry in Mexico." *World Development* 21, no. 1:67–80.

Winch, Donald. 1983. "Adam Smith's 'Enduring Particular Result.'" *Wealth and Virtue*, ed. Istvan Hont and Michael Ignatieff. 253–70.

Wolf, Eric R. 1966. "Kinship, Friendship, and Patron-Client Relations in Complex Societies." *The Social Anthropology of Complex Societies*, ed. Michael Banton. London: Tavistock. 1–22.

——. 1999. *Envisioning Power: Ideologies of Dominance and Crisis*. Berkeley: University of California Press.

——. 2001. *Pathways of Power: Building an Anthropology of the Modern World*. Berkeley: University of California Press.

Wood, Alfred C. 1964. *A History of the Levant Company*. New York: Barnes and Noble.

World Bank. 1991a. "Staff Appraisal Report: Arab Republic of Egypt, Social Fund Project." Population and Human Resources, Country Department III: Europe, Middle East, and North Africa. Report No 9561-EGT. 28 May.

——. 1991b. *Egypt: Alleviating Poverty during Structural Adjustment*. Washington: World Bank.

——. 1994. *Private Sector Development in Egypt: The Status and the Challenges*. Prepared for the Conference "Private Sector Development in Egypt: Investing in the Future," Cairo, 9–10 October.

——. 2001. *World Development Report 2000/2001: Attacking Poverty*. Washington: World Bank.

Zaalouk, Malak. 1989. *Power, Class, and Foreign Capital in Egypt: The Rise of the New Bourgeoisie*. London: Zed.

INDEX

in, 156–57; loss in, 152–56; male kin in, 127–28; microenterprises vs., 15–16; money flow from, 129–32; neoliberalism and, 142–47; as obstacle to development, 85; as part of network, 149–52; policies toward, 14–15; power in, 101; as practice, 96; as property, 136; reemergence of, 62; relationships within, 115, 145; revoking licenses of, 42; during Second World War, 62; sending work away from, 153–54; separating from home, 133–34; skill vs. authority in, 117; as "small enterprises," 46; sounds and snapshots of, 39–41; state officials and, 140–41; value production in, 9, 137–66. *See also* Craftsmen; Masters

World Bank: caricatures of, 34–35; on Egyptian economy, 85–86, 146; free markets imposed by, 6; governmentality and, 93–94; government statistics and, 77; informal economy and, 80, 82–83; information gathering and, 85;

microenterprises funded by, 197; microlending by, 193–94; "ownership" of development programs and, 173–74; SAPS enforced by, 74. *See also* Social Fund for Development

World Trade Organization, 92

Youth Entrepreneurs Society, 82

Youth graduates, 3; craftsmen on, 87; experience of space among, 47–48; housing for, 52–54; microenterprises of, 46; model market and, 98–99; move to el-Hirafiyeen by, 53–54; NGO of, 175, 191–92, 202–8; short-term gain and, 11; Social Fund money and, 49; tax exemptions for, 178. *See also* Entrepreneurs; Microentrepreneurs; Microenterprises

Zeitoun, el- (neighborhood), 41

Zhou, Yu, 84

Julia Elyachar is a research fellow at the Institute of Anthropological and Spatial Studies, Scientific Research Centre, Slovene Academy of Sciences and Arts, Ljubljana, Slovenia.

Library of Congress Cataloging-in-Publication Data

Elyachar, Julia, 1961–
Markets of dispossession : NGOS, economic development, and the state in Cairo / Julia Elyachar.
p. cm. — (Politics, history, and culture)
Includes bibliographical references and index.
ISBN 0-8223-3583-2 (cloth : alk. paper)
ISBN 0-8223-3571-9 (pbk. : alk. paper)
1. Cairo (Egypt)—Economic conditions. 2. Urban poor—Egypt—Cairo.
3. Entrepreneurship—Egypt—Cairo. 4. Social networks—Egypt—Cairo.
5. Business networks—Egypt—Cairo. 6. New business enterprises—Egypt—
Cairo. 7. Non-governmental organizations—Egypt—Cairo. I. Title. II. Series.
HC830.Z7C338   2005
330.962'16055—dc22   2005009916